The Saudi Swindle

How the Deception Surrounding Saudi Oil Gave Rise to the
Green New Steal, the Looting of Nations, and a Global Lockdown

By Susan Bradford
(c) 2024

ISBN: 9798328310154
(c) 2024 Susan Bradford
All Rights Reserved

Biography

Susan Bradford has written a series of books on the Deep State – the totality of which will provide readers with complete understanding on the forces shaping the world. She has also ghost written and edited a number of books and articles.

Bradford holds a BA in English from UC Irvine, an MA in International Relations from the University of Essex, and postgraduate certificate in public international law from the University of Helsinki. She spent her junior year abroad studying at the University of St. Andrews in Scotland.

Bradford began her career as an intern for CBS-TV News in Los Angeles before joining City News Service as a reporter, covering Hollywood and the police beat. She worked as production assistant for the PBS Red Car Film project in which she interviewed the leading anti-trust attorney in the federal government's case against Standard Oil et al in the Red City line case; and news writer for KNX (CBS) news radio before pursuing postgraduate work in England .

During her postgraduate matriculation, Bradford founded and edited the *European Review,* which became the departmental publication for the Centre for European Studies at Essex University. In addition to soliciting, editing, and publishing contributions from leading academics and heads of state on evolving Atlantic Alliance and European integration, Bradford covered, as foreign correspondent, the Council of Madrid in Europe which launched the euro; an anti-NATO debate in the Russian state Duma; and the Britain in the World conference. She also scored an interview with Baron Robert Rothschild, one of the architects of the European Coal and Steel Community, a precursor to the EU.

Concurrently, she worked as Senior Research Fellow for the Atlantic Council of the UK while representing Essex University on the NATO Universities Advisory Committee. She represented the ACUK before the Euro-Atlantic Group – and the Standing Conferences of Atlantic Organizations.

After completing her Master's degree, she lived for a while in London, working for a summer, with UK Shadow Foreign Secretary Michael Howard as speech writer.

Upon returning to the United States, she worked for Fox News Channel as producer, progressed to Voice of America's assignments editor, and then wrote speeches for Korean Ambassador Sung Chul Yang.

Republican superlobbyist Jack Abramoff granted Bradford the exclusive to write a book about the federal probe into his lobbying activities, providing her access into the networks, financial relationships, and strategies behind the transnational crime syndicate that has both overtaken the United States and the world.

Now a frequent guest on podcasts and other interview shows, Bradford is a public speaker, prolific author, and investigative journalist, who loves God, family, and country.

Bradford's biography is maintained in Marquis' *Who's Who in the World, Who's Who in America*, and *Who's Who Among American Women*.

Books by Bradford
www.susanbradford.org

Taking Back America

The 2020 Election Steal ... and Cover Up

Executive Summary of the Theft of U.S. Assets and Corruption of the Department of Justice

The End of Globalism

Dethroned

Royal Blood Lies

Fl33c3d

Tartar Treachery

Jack Abramoff, Rothschild Zionist

The Shadow Dragon

United Church of Heist

The Second American Revolution

Lynched

The Full Court Press

The Tribes that Rockefeller Built

UnMasked: The Coronavirus Story

among others....

Table of Contents

Author's Brief _____ 11

Origins of the Syndicate _____ 12

    Enslaving the American People _____ 23
    Genesis of the Fed _____ 28
    The South Sea Company _____ *31*

Securing Saudi Oil _____ 36

    War for Saudi Oil _____ 38

The Rise of the National Crime Syndicate _____ 42

    The Syndicate Takes Over China _____ *50*
    Yale in China _____ *56*
    Wall Street Bankrolls the Russian Revolution _____ *58*

Inside the Central Banks _____ 64

    The Saudi Central Bank _____ 65

Launching the Petrodollar _____ 69

    Sabotaging the Saudi Oil Fields _____ 76
    The Carlyle Group and Crony Capitalism _____ *80*
    A Native-American OPEC _____ *84*
    Filipino Kleptocrats Get in on the Game _____ *91*

The Decade of Greed _____ 97

    Revolutionaries of the Right _____ 97
    Iran-Contra, Marc Rich, and the Oligarchs _____ 104
    Kleptocrats in the Philippines _____ 107
    NarcoDollars, Junk Bonds, and Casinos _____ 109
    The Tribal Connection _____ 112

Christianity as a Trojan Horse for Globalism___115
Opening the Gates of Hell___120
*The City of London Does Banking with the Bolsheviks*___*124*

The Syndicate Goes Global___127

The Harvard Connection___131
Abramoff, Soros, and Gates___145
Russian Influence___146
*Establishing a Bank Holding Company for Gates*___*147*
*Microsoft and Human Trafficking*___*148*
*Harvard's Stolen Patent*___*151*

The Syndicate's Mask Slips___154

The Best Laid Plans___154
Taking a Page out of the Oligarch Playbook___157
The Trump Connection___163
Microsoft Seeks Cover___166
*Wells Fargo, Bill Gates, and the Saudis*___*169*
*A Closer Look at Citadel*___*173*

Saudi Arabia Comes Clean___178

Saudi Arabia Realigns Oil Priorities___185
Strange Coincidences___191
The Saudis Lead the Way___196

Betrayal of Trust and Innocence___199

Launching Microsoft___211
Microsoft in China___214

The Green Years___216

Green Boondoggles___222
The Sudden Death of Simmons___225
Keeping the Agenda on Track___231

    Climate Bond Partners   *235*

Pandemic as Panacea   **240**

    Saudi Political Consultants   251
    Saudi Investments   252
    Towards a New Normal   257
    The Next Pandemic, Permanent Lockdowns   *266*
    Hamilton's Technocrats   *271*

Building BRICs for the New Abnormal   **284**

Solutions: Let's End this Madness!   **296**

Author's Brief

    The petro-dollar was a linchpin in the development of the world. With Saudi Arabia intrinsically linked to the development of the world for corporations, the United States established itself as a global hegemon; Saudi oil provided the cheap oil needed to drive progress for corporations to dominate markets worldwide. With the World Bank setting global oil prices, the petro-dollar provided cheap, accessible oil with which to develop the world. With the ability to print unlimited amounts of dollars, the elites could bankroll businesses with public funds, and ship the goods anywhere through an elaborate shipping system while the politically connected helped themselves to the profits. The elites were in the process of acquiring the assets of the world while the public was left holding the debt.

    The agenda stalled once the Saudis hit "peak oil," at which point, global planners had to go back to the drawing board and come up with a new plan to keep a global agenda centuries in the making on track.

    Saudi Arabia had overproduced its oil fields, dramatically curtailing anticipated supplies of cheap oil. With growing awareness among elite circles that globalism needed to change course to reach its final destination, global planners within the City of London changed course in a manner riddled with deceptions.

    The rise of BRICS, the government's response to the War on Terrorism, climate emergencies, and the global pandemic lockdown were all manifestation of a strategy global planners pursued to move humanity towards a new normal within a post-Saudi oil global economy.

    This book will explore the Saudi swindle, revealing the forces, agenda, history and networks behind BRICS, the Green agenda, the death of the petro-dollar, and the rise of 15-Minute Smart Cities, with all the breathless urgency explained. Bringing the pirates back to port requires that we identify who they are, the routes through which they ply their trade, and the injury they have inflicted upon humanity.

    With that, let us begin.....

I.
Origins of the Syndicate

"Nip the shoots of arbitrary power in the bud, is the only
maxim which can ever preserve the liberties of any people.
When the people give way, their deceivers, betrayers, and destroyers
press upon them so fast that there is no resisting afterwards.
The nature of encroachment is to, grow every day more encroaching, like
a cancer; it eats faster and faster every hour."

President John Adams
American Founding Father

The American author John Steinbeck reminds us that the best laid plans of mice and men often go awry. And so it was with the Rothschilds. Many efforts have been made to document the crimes of this powerful banking family, with a view to coming to terms with how the United States – a beacon of light, freedom, and God's grace throughout the world – was lost to criminals.

The Rothschilds rose to power as financial advisors to the Vatican, Christian Monarchs, and other world leaders. Within this trusted role, they lent money at usurious rates, pitted nations against each other and bankrolled both sides to generate debt for nations and revolutions, with a view to crushing, destroying, and ultimately looting nations to advance Rothschild power.

They financed wars, betrayed their benefactors, crashed and rigged markets, and engaged in every unhanded anti-competitive tactic and bad faith to eliminate competition to their enterprise. It wasn't enough they had to be prosperous and successful; everyone else had to be destroyed in the process. Retaining control required them to manage public perception, to bury knowledge of their treachery, discredit and eliminate their critics while holding all reins of power to prevent anyone from successfully challenging them. This required a careful balancing to act, to control without being seen as the controller. Thus, countries they claimed necessarily slipped into dictatorships; and corporations and nations were run by proxies.

During the Napoleonic Wars, the Rothschilds took specific aim at the British Monarchy and the Vatican. After threatening both with attacks at the hands of Napoleon dictator Napoleon Bonaparte, Rothschild offered to finance a defense and military counter-offensive, placing both into debt and under the financial control of the dynasty. While others were going about their lives, the desperately covetous Rothschilds, a deranged, if maniacally clever family that had somehow managed to insinuate itself into European aristocratic circles, began to destroy and undermine Christian society in ways that were simply inconceivable to others as part of an effort to claim the possessions of European rulers for itself.

The Napoleonic Wars proved to be a watershed in Rothschild power. While targeting the British empire, Rothschild deceived the British elite about the outcome of the Battle of Waterloo, sending the stock market into a nosedive at which point Rothschild bought British stocks for pennies on the dollar. By the time the truth surrounding the crushing defeat of Napoleon made its way back to England, the stock market was soaring, transforming the dynasty overnight into one of the wealthiest families in Europe, all based upon a lie. This twist of fortune might not have been so ominous had the Rothschilds been genuinely honorable people, rather than psychopaths nursing a grudge born out of obvious feelings of inferiority in which they sought to destroy and fleece others so that they alone would emerge as rulers of the world with everyone else crushed under their feet.

Queen Victoria was reputedly the first Rothschild bloodline to serve as British sovereign. According to Royal historians, the Rothschilds accepted the mythical Jesus bloodline as a qualifier to rule. As part of an effort to claim the mythical bloodline, they secured a Rothschild as Queen. Queen Victoria was then impregnated by George of Cumberland, an aristocrat who allegedly held the sacred Jesus bloodline, Royal historians maintain. Rothschild's usurpation of the British Monarchy, "the defender of the faith" and its scheme to breed Rothschilds into the Jesus bloodline constitute "Victoria's secret," the inspiration behind the name of a company led by Les Wexler, a cohort of Jeffrey Epstein, a Mossad operative running a pedophile compromise ring on behalf of the Rothschild crime syndicate.

The alleged Jesus-bloodline child was sent away into hiding so that the Rothschilds could deliver the Messiah, without widespread knowledge of its Rothschild origins, once their 200-year contract with the Crown ended. Through the Scofield Bible, they peddled a prophecy that "Jesus" would return to rule over humanity for a millennia. With vast wealth and influence at their disposal, the Rothschilds endeavored to manipulate society from the shadows to fulfill prophecy – including the erection of a Third Temple in Jerusalem and return of a "Messiah" of their creation, ensuring their right to rule the world in perpetuity, under the moral authority of a Christ figure recognized by all.

This dastardly scheme is arguably among the reasons the Rothschilds are aligned with the religious right, many of whom believe in the highly marketed prophecy which entails the return of the Messiah, following Armageddon and the destruction of the world (at Rothschild hands).

The criminal elites expected to rise from the ashes (underground bases) to inherit the world after their enemies perished. Rothschild even established a division devoted to the coordinating events to fulfill their version of Biblical prophecy, the "Esoteric CIA," which the Rothschilds had established for this purpose.

Toward the end of the 19th century, early 20th, the Rothschilds conceived a plan to absorb the wealth and power of the world while enslaving everyone else. With their mind fixed singlemindely on this goal, the Rothschilds endeavored to consolidate their position while undercutting the competition.

According to Royal historians, Victoria's children were all sired by a Rothschild, presumably Nathan Rothschild; upon reaching the age of maturity, they were married off and bred into Christian Royal families throughout Europe. These arrangements created an opportunity for Rothschild to insinuate itself into Christian Royal families before eliminating them. The Rothschilds embarked upon a campaign to destroy any and all rival claims to power, all the while maintaining a public front of respectability. Royal historians alleged that Rothschild paid assassins to hunt down and eliminate Christian aristocrats and rulers who held the sacred bloodline or might challenge their power, clearing the path for Rothschild's exclusive claim to global governance.

Leaving nothing to chance, the Rothschilds launched a secret breeding program in which Rothschild bloodlines were placed into obscure families and provided shadow support and funding while guided into positions of power to lead and corrupt nations on behalf of the dynasty, Royal historians report. Nazi Fuhrer Adolf Hitler, Prime Minister Winston Churchill, President Bill Clinton, Soviet Premier Joseph Stalin, and Communist leader Mao Tse-tung were allegedly produced through this secret breeding program.

Given this track record, the reader should not be surprised to learn that the international crime syndicate that has spread crime, drugs, and vice throughout the world is led by Rothschild.

Opium was a drug traditionally used among the initiated, to achieve higher states of spiritual consciousness – and in wars, to relieve pain. Applications were carefully administered by physicians to avoid misuse and addictions. For the Rothschilds, opium was a means to make more money and weaken the resolve of the populace through addiction, rendering nations easier to conquer.

The Venetians, among other Vatican-aligned merchants, engaged in arms, human, and drug trafficking while establishing monopolies for their commercial enterprise, with the support of vicious, blood-thirsty mercenaries drawn from the ranks of Khazars, Mongols, and Turks.

After the Venetian maritime empire fell, its pirates infiltrated the East India Company (EIC), which Queen Elizabeth I had chartered in 1600 for the Jewish Merchants of London to expand markets for the British Empire. The Venetians transformed the EIC into a vehicle for imperialist conquest and monopoly. EIC pirates confronted new markets with military might, slaying those who got in the way. After subduing the territory, the EIC established an administrative authority over it to protect and manage the EIC's burgeoning markets. Conquered territories were looted of treasures, wealth, and resources, with one-sided arrangements designed to enrich the merchants and the kingdoms supporting them.

According to *Dope, Inc.* the EIC's "opium trade constituted a sizable portion of the war chest that financed Britain's deployment of (the Rothschild-backed) Hessian mercenaries into North American to crush the rebellion" against exploitative Rothschild banking principles – namely Rothschild's efforts to prevent the American colonies from printing their own money. Upon discovering colonial prosperity, Rothschild decided to put an end to it by forcing colonists to take loans from the Rothschild-controlled Bank of England – thereby placing them in debt – and under the financial control of Rothschild.

Up to this point, Britain and the colonies enjoyed a harmonious relationship – one based upon mutual reward and trust. Disputes between them were easily resolved through diplomatic channels. Severing colonies from kingdoms was a Rothschild tactic to weaken and destabilize empires – often through wars and "revolutions" the dynasty prompted, financed, and managed to achieve a pre-determined outcome which resulted in both sides being indebted to Rothschild.

The young colonies rejected Rothschild's financial meddling and "colonial looting policies," *Dope, Inc.* reports, but the Rothschilds were not easily dissuaded. The EIC, which traded with the colonies, consistently used drugs and poisons against nations and their people to weaken them for conquest, creating a powerful, well-heeled network of pirates.

During the reign of the Rothschild Queen Victoria, Great Britain waged opium wars against China to "soften" the Chinese for British imperial conquest and generate revenue to fund the British empire. During the "British drugging of the Chinese population," a Chinese leader sent correspondence to the Queen, asking her "if she would allow the importation of such a poisonous substance into her own country," *Dope, Inc.* reports. He then requested that she "forbid her subjects to bring it into his. Narcotics traffic was the business of organized crime during the 19th century no less than in the 20th, and Britain's Opium War cabinet spun out a web of criminal connections that crisscrossed the globe."

The EIC established a monopoly on the opium trade in the new world and around the globe, and increasingly used poisons and drugs, including vaccines, to subdue targeted populations for imperial conquest and targeted markets. Rothschild used the resources, manpower, and assets of the British Empire for this purpose. Rather than strengthen the British Empire, the Rothschilds weakened it from within to build another from which it could expand and consolidate its power, and then extract resources to target other nations for conquest and endless looting.

Baring Brothers, a prominent British merchant bank, "remodeled the old East India Company as an instrument for the opium traffic," *Dope, Inc.* reports. "The Baring family formed a partnership, through marriage, with Sen. William Bingham, a delegate to the Continental Congress and reportedly one of the richest men in the United States." Bingham acquired his fortune as an owner of privateers – that is, vessels engaged in maritime warfare under a commission of war, or "robbery under arms" in seaborne trade.

Barings went on to establish the Hong Kong and Shanghai Bank of China (HSBC), which has been implicated in drug trafficking, money laundering, and accounts associated with the Jeffrey Epstein pedophile network. HSBC, which financed the opium trade, worked closely with the House of Morgan (JP Morgan). Morgan, in turn, profited handsomely from the opium trade. Morgan Guaranty Trust financed the Bolshevik Revolution in Russia and ranked among prominent "British dope banks," *Dope, Inc.* reports.

Since 1838, the House of Morgan was banker to Standard Oil. Standard Oil was established by John D. Rockefeller, America's first billionaire and robber baron whose family served as the shadow power behind the United States in service to Rothschild. The House of Morgan was launched in London by George Peabody, who established modern philanthropy as a cover and strategy to amass and protect private wealth. In addition to establishing "international credit" (i.e. debt) for the United States, he recruited Junius Spencer Morgan, the father of J.P. Morgan, the founder of the House of Morgan, as a partner in 1854 – establishing a global financial services firm which became J.P. Morgan & Co.

Peabody worked with the Rothschilds, revealing, as Eustace Mullins reports, that the Morgans were Rothschild agents who served as proxies, or useful idiots, behind which Rothschild advanced its financial agenda. The House of Morgan was reportedly assigned the role of transporting gold in and out of the United States as Rothschild moved to corner the world's gold supply. The Rothschilds set the daily price of gold at the N.M. Rothschild Bank until 2004.

The Chairman of Morgan et Cie, the House of Morgan's international division, served on the Council of the Royal Institute of International Affairs (RIIA) – a product of Rothschild's Round Table, which mapped out Rothschild strategies and designs to consolidate the world's wealth and power within the hands of the so-called elites, principally themselves, starting with the re-colonization of the United States. The RIIA charted international opium trading routes, *Dope, Inc.* reports. Morgan Guaranty Trust held a 40 percent stake in Morgan Grenfell. Lord Catto, the Chairman of Morgan Grenfell, sat on the London Committee of HSBC, reflecting a confluence of interests among them.

A registered charity of the Rothschild-controlled British Monarchy, the RIIA was bankrolled by the Bank of America, JP Morgan Chase, Citigroup, and Wells Fargo. Its sister organization in the United States was the Council on Foreign Relations, "the central planning and recruitment agency for Britain's one world empire," *Dope, Inc.* reports. These think tanks, which assumed an air of respectability among the public, were "controlled by a single group of evil men whose names and organizational affiliations (and) whose intimate ties of ownership, family, and political collaboration go back 200 years." The Italian-American mafia reported directly to Prime Minister Benjamin Disraeli, who was bankrolled by Nathan Rothschild and his brother-in-law, Moses Montefiore.

The RIIA is an organization through which the Knights of St. John Jerusalem, the Knights of Malta, Knights Templar, and the Scottish Freemason coordinate their strategies on behalf of the House of Rothschild. The Rothschild Queen Victoria "reconstituted the Most Venerable Order" in the 1880's as the Protestant branch of the Knights of Malta. The Scottish freemasons trace to the Knights of St. John who drew from "the wisdom of the East," the origins of the occult and aspects of the mystery schools that Christianity has characterized as "Satanic."

St. John the Baptist, who baptized Jesus, and St. John the Evangelist, an Apostle, are the patron saints of freemasonry. Once Rothschild acquired contractual and financial control of the Crown, freemasonry took on a decidedly sinister character.

From colonial days to the founding of the United States, the American people and its leadership have resisted Rothschild treason. While running for President in 1828, Andrew Jackson challenged the international bankers, telling them: "You are a den of vipers. I intend to expose you and by Eternal God I will rout you out. If the people understood the rank injustices of our money and banking system there would be a revolution before morning."

In 1832, Jackson vetoed a bill that discontinued the Second Bank of the United States, which was chartered after the War of 1812 to help the United States finance another (Rothschild)-instigated war. "The Act seems to be predicated on an erroneous idea that the present shareholders have a prescriptive right to not only the favor, but the bounty of the government," Jackson said. "For their benefit does this Act exclude the whole American people from competition in the purchase of this monopoly."

The bank was perceived as a fourth branch of government around which "money power" concentrated. Among the allegations was that the bank had provided preferential loans to speculators and merchants, used its money to bribe politicians, and undermined America's free and independent press in favor of propaganda and slanted coverage.

The Rothschild-controlled *Times of London* countered, "If (Jackson's) mischievous policy, which had its origins in the North American Republic, should become indurated down to a fixture, then that Government will furnish its own money without cost. It will pay off its debts and be without debt. It will have all the money necessary to carry on its commerce. It will become prosperous beyond precedent in the history of the civilized governments of the world. The brains and the wealth of all countries will go to North America. That government must be destroyed, or it will destroy every monarchy on the globe."

Another Rothschild scheme involved abolishing slavery in the United States in order to protect British cotton investments in Egypt which could not compete with America's cotton plantations. America's cotton plantations exploited cheap labor with slaves trafficked to America by the Rothschild-backed EIC.

Bear in mind, that Christians, including the American colonists, were opposed to slavery on grounds that no man (or woman) should be enslaved and that all people are equal in the eyes of God. The slaves were imported to the United States to support Rothschild's cotton trade. As part of this trade, cotton was produced in North America, shipped to a British textile manufacturer which exploited cheap labor to produce clothing which was sold overseas to merchants who paid for it from proceeds of opium sales.

When British merchants complained their Egyptian cotton-growers were unable to compete with their American counterparts, Rothschild arranged to end the institution of slavery in the United States. The southern plantation owners (the dynasty's network of merchants) were promised that they would be reimbursed for the loss of their slaves through a generous gift from the British government, financed with a loan provided by Rothschild-- which placed the British people in debt.

The Rothschilds and their agents agitated for Civil War in the United States to end the institution of slavery, with the promise that the former slaves would be given their own land. As is the pattern, Rothschild promises were broken. After the Civil War, the newly freed slaves returned to the plantation as indentured servants and cheap labor.

The Rothschilds used the Civil War to break the United States apart and claim the territories for their dynasty – but were blocked by the Russians who threatened to send troops, if they dared, thereby marking Russian rulers for elimination for interfering with Rothschild plans.

In 1833, Prime Minister Earl Grey, a faithful devotee of Queen Victoria, passed the Slavery Abolition Act, which expanded the jurisdiction of the Slave Trade Act of 1807. The legislation rendered the purchase and ownership of slaves illegal within the British Empire – with the exception of "territories in the possession of the East India Company," *Dope, Inc.* reports.

By 1835, President Andrew Jackson paid off the national debt, releasing the United States from Rothschild financial bondage. An assassination attempt was then made against Jackson's life. The President of the U.S. Bank, Nicholas Biddle, who was an agent for the House of Rothschild of Paris, then proceeded to undercut Jackson's efforts by severing funding to the U.S. Government in 1842, spurring a depression.

Meanwhile, Rothschild and Montefiore moved ahead with plans to reimburse the Southern plantation owners for the loss of their slaves. To this end, the men "forged an agreement with the chancellor of the exchequer to loan the British government £15 million, with the government adding £5 million later; this amount reflected 40 percent of the government's annual income, or what would be equivalent to £300 billion today," *Dope, Inc.* reports.

"You might expect this so-called slave compensation to have gone to the freed slaves to redress the injustices they suffered," *The Guardian* reports. "Instead, the money went exclusively to the owners of slaves, who were being compensated for the loss of what had, until then, been considered their property. Not a single shilling of reparation, nor a single word of apology, has ever been granted by the British state (or the Rothschilds) to the people it enslaved, or their descendants." Instead Rothschild blamed white Christians for slavery and weaponized African-Americans against them and their society even though Christianity forbade slavery, many Christian slave-owners rejected the institutions, and sought to free their slaves at the first opportunity.

British taxes were used to subsidize slave owners and their descendants for generations – a money grab that ended in 2015, the year Rothschild's 200-year contractual control of the Crown came to an end; the total redemption value of debt incurred to bankroll former slave owners reached a reported £218,338,715. "Generations of Britons have been implicated in a legacy of financial support for one of the world's most egregious crimes against humanity," *The Guardian* reports. "For the

15th to the 19th centuries, more than 11 million shackled black captives were forcibly transported to the Americas."

FOIA reports reflect that the British government paid into over 11,000 accounts over the course of the Slavery Abolition loan, which was "rebundled with other government debt many times, and never canceled or repudiated."

The University College London compiled a list of over 46,000 current individuals and groups who have received government payouts related to the abolition of slavery – including powerful British families who were being subsidized by tax-slaves. Such accounts abound whereby governments are forced to subsidize seemingly high-minded causes and contracts that warrant lavish payouts that wind up in the hands of politically-connected individuals.

The cotton trade in the South was intertwined with the British opium trade and the Rothschild crime syndicate – and played a key role in financing the expansion of the British empire under Rothschild. "Opium was the final stage in the demand cycle for British- financed and slave-produced cotton," *Dope, Inc.* reports. "British firms brought cotton to Liverpool. From there, it was spun and worked up into cloth in mills in the north of England, employing unskilled child and female labor at extremely low wages. The finished cotton goods were then exported to India, in a process that destroyed the existing cloth industry, causing widespread privation. India paid for its imported cloth (and railway cars to carry the cloth, and other British goods) with the proceeds of Bengali opium exports to China. Without the final demand of Chinese opium sales, the entire world structure of British trade would have collapsed."

Cotton was Britain's biggest import, transforming Britain into the "workshop of the world;" slave labor fueled the British Empire. The cotton industry peaked before the First World War. "By the time shots were fired on Fort Sumter in April 1861, cotton was the core ingredient of the world's most important manufacturing industry," *The Atlantic* reports. "The manufacture of cotton yarn and cloth had grown into 'the greatest industry that ever had or could by possibility have ever existed in any age or country,' according to the self-congratulatory but essentially accurate account of British cotton merchant John Benjamin Smith. By multiple measures - the sheer numbers employed, the value of output, profitability —the cotton empire had no parallel."

Rothschild backed the Abolition movement and instigated the Civil War, pitting brother against brother – and the nation against itself, causing blood to run on the streets. In turn, society was needlessly devastated, families were uprooted, and the nation was plunged into debt – to Rothschild. The Rothschild's hand in the Civil War is documented in a Rothschild biography that references a London meeting where an "International Banking Syndicate" decided to pit the American North against the South as part of a "divide and conquer" strategy. German Chancellor Otto von Bismarck even remarked, "The division of the United States into federations of equal force was decided long before the Civil War. These bankers were afraid that the United States…would upset their financial domination over the world. The voice of the Rothschilds prevailed."

The Rothschild crime syndicate expanded into North America by way of the Scottish Rite for Freemasonry, which promoted the global slave and opium trade. For example, the Viceroy to India, James Bruce, a relation of Scottish Rite Freemason founder Sir Robert the Bruce, supervised the Caribbean slave trade as Jamaican Governor General from 1842 to 1846; he was then appointed Britain's Ambassador to China during the Second Opium War.

In 1843, the Scottish rite established the B'nai B'rith (also known as the Constitutional Grand Lodge of the Order of the Sons of the Covenant) in Manhattan. The group was described by the *Executive Intelligence Review* as a "covert intelligence front for the Montefiores and Rothschilds."

Meanwhile, in Europe, revolution was raging across the continent, destabilizing Christian society while revolutionaries targeted, looted, and assassinated Christian leaders and overthrew Christian governments, replacing them with Rothschild puppet regimes.

Rothshild networks then insinuated throughout society and into leadership positions and throughout the trades. The dirty tricks arm of the Scottish freemasonry became the Order of Zion, founded by London based "Hofjuden," or "court Jews," whose families trace back to the establishment of the Bank of England, which was established by Scottish freemasons – and before that, "to an alliance with the piratical financiers of post-Renaissance Genoa," *Dope, Inc.* reports

The Order of Zion answered to foreign financial interests within the British Board of Deputies whose President was Lord Lionel Walter

Rothschild to whom the Balfour Declaration was addressed, promising him Israel as a home for the Jews. Montefiore presided over the Order of Zion, which established the leadership of the Confederate South which represented the slave owners, *Dope Inc.* reports.

As President, Abraham Lincoln had promised to rescind the 1863 National Banking Act, which reinstated Rothschild's private central bank. Before he could fulfill this promise, Lincoln wsa struck down at Ford Theater. The trigger man was John Wilkes Booth, who had just met with Simon Wolf, who presided over the B'nai B'rith in Washington, DC. According to *Dope, Inc.,* Judah Benjamin, a leader in the Order of Zion leader, was among the individuals who ordered the assassination. Alluding to the foreign network working behind the scenes to subvert the United States, the President's granddaughter writes in *This One Mad Ac*t that Booth had met with "mysterious Europeans" before the assassination.

While the cotton plantation owners received a generous, multi-generational payout from the British government, the slaves were denied their promised land, and forced to return to a life of toil on the plantations for meager wages, minus the protections and support they had previously enjoyed as slaves – such as room, board, and amenities. At the same time, the American people who had spilled their blood to end the evil institution of slavery were enslaved through debt and then blamed for an institution they had rejected.

While Lincoln has been celebrated as one of the greatest Presidents who ever lived, according to historians, he too was a British agent and President not of the United States, but of a Rothschild corporation dba the U.S. federal government, under color-of-law.

Enslaving the American People

In March, 1861 the Southern States walked out of Congress and in so doing destroyed the original union created by the Articles of Confederation (1781), Alaska Common Law Judge Anna Von Reitz writes. The syndicate "promptly wrote their own articles and re-created a union of Confederate States of America thereby eroding states rights," she writes. "(To) this day, it is the only actual and lawful union of sovereign states left standing on this continent. The Northern States under Lincoln quickly devolved into a military dictatorship. Lincoln assumed the role of Commander-in-Chief and ordered the members of Congress back into session. They still serve at the President's pleasure" – that is, the President of a Rothschild-created corporation, rather than a true representative government.

During the Civil War, the nation was torn apart, with Americans pitted against their own neighbors, brother against brother, and countrymen against themselves at the cost of lives, livelihoods, and limbs. Meanwhile, Lehman bankers were generating a fortune in blood money, smuggling arms to the South, their constituents, and cotton, the syndicate's product, to the North.

The war plunged the nation into debt that was valued then at more than $100 million to the bankers for a war that had never received the required approval from Congress to fight in the first place. The debt was generated by the Rothschild corporation dba as the federal government and was not the responsibility of the American people and yet the bankers acted as if the burden was America's to bear.

After the Civil War, the 1863 National Banking Act reinstated a private central bank. According to Von Reitz, the American people have been deceived on many accounts on the Civil War and other matters by the financial interests surrounding the City of London, which all lead back to Rothschild and its underhanded schemes to fleece the American people. Neither Lincoln nor the Civil War are what the American people were led to believe they were.

In 1868, Gen. Ulysses Grant, who was named Hiram Grant, at birth, had led the Union to "victory" during the Civil War, established a British Crown Corporation in Scotland called "The United States of America, Incorporated," Von Reitz writes. "And from there on, the only big change in the operation of this big con game against the actual American government and the people of our states and against our Constitution, is the entry of the Roman Catholic Church to take part in the same fraud for a share of the takings in 1921."

Lincoln "suspended the right of Habeas Corpus for the U.S. citizens and also pretended to have authority to suspend the Constitution of the United States of America and replace it with the Lieber code," Von Reitz writes. Lincoln was never the "President of our Federation of States."

Rather, he was *a* President of a corporation, but not *the* President of the confederation of united states. A new British corporation was established in 1868 to replace the United States of America Corporation

Lincoln had bankrupted in 1863; the new Scottish commercial corporation called itself The United States of America, Incorporated as a means to "gain access to the credit (of the American people) much the way any credit card hacker does," she writes.

This corporation, in turn, went bankrupt in 1907.

The legacy of the Civil War, Von Reitz writes, was the enslavement of "everyone in a modern system of commercial feudalism that was engineered in Great Britain by Benjamin Disraeli as a means to fund the Raj in India and vastly increase the wealth and political power of Queen Victoria. What we call the American Civil War, or War of Secession, was, in fact, an illegal commercial mercenary war for profit staged on our shores by two foreign commercial companies vying for control of our commerce and our natural resources (between Dutch India Company and the British Crown). This time, the Brits nominally won, with the South left in ruins and the North left in bankruptcy and the American people and their states saddled again with the expense of the conflict."

Fraud vitiates contracts, essentially rendering them null and void, she writes. Therefore it would appear that the fraud the Rothschilds perpetuated upon the United States can legally be undone.

Moreover, Von Reitz maintains that Lincoln was not even the President of the republic. "Lincoln was a British Crown agent and an attorney who did not meet the requirements to be President of the united States of America, nor even President of the United States of America - but who was eligible to serve as President of the United States, and in that foreign, private, corporate office.

"Lincoln issued a phony declaration of war to start the bloodiest (mercenary) conflict in our nation's history. Everyone should have known that a Declaration of War by our own Congress was required, but millions of naive Americans didn't notice the absence of a proper Declaration from the American Congress. They accepted the words and deeds of a foreign corporation President, mistaking Lincoln for their President. He was the Queen's President instead. Lincoln followed up by ruining the Southern State of State organizations and bankrupting their Northern counterparts, replacing them, on an emergency basis, with British Territorial business organizations instead. In this way, the Brits gained an illegal control of our State's business functions."

How did he enslave Americans? According to Von Reitz, "Lincoln launched the Greenbacks, a foreign military scrip that based its value on the lives and energy of British Territorial U.S. Citizens and sold the U.S. Citizens into bondage and indentured servitude for periods of 10 or 40 years, in exchange for gold exchanged for Greenbacks. The scheme worked like this: Lincoln's Government issued gold-backed bonds that promised a high rate of return after either ten or forty years, which were called 1040 Bonds. Yes, the same 1040 you are familiar with. However, in order to buy these bonds, you had to first exchange your gold or gold certificates for the new scrip, and use Greenbacks to buy these new bonds.

"When these bonds matured and investors sought to redeem them (cash them in for the return of their gold plus more gold as profit) General Sherman asked them what they used to purchase the bonds? Why, Greenbacks, of course. Then why should you expect anything but Greenbacks in return?

"Their answer, that they had been promised gold-backed bonds, was ignored. By voluntarily using the private military scrip to buy the bonds, they had also given up their gold and their right to demand gold in return. They were snookered by the treasonous Lincoln Administration and the equally crooked and treasonous British Territorial U.S. Generals supporting all this fraud and oppression."

"Lincoln's greatest act of fraud came in 1863, when he adopted the so-called Lieber Code otherwise known as General Order 100, and began issuing Executive Orders as Commander in Chief, and claiming non-existent Emergency Powers," she writes. "Just after bankrupting the Northern State of State business organizations that were members of the original Confederation, Lincoln entrusted the nation's fate and its money to the military and claimed to set aside the Constitution (the one he was working under anyway) and the Public Laws of the Federal Republic and all other laws, except for the Lieber Code. Fortunately for all of us, Lincoln had no such authority ever granted to him in any office, Public or private, and a criminal act of usurpation, fraud, and breach of treaty, trust, and contract is utterly void."

What is the ultimate agenda of the syndicate? According to Von Reitz: "They propose to steal the private wealth of Americans (just as they did via the Greenbacks Scheme) and our so-called Trust Funds and property interests. They propose to give our land (which they don't own any interest in) to the Lakota Sioux Nation, and they propose to make us use a worthless digital coinage --- still in violation of the Constitution --- and they propose to continue to issue fiat money and the only basis of value their fiat money has relies on peonage, enslavement, and extortion. These miscreants propose to simply change hands, left to right, from one group of pirates in possession of our stolen property, to another group of pirates in secondary possession of our stolen property--- and that means, building on more sand, more lies, more fraud. Everything must revert to the actual owners (States) and the actual sovereigns (people) of this country and the cadastral survey, physical landmarks, and United States Land Patents must be honored as private assets."

The Breach of Trust and fraud by officers of "Her Royal Majesty Victoria counts as one of the greatest crimes in history and it has continued to plague and confuse this nation and the world ever since. At the end of the war, the perpetrators of these crimes pretended to abolish slavery, while in fact enshrining slavery as a permanent part their government."

Whether the Rothschilds orchestrated the assassination of President Lincoln and spurred the Civil War or not is a question for another book. Whatever the case, the dynasty has sought to hide and obfuscate the details surrounding this act. It appears that the Rothschilds have attempted to obscure their role. Rothschild dynasty biographer, Niall Ferguson observed a "substantial and unexplained gap" in the family's private correspondence between 1854 and 1860. All copies of outgoing letters penned by the Rothschilds of London during the Civil War period "were destroyed at the orders of successive partners," he writes. If they had done nothing wrong, illegal, or damning during that period, why hide it, particularly when the family has marketed itself the world over as the greatest benefactors of mankind and sought to document their so-called greatness in books, films, and museums for all to marvel at in awe.

Tellingly, after Lincoln was slain, Salmon Rothschild, whose family emerged from the ghettos, snidely remarked of the President: "He rejects all forms of compromise. He has the appearance of a peasant and can only tell barroom stories." Of the loss of over 500,000 American lives to the Rothschild-orchestrated Civil War, Jacob Rothschild told Henry Sanford, the U.S. Minister to Belgium: "When your patient is desperately sick, you try desperate measures, even bloodletting."

Genesis of the Fed

At the turn of the 20th century, the Rothschilds had conceived a vision for the British Empire – one that involved eliminating Germany as a competitor to British industry; restoring the United States to colonial status, curtailing Russian commercial dominance, and establishing a global monopoly on wealth, power, and commerce. One of the vehicles through which the Rothschild crime syndicate established financial control over the United States was through the Federal Reserve (central banking) system. The campaign to establish the Fed was bankrolled by Standard Oil founder John D. Rockefeller, an agent of Rothschild and the Fed's largest shareholder.

In 1912, the United States of America – that is, the Trust Management Organization (the U.S. corporation) was purchased by a "consortium of banks (dba) the Federal Reserve," Neil Keenan's writes in *Securing the Global Collateral Accounts*. "By 1913 they had pushed through the Federal Reserve Act and via legal tender laws, began a purposeful agenda to devalue the American dollar and bankrupt the original corporation (dba) the United States of America, Inc."

Once the Federal Reserve was established as the nation's central bank, it was granted stewardship of the nation's gold by the corporation dba as the federal government. Upon acquiring possession of the gold, which was deposited at Ft. Knox, the Rockefellers allegedly absconded with it. "Through control, direct and indirect of both the Federal Reserve and the top officials of the U.S. Treasury, David Rockefeller was able to remove it," said Export-Import counsel Peter Beter, who served under President John F. Kennedy. "American dollars transformed into IOUs from the Fed (and) the U.S. Mint, a branch of the Treasury Department, (was) reduced to a mere printing press for dollars."

The Federal Reserve System, Keenan writes, is financially owned and controlled by the Crown Temple in the City of London from Switzerland, "the home and legal original for the charters of the United Nations, the International Monetary Fund, the World Trade Organization, and most importantly, the Bank of International Settlements."

The 1929 stock market crash was reportedly engineered by these interests so that America's stock could be purchased for pennies on the dollar, reflecting a strategy pursued by Rothschild against Britain during the Napoleonic Wars. By employing this scheme in the United States, the

Rothschilds were able to purchase majority shares in America's corporations, thereby providing the dynasty a controlling interest in them.

A report published by the University of New Mexico by an oil industry insider with connections to the House of Saud, reported that eighty percent of the ownership of the New York Federal Reserve Bank, was controlled by eight families, including Goldman Sachs, the Rockefellers, Lehmans, and Kuhn Loebs of New York, the Rothschilds, the Lazards, and Israel Moses Seif.

The report also establishes that ten banks control all twelve Federal Reserve Banks, including N.M Rothschild of London, the Rothschild Bank of Berlin, the Warburg Bank of Hamburg, the Warburg Bank of Amsterdam, Lehman Brothers of New York, Lazard Brothers of Paris, Kuhn Loeb Bank of New York, Israel Moses Seif Bank of Italy, Goldman Sachs of New York, and JP Morgan Chase Bank of New York.

The Federal Reserve Act was conceived on Jekyll Island in 1909 and passed on Christmas eve in 1913. If the American republic, as established by the nation's founders, were properly functioning, then the Federal Reserve Act could never have passed as it never received a quorum.

Congress adjourned on the 20th of December – days before the Federal Reserve Act was submitted to Congress and when members of both chambers, "except for a few Senators who had been hand picked to stay long enough to pass the Act, left for their homes for the Christmas Holidays," Texas Congressman Sam Rayburn writes in a letter.

On December 24, Senators Carter Glass and Nelson Aldrich submitted the Federal Reserve Act to President Woodrow Wilson for a signature even though a quorum had never received, read, reviewed, or voted on the legislation. Upon receiving the bill, President Woodrow Wilson promptly signed it into law. According to Myron Fagan, the legislation served the purpose of wrestling control of U.S. money "out of Congress and to an international system to enable (international bankers, led by the House of Rothschild), to loot the country's assets,"

The usurpers then lied about the bill, claiming in newspapers that a majority of the members of the U.S. Senate and the House of Representatives had voted in favor of it. The truth was, only two members of the Senate had signed off on when Congress was in recess. The bill did not have a companion bill presented or passed in the House. The required majority hadn't been obtained. Moreover, he writes, the Federal Reserve

Act was neither constitutional nor legal – since the U.S Constitution codifies that the the right to regulate the U.S. monetary system is the exclusive preserve of Congress, not a privately owned bank.

Over the years, the U.S. Supreme Court has consistently affirmed that only Congress has the constitutional right to print money, as written in the Article 1, Section 8, Paragraph 5 of the U.S. Constitution; "Congress shall have the power to coin (also print) money and regulate the value thereof."

The bill was presented and signed off on by Rothschild agents who were employees of a Rothschild corporation, not the representative government established by the Founding Fathers. Most people simply were unaware that the nation had been hijacked as the syndicate lent the impression that business was carrying on as usual, with a fully functioning system of checks and balances, which had been neutralized. That the syndicate had to lie about the votes it never received – and the fact that no Congressman attempted to repeal the legislation or contest its legitimacy, reflects that the federal government was, by then, operating under color of law.

Fagan blames Congress for not repealing the law, but if the legislation had not even passed in the first place, how could it be repealed? Arguably, it shouldn't have taken effect. It could only have taken effect if by virtue of the fact that the federal government had, by then, transformed into a Rothschild corporation and was therefore merely executing a corporate directive.

In a revealing interview, a reporter asked Federal Reserve Chairman Alan Greenspan what the "proper relationship" should be "between the Chairman of the Fed and a President of the United States" to which Greenspan responded: "The Federal Reserve is an independent agency. And that means basically that, uh, there is no other agency of government which can overrule actions that we take."

But the Fed essentially created itself. No act of Congress, legitimate or otherwise, ever established it, reflecting that the United Stated had fallen into the clutches of predatory foreign bankers.

Once Wilson signed the legislation, the House of Rothschild was granted "license to commit every act of lawlessness," including "the federal income tax," Fagan writes, attributing to the dynasty "every Depression, practically every bank failure, and the terrible, and utterly unnecessary national debt, and the poverty of the vast majority of our people while vast amounts of the produce of our nation are being deliberately and intentionally destroyed."

The South Sea Company

When the Federal Reserve was established, foreign bankers surrounding the City of London had not invented the mouse trap. Rather they were replicating a centuries-old scheme honed to perfection among British bankers, merchants, and freemasons to generate untold wealth for themselves through government debt – a practice in which America's founders were well aware and against which they erected protective barriers.

By allowing England's illegal re-colonization of the United States, the British financial freemasonic aristocracy has been allowed to take root in the United States and spread, like cancer, to the point of strangling a nation established as a financially sound, prosperous confederation of states united under a representative federal government restrained by a carefully constructed constitution which enshrined the rights of it citizenry in a Bill of Rights.

The origins of the modern day economic bubble trace back to the South Sea Company, a privately owned joint-stock company competing against the Bank of England for the opportunity to finance the debt of the British government. The South Sea Company and the Bank of England provided the templates upon which the Federal Reserve was modeled.

The idea conceived by the rapacious bankers was to print money out of thin air; extend loans with interest; and control the finances of the nation while manipulating foreign affairs in such a way as to enhance their profit margins and expand their markets.

The South Sea Bubble is dramatized in David Liss' compelling, must-read mystery novel, Conspiracy of Paper, *which breathes life into familiar financial fraud, placing it in the 18th century, raising questions of whether bankers have forgotten history or whether they have studied it and refined old strategies to perfection.*

The South Sea Company (SSC) was established as a join-stock company and public-private partnership in 1711 to consolidate and finance the British national debt. Like the East India Company, the SSC profited from the slave trade. Debt was generated through war and miscellaneous expenditures acquired while seeking markets and resources overseas.

Headquartered at Threadneedle Street at the center of the City of London, the SSC specialized in insider trading. By exploiting its access to government and by bribing government officials, the SSC purchased its own shares with its own money to pump up its value and create the illusion of profits that were illusory while hyping opportunities to generate wealth. They relied upon insider knowledge to purchase debt before government debt consolidations, enabling them to make quick profits and get out before everyone else lost their collective shirts.

The British government relied heavily upon private financing long before Rothschild got into the game. Its techniques were supported by such institutions as Hoare's Bank, whose owners were associated with the Society for Promoting Christian Knowledge, a Christian-based charity dedicated to increasing the awareness of the Christian faith throughout the world. Established as C. Hoare & Co., Hoare's Bank is one of Great Britain's oldest privately owned banks.

The primary bank and lender of choice for the British government was the Bank of England. Established in 1694 as a private bank, the Bank of England was a private institution; its ownership was held by private shareholders, including wealthy individuals and members of the nobility. As England's central bank, the Bank of England has managed the national debt and provided financial stability.

In 1710, the British government was dissatisfied with the service it was receiving from the Bank of England, which had established a monopoly as government lender.

The Chancellor of the Exchequer sought out alternatives for its debt management while Britain struggled to meet its financial obligations. Debt was accumulating from two simultaneous wars, among other obligations, including payroll for the British Army.

The Chancellor attempted to consolidate the debt, as the Bank of England had done previously; it therefore created the South Sea Company for this purpose. The creditors were required to surrender their debt to the new company which promised to issue new shares in the SSC at the same value.

The British government agreed to make an annual payment to the SSC at interest and distribute payments to shareholders as dividends.

While marketing opportunities for great wealth, the SSC was aware that it did not have money to invest and that the government was unable to honor its debt. New investors helped the SSC service loans and buy time while the bankers made out like bandits.

The SSC was one of a number of joint-stock companies making unsubstantiated, fraudulent, claims in order to raise money. Some companies lacked legal basis while others, like the Hollow Sword Blade - the SSCs banker - used existing companies for purposes contrary to their founding charters. For example, The York Buildings Company, which was established to deliver water, was acquired by Case Billingsley who repurposed the company to confiscate Jacobite estates so that it could purchase an insurance company.

The schemes perpetuated by British bankers, Christian and Jewish alike, were replicated many times over, deceptions and all, by the Rockefellers, Rothschilds, and their affiliated bankers and corporations in United States and around the world. Modern international bankers have used these antecedents as templates, strategies, and inspirations to enrich themselves and establish monopolies through public-private partnerships while devastating nations and their citizens and separating them of their wealth.

The more wars, contracts, projects, and schemes they could finagle with and through the government, the more markets they could rig, insider tracks they could acquire, and debt they could finance, the wealthier they could become.

The people who served as intermediaries between brokers and British society were called Stock Jobbers whose tricks of the trade were documented in such publications as The Anatomy of Exchange Alley and The Villainy of Stock Jobbers Detected.

One of their strategies involved forging interdependent relationships among the government, British Monarchy, and company, creating companies that were deemed "too big to fail" and were therefore exempted from strict oversight and kept afloat by any means and deception necessary; in turn, they left others holding the tab for their greed, incompetence, mismanagement, and debt. Other schemes involved transforming government debt into shares of a company and then marketing the shares for profit.

The South Sea company ultimately collapsed in 1720.

This is year in which the South Sea Company proposed a scheme to assume British national debt in exchange for government annuities, leading to a speculative frenzy. Investors bought shares in the company with the expectations of quick profits. A financial bubble followed, leading many to financial ruin while sparking a national financial crisis.

The collapse of the South Sea Company contributed to the Bank of England's growing influence as a stabilizing force in the English financial system.

Coincidentally, the idea for the SSC was conceived by William Paterson, the founder of the Bank of England and member of the Scottish Rite of Freemasons – a secret society that ultimately gave rise to the underhanded financial schemes that recaptured the United States as a British colony centuries later.

After the South Sea Company collapsed, the Bank of England became the exclusive banker to the British government, like the Federal Reserve. The Bank of England then was nationalized, as the Fed is now.

America's founders specifically limited the right to print money to Congress to prevent bubbles and to force the government to operate within a budget while ensuring the American people were not enslaved by debt.

Paterson made his fortune through the slave trade – and the Worshipful Merchant Taylors Company. Originally known as the Guild and Fraternity of St. John the Baptist in the City of London, which was incorporated under a Royal charter in 1327, the Merchants transformed from a tailoring society into a philanthropic and social group associated with Savile Row.

Its membership included "radical Protestants and Catholics," who were dedicated to St. John the Baptist, a Jewish antecedent and cousin of Jesus.

Both the Jewish St. John the Baptist and St. John the Evangelist, an apostle, are the patron saints of freemasonry.

In the Gospel of St. John it is written: "In the beginning was the word, and the word was with God, and the word was God." The masonic "word," refers to the secrets of freemasonry, including protection (privileges) for the brotherhood and access to work (by way monopolies and through exclusive, inside channels), approaches antithetical to the free society envisioned by the founders of the United States, despite their freemasonic heritage.

The Bank of England was nationalized in 1946. In 1998, the bank became an independent public organization wholly owned by the Treasury Solicitor on behalf of the government, but with a mandate to support the economic policies of the government. It was afforded independence to maintain price stability.

In the late 1990's, when the petrodollar was waning and the Saudi central bank was on the rise, the British government awarded the bank the freedom to set interest rates, "helping to make central bankers the most powerful financial actors in the world, not only setting rates, but also buying trillions of dollars worth of assets, targeting exchange rates and managing economic cycles," the Economist *reports.*

II.
Securing Saudi Oil

"There are two ways to conquer and enslave a country. One is by the sword.
The other is by debt. Always stand on principle, even if you stand alone."

President John Adams
American Founding Father

By the end of the 19th century, Standard Oil founder John D. Rockefeller had achieved billionaire status. Backed by bankers with London connections, like J.P. Morgan, the Rockefellers aligned with other robber barons to pursue "public policy for private gain," with a view to establishing a global monopoly on wealth and power.

In 1917, Harry St. John Birdger Philby discovered oil on the Saudi peninsula. The father of Kim Philby, a member of the British Secret Service who provided intelligence to the British government, the elder Philby spied for Soviet Premier Joseph Stalin. The younger Philby cultivated Flora Solomon, a daughter of Russian banker and gold dealer Grigori Bensenson, who had made his fortune in Baku oil. The Baku region attracted leading petroleum companies from around the world. As Prime Minister Winston Churchill once quipped, "If oil is a queen, Baku is her throne."

A Rothschild relation, Philby worked for the KGB to "destroy imperialism" – that is, to crush empires so that the City of London could claim their colonial interests for Rothschild.

During the Russian Revolution, the Communists were directed to destroy Russia's oil industry. Afterward, the doors to the Soviet Empire flung open for Rockefeller to restore the fields and establish a monopoly for Standard Oil, with the competition effectively obliterated. The Rockefellers consolidated a base of power within the Kremlin and established dominion over Soviet oil which then produced nearly 30 percent of the world's supply.

For a while, the British aristocracy believed that Rothschild was ruthlessly working on their behalf, to help them all grow rich, perhaps not appreciating Rothschild's double play – that of saying one thing and doing another, and playing all players in the game of monopoly against each other until the dynasty remained the last player standing.

The City of London followed up on Philby's discovery to claim the oil on the Saudi peninsula while Rothschild set its sights on the conquest of the United States. With assistance from the British, Ibn Sa'ud became King of the newly created Kingdom of Saudi Arabia and established a Privy Council in the pattern of the British Monarchy, with Philby as his advisor.

By this time, "several American companies were interested in testing the oil potential of this realm," Matthew Simmons writes in *Twilight in the Desert.* "(The King) was also growing desperate to find new sources of revenue to replace the declining fees collected from dwindling numbers of pilgrims journeying to Mecca.

"Philby told the King that Arabia was 'like a man sleeping atop buried treasure' and suggested (he) take steps to develop Saudi mineral resources. (The) King responded that he would give a mineral or oil concession (in exchange) for one million British pounds."

Eager to tap Saudi oil, Philby arranged a meeting between the Saudi Royals and Charles Crane, an American multi-millionaire from the Crane Plumbing family. With an opening created for the Americans, Standard Oil of California (SoCal) convinced the Saudis to allow a subsidiary, the Bahrain Petroleum Company, to explore oil in the region. Through exploration, the oil men discovered the extent of Saudi Arabia's oil resources. The oil fields were large enough to fuel the development of the world.

In 1933, SoCal was granted a concession to drill oil on the Peninsula. After the Americans were directed to turn in their gold to the federal government, the Saudis were loaned 50,000 pounds of gold. In turn, the oil executives agreed to pay the Saudis £1 for every ton of oil produced.

After securing the exclusive rights to explore and produce oil in the region, SoCal transformed the kingdom into the most important oil producer on the planet. Four of the "Seven Sisters," including Exxon, Shell, British Petroleum, Mobil, Chevron, Texaco, and Gulf became the sole owners of the newly formed Saudi oil company, Aramco, a position they held until the Saudi oil company was nationalized.

War for Saudi Oil

The Rothschilds generally worked through, rather than on behalf of nations. Their strategy needed to be executed in such a way that the public and anyone else who could obstruct their plans remained oblivious to the agenda afoot. Strategies were advanced behind the banner of high-minded rhetoric that often cloaked an insidious, self-serving agenda. Indeed Rothschild had no qualms about destroying the nations that were foolish enough to engage them. The dynasty pit nation against nation while bankrolling and managing all sides. Through the skirmish, the dynasty amassed a tremendous fortune while the other players advanced towards a pre-determined outcome that eventually led to their doom.

By the turn of the 20th century, the Rothschilds had consolidated power around the City of London. . They controlled the Crown – its affiliated media, government, and intelligence networks. After having built up British industry, the Rothschilds proceeded to destroy it in order to rebuild it under the dynasty's control. While citizens remained loyal to their own country, the Rothschilds were only loyal to themselves. Once an interest of ally had served the dynasty's purpose, it was put out to pasture.

Few were aware of the machinations of the dynasty since they worked through proxies and controlled public perception through the media. Healthy, morally upright individuals who tended to hold positions of responsibility could not conceive of or anticipate the sheer evil and degeneracy of the Rothschilds, who had billed themselves as the benefactors of mankind.

After having built up German and British industry, the Rothschilds then pit the nations against each other in a contest for market dominance, and then used that contest to separate Saudi oil from the British and hand it over to the United States, its next mark.

For centuries, the British enjoyed amicable relations with the Arabs. Rothschild was keen to disrupt these relationships with a view to placing its own compliant assets into positions of power throughout its expanding sphere of influence.

The transfer of Saudi oil from the Brits to the Rockefellers, a powerful U.S. proxy, occurred under the cover of the World Wars. By this point, the United States held the potential to overtake the British Empire as a global power, and so the Rothschilds were all too keen to hasten the demise of the British and build up the United States, until this nation had served its purpose at which point it too would be discarded.

As far as the Rothschild's were concerned, the British Empire had outlived its usefulness, and so the United States, its next target, was manipulated into a war that would further entrap it within a Rothschild spiderweb.

With a view to seizing Saudi oil, the Rockefellers built up Germany as a threat to Britain – through a plan conceived in the city of London. The terrified British appealed to the appeal to the Americans to enter the war on its behalf. Rockefeller, the shadow power behind the federal government, agreed to convince the United States to join the war as long as the Brits surrendered control of Saudi oil, a concession the Brits reluctantly made.

Under the cover of war, Rockefeller merged German companies into IG Farben and then seized markets the British had abandoned for itself. In 1929, Rockefeller established a cartel between IG Farben and Standard Oil of New Jersey to prevent the companies from competing against each other. While Rockefeller served as the shadow power and advisor behind the U.S. federal government, IG Farben operated exclusively to the benefit of the Germans and to the disadvantage of the United States, effectively placing the Rockefellers in a position of committing treason as they harvested the wealth, power, resources, and manpower of the United States to advance Rothschild power around the globe.

Once the Germans were defeated, the bitter Brits obstructed Standard Oil's efforts to gain access to the Saudi oil. Unable to tap the lucrative Saudi oil fields, the Rockefellers built up Nazi Germany and then pit Germany against the British, leading the Brits to appeal for U.S. support once again. Rockefeller offered to convince a reluctant United States to enter the war – but only if the Brits surrendered Saudi oil and cleared the passage for Standard Oil to drill in the Kingdom, terms to which the British agreed. Hitler's Germany never would have acquired the power it had had the Rockefellers not provided the fuel for its rampage through Europe.

Once the new terms had been established, the Rockefellers unleashed the military might of the United States to crush Nazi Germany while generating lucrative government contracts for itself and its corporate allies, before, during, and after the war. Nazi scientists acquired access to powerful ancient tech by way of China and were then recruited into the U.S. military industrial complex while Nazis planned the Fourth Reich from Madrid, with a view to establishing a global dictatorship.

Control of Saudi oil made the Rockefellers even wealthier than before. Not only had this acquisition cost them nothing, but this result came at the expense of millions of innocent lives, a loss of $4.1 trillion (based upon the current value of the dollar), and the erosion of national sovereignty, rendering the United States increasingly vulnerable to foreign intrigue. While Standard Oil developed Saudi oil, the Saudis reportedly financed Rockefeller's multinationals and their expansion throughout the world, with oil proceeds, at 5 cents a barrel.

The Bretton Woods financial system was launched in 1944 to establish an international monetary and financial order among independent sovereign nations. The United Nations Monetary and Financial Conference (or Bretton Woods conference) was held in Bretton Woods, New Hampshire, a state Pandora Box whistle blower Mike Gill has identified as a key linchpin in international money laundering, drug running, and transnational crime.

The conference launched the International Bank for Reconstruction and Development, which became part of the World Bank Group; and the International Monetary Fund. The World Bank extended loans to the Third World – through which concessions were granted to the shadow elite who acquired and dominated markets around the world through public-private partnerships.

In 1947, the World Bank suggested that Ibn Saud be the source of development loans instead of the U.S. Export-Import Bank – the Saudi King enthusiastically agreed to this role. Ibn Saud was opposed to Zionism – and by extension, the Rothschilds, unaware that the Rothschild Zionists were in control of the United States through proxy. While fond of Jews, who were "good friends of the Arabs," he rejected Rothschild Zionism – as did many prominent Jews within the United States, including acclaimed physicist Albert Einstein.

In 1957, Saudi Arabia became development partner of the World Bank, providing the institution the oil and resources it needed to develop the Third World so that corporations could tap those markets. The U.S, dollar, which was backed by gold, became the global reserve currency – while Rothschild controlled the value of gold through its gold exchanges in London, and the World Bank determined the price of oil in global markets. With the dollar now unleashed, the financial interests around the City of London, which controlled the Federal Reserve, were able to print money, backed by gold, that was then distributed around the world for "development" purposes, thereby helping politically-connected corporations corner markets by way of lucrative government contracts that enriched a few while the many were left holding the debt.

With the European continent ravaged by war, the Rothschilds blamed nationalism, rather than themselves. To avoid the horrors of war, nations must pool their resources, surrender their sovereignty, and become interdependent, Rothschild advised as the dynasty established governing bureaucracies around them. Rothschild established the European Coal and Steel Community, as a nascent common market and precursor to the European Union which would be governed by unelected European bureaucrats. A European Central Bank followed after. A London Gold Pool Agreement was established in 1961 with the goal of "coordinating the gold operations in London of certain European central banks and the Federal Reserve Bank of New York.

III.
The Rise of the National Crime Syndicate

"Remember, democracy never lasts long. It soon wastes, exhausts, and murders itself. There never was a democracy yet that did not commit suicide."

President John Adams
American Founding Father

"Without the (Anti-Defamation League)'s undaunted public relations work on behalf of organized crime, the United States would never have been flooded with illegal drugs, and gangsters (would) have long ago have been carted off to the penitentiary," the editors of the *Executive Intelligence Review* (*EIR*) report in the *Ugly Truth about the ADL* (Anti-Defamation League).

The Rothschild crime syndicate is an extension of the Scottish Rite of Freemasonry, which established the ADL and the B'nai B'rith in the United States to project its influence. While planned from the City of London, the U.S. Civil War, the Chinese Communist Revolution, the Russian Revolution, the World Wars, the assassination of American leaders, race wars, terrorism – and in international human trafficking, child exploitation, drug and arms trafficking, societal destabilization, and the looting of nations, companies, and assets of citizens reflected the networks and coordination of the freemasons (and Jesuits), reflecting a single-mindedness of purpose that extended into the banking system.

In 1913, Chicago attorney Sigmund Livingston assumed leadership of the Anti-Defamation League (ADL) of B'nai B'rith. Reflecting the syndicate's network of interests, Livingston's clients included Alton Railways - a company owned by William Moore, an Episcopalian who partnered with JP Morgan, the banker to the robber barons who served the interests of the City of London. Moore's family sat on the Board of IBM – an American multinational which provided the technology Nazis used to track and trace Jews in concentration camps. In fact, IBM owes its market dominance to its early collaboration with the Nazis.

In 1903, the Moores established the Bankers Trust Company (BTC), which holds the reserves of other banks and trust companies –

and loans them money. Within 12 years, the Bankers Trust had grown to process over $30 billion in business. Among its Presidents was Benjamin Strong, Jr., the first governor of the Federal Bank of New York and a founder of the Federal Reserve System, which drew its inspiration from the Bank of England (BOE), which was established by the Scottish Rite of Freemasonry as a private bank entrusted to private shareholders.

In 1999, Deutsche Bank acquired BTC and spun off its Trust and Custody division to State Street Corporation four years later. JP Morgan, the banker of choice for the robber barons, retained voting power and a controlling interest in the company.

The Moore family bankrolled the ADL, According to ADL National Director Jonathan Greenblatt, the organization works closely with the FBI and has established relationships with all social media, including Twitter, etc. to track and trace "extremism," particularly with regards to antisemitism.

August Belmont worked on Rothschild's behalf to position British bankers and their freemasonic corporate representatives into key positions throughout Wall Street. Reflecting the syndicate's shadow hand, Kenneth Bialkin, an ADL executive and senior partner at Willkie Farr and Gallagher, provided defense for criminals implicated in money laundering. Willkie Farr & Gallagher reportedly engineered Robert Vesco's takeover of the Investor Overseas Service (IOS), a Swiss-based mutual funded established by the Rothschild family.

Through these networks, drugs flooded into the United States, serving a purpose similar to that which the Rothschild-controlled British Crown waged against the Chinese – that of weakening the resolve of the nation and its people, to soften them up for conquest. "Bialkin's real claim to fame is that he was a central figure in the doping of America," *EIR* reports. "Without Kenneth Bialkin's behind-the-scenes legal maneuvering, the Medellin Cartel (of Colombia) would have had a far more difficult time establishing a beachhead in the United States."

On the island of Aruba Dutch, the Sicilian Mafia and Colombia's Medellin cartel joined forces. Narcodollars then began flooding through Milan's banking system, stock market, and legitimate business—"rivers of it," according to Con-findustria, the Italian manufacturers' association.

The founder of the National Crime Syndicate and Murder Inc. was Meyer Lansky, who trained assassins for George H.W. Bush, another member of the syndicate. When Lansky decided to shift the center of underground banking operations from Switzerland to the Caribbean as part of the planned expansion of cocaine and marijuana smuggling into the United States, ADL and Bialkin engineered the move as part of a "planned expansion of cocaine and marijuana smuggling into the United States." *EIR* reports. Lansky used the IOS as a front group.

Tibor Rosembaum, a senior officer with the Mossad (Israeli intelligence) who linked with Lansky through Resorts International, owned the International Credit Bank (BCI's), which partnered with the IOS, *EIR* reports. BCI's office manager, Sylvain Ferdman, was Lansky's bagman, according to *Life* magazine.

Lansky cultivated the booze-distributing Bronfman family and launched his first offshore gambling, narcotics, and money laundering operation in Cuba where the syndicate conspired to promote vice to destroy the virtuous Judaeo-Christian United States as Rothschild advanced its plan to build its kingdom on the ashes of the world.

The Bronfmans were linked to the Rothschilds through marriage. In 1920, Lansky aligned with "Britain's dope-trading Keswick family," who founded Hongkong and Shanghai Bank of China (HSBC), which has laundered over $10 billion narcotics proceeds, according to *Dope, Inc.* As will later be discussed, HSBC has deep ties into the proverbial Deep State and Jeffrey Epstein pedophile operation.

Dope, opium, and other drugs were trafficked around the world through these channels. The Bronfman family founded Seagram's as a "legitimate" whiskey empire" after the U.S. Treasury Department "cut a deal with Sam and Abe Bronfman, (enabling) them to pay several million dollars in back taxes in return for whitewashing their decade of big-time crimes," *EIR* reports.

As newly minted multi-millionaires, the Bronfmans transformed the World Jewish Congress into an international arm of the ADL, *EIR* reports, adding that Lansky established Murder Inc. to "enforce the creation of a National Crime Syndicate overseeing the Prohibition-era illegal liquor and narcotics traffic."

Lansky enlisted Cuba and the Castros into the drug trafficking operation on behalf of the crime syndicate with a view to undermining and crushing the United States, Joseph Douglass writes in *Red Cocaine*. "Cuba's General Arnaldo Ochoa Sanchez was found guilty of helping Colombia's Medellin drug cartel smuggle cocaine into the United States," he writes. "The star witness was General Raul Castro, the Minister of

Defense, and Fidel Castro's brother, deputy, and expected successor. Several defectors had previously reported strong ties between Cuba and the cartels."

The Cuban Communists Americas Department was assigned "special responsibility for sabotage and subversion throughout the Western hemisphere," he writes.

Cuba is the primary sponsor of Colombia's M-19 guerrilla revolutionaries and is the military/terrorist arm of Colombia's Communist Party, the Revolutionary Armed Forces of Colombia (FARC), both of which produce and traffic narcotics. The U.S. and Colombian militaries partner on combined military exercises while drugs flood across the U.S.-Mexican border and the federal government mysteriously remains "powerless" to combat it.

In the 1960's, Raul Castro, first secretary of the Communist Party of Cuba and brother of Cuban dictator Fidel Castro, engaged the Soviets, leading the USSR to direct Czechoslovakia "to work with the Cubans to pave the way for an eventual Soviet takeover of Cuba," Douglass writes. "The Soviets wanted Czechoslovakia to take the lead, hiding the role of the Soviet Union. They did not want Fidel Castro to be aware of the Soviet operation to infiltrate and take over Cuba, and they did not want the United States to be alerted to what was happening." In this way, Castro served as a proxy for the Czechs who were proxies for the Soviets who were proxies for the crime syndicate led by Rothschild.

Czechoslovakia trained Cubans in military planning and operations, supplied the equipment, and organized Cuban intelligence and counter-intelligence, which was based upon British intelligence, which was based upon Jesuit intelligence, which was based upon Mongolian intelligence – and which has since become the basis for intelligence operations throughout the world, all of which ultimately serve, answer to, and work on behalf of Rothschild.

Cuba became a center of revolutionary activity in the West, allowing the Czechs, as proxy for the Soviets, "to establish an intelligence station in Cuba," Douglass writes. Rumors abound suggesting that Canadian Prime Minister Justin Trudeau is the biological son of Fidel Castro. Whether or not Trudeau is Castro's biological son, the Canadian Prime Minister is bound by oath to serve the British Monarchy, which has been controlled by Rothschild since 1815.

After the Cubans were trained to serve as Soviet intelligence assets, they received instructions from Moscow, via Czechoslovakia, to "infiltrate the United States and all Latin America, to produce and distribute drugs and narcotics," Douglass writes.

The Soviets promoted peaceful co-existence, a strategy intended not to befriend the United States but to hasten its demise. Drugs were a key part of this strategy. Cuba established drug operations in Colombia. The Soviets infiltrated drug and intelligence networks throughout the world and then set up Cuban operations throughout Latin America. "The Soviets ordered the formation of production and distribution networks all over the region – this one organized directly selected by East European intelligence service," Douglass writes. Between 1960 and 1965, the Soviet intelligence services, which answered to Moscow, established drug production, distribution, and money laundering operations throughout South, Central, and North America.

The Soviets targeted America's schools, which provided a high standard of education and moral instruction for children throughout the nation. "American schools were high priority targets because this was where the future leaders of the bourgeoisie were to be found," Douglass writes. "Another high priority target (the Soviets) identified was the American work ethic, pride, and loyalty, all of which would be undermined through drugs. Drugs and narcotics would lead to a decrease in the influence of religions (and) under certain conditions, could be used to create chaos."

The Soviets – and their shadow controllers -- established a distance between themselves and the drug operations, just as Rothschild established a distance between itself and its proxies. "Throughout Latin America, for example, while Soviet Bloc intelligence agents exercised overall control and direction, indigenous personnel were heavily relied upon to run the actual operations," Douglass writes. "Religions were viewed as an especially dangerous force within socialist countries and in all countries being prepared for revolution, given the conflict between Marxist and religious morality."

Cuba was the operational center for drug trafficking and training of revolutionary terrorists in the Caribbean, Douglass writes, conceding that "in Colombia, the Marxist M-19 revolutionaries have close ties to Cuba and various drug-traffickers, of which the most highly publicized over the years has been the organization known as the Medellin Cartel."

Claire Sterling writes in *The Threat of the New Global Network of Organized Crime* that "cooperation between criminal operatives of U.S. and Israeli intelligence can be traced back to the assistance provided to the CIA by the Meyer Lansky crime syndicate from Chicago, with which the CIA was cooperating from an early stage of its existence. (The) resulting lucrative joint Lansky-CIA international drug racketeering operations thrived against the background of deep US involvement in Southeast Asia."

According to *Dope, Inc.*, the world's illegal drug trade is "controlled by a single group of evil men," reflecting centuries of collaboration. "How is it possible that $200 billion and up in dirty money, crisscrossing international borders, can remain outside the control of the law? Only one possible answer can be admitted: a huge chunk of international banking and related financial operations have been created solely to manage dirty money. More than that, this chunk of international banking enjoys the sovereign protection a few governments."

Dope, Inc. reports that "the origin of the London-Peking joint-drug running venture in the Far East (is) the wartime deal between the Royal Institute of International Affairs and Chou En-lai."

The elite considered China the greatest prize in which to expand their markets. At the Yalta conference, which concluded World War II, Prime Minister Winston Churchill, Soviet Premier Joseph Stalin, and President Franklin Delano Roosevelt, all of whom were heavily influenced by financial interests surrounding the City of London, committed their respective nations to elevating Communist China to leader of the New World Order while relegating the United States to a bankrupt, welfare state. Henry Kissinger, a German-Jew who had been recruited as an intelligence asset during World War II was sent to the United States to fulfill this mandate on behalf of British imperialist designs.

British Prime Minister Lord Alec Douglas-Home, who advocated opening China to the West, trained Kissinger for the role he would play on the world stage. Among Douglas-Home's colleagues was Lord Bertrand Russell, a socialist who trained Chinese Communist leader Mao Tse-tung and (future Chinese Premier) Chou En Lai – Chinese leaders with whom Kissinger would engage in diplomacy as Secretary of State.

Documents released by the State Department in 1978 reflect that "the creation of the People's Republic of China included an alliance between the British dope-runners and the Chinese dope-runners," negotiated on the British side by Sir John Henry Keswick, whose family founded HSBC bank; and on the Chinese side by Chou En-lai, *Dope, Inc.* reports. The Chinese mafia were disbursed throughout the opium trade as drugs were trafficked throughout the Far East and throughout the Chinese expatriate community.

The Rothschilds effectively weaponized drugs against humanity. During the Communist Chinese Revolution, after drugs had weakened China for British imperial conquest, Mao weaponized drugs against his own people. "Mao's strategy was simple," Douglass writes. "Use drugs to soften a target area. Then, after a captured region had been secured, outlaw the use of all narcotics and impose strict controls to ensure that the poppies remained exclusively an instrument of the state for use against its enemies. (As) soon as Mao had totally secured mainland China in 1949, opium production was nationalized and trafficking of narcotics, targeted against non-Communist states, became a formal activity of the new Communist state, the People's Republic of China."

Just as the Cubans and Soviets aligned against the United States – so too did the British and Chinese – all of whom took instruction from the City of London. "The Chinese knew it and said so, and the British knew it, and said so, and American diplomats cabled home that the United States had been shafted," *Dope, Inc.* reports.

The British were behind the pro-Maoist propaganda "which began far before the Communists took over (China)," *Dope, Inc.* reports. The British celebrated leading members of Communist Chinese Party. The British and Maoists also partnered to establish the financial infrastructure of "what would later underwrite the Far East narcotics traffic."

Even before the Civil War, the Rothschild crime syndicate was trafficking Chinese slaves into the United States. "The same British trading companies behind the slave trade into the South were running a fantastic market in Chinese indentured servants into the West Coast," *Dope, Inc.* reports. "In 1846 alone, 117,000 (Chinese) coolies were brought into the country, feeding an opium trade estimated at nearly 230,000 pounds of gum opium and over 53,000 pounds of prepared (smoking) opium."

Within every country within which the Rothschild syndicate extended its claws, revolutionary activity exploded along with crime; human, drugs, and arms trafficking; money laundering; looting;

subversion; chaos. Criminal gangs and mafia took hold and proliferated within their controlled regions. "The Italian, Jewish, Ch'ao Chou Chinese, and other ethnic minorities that figure in aspects of the narcotics traffic were aligned with the British establishment," *Dope, Inc.* reports.

Even Giuseppe Mazzini, an Italian revolutionary who was credited with establishing the Italian mafia in the United States, served the Rothschild crime syndicate. The Italian mafia built itself upon the foundation laid by the B'nai B'rith and other tributaries of the syndicate. "A dynasty that has controlled Britain for hundreds of years, enjoys virtually all major positions of corporate and political power, and believes that making events happen from behind the scenes is as natural and ordinary as afternoon tea," *Dope, Inc.* reports of the seamless coordination. "When the chairmen of the boards of Britain's leading banks, trading houses, and mining companies show up at the same weddings and christenings (and bar mitzvahs) as the chiefs of British intelligence and various government ministries, there is no need for the formal trappings of conspiracy."

At the direction of British Prime Minister Benjamin Disraeli, who was bankrolled by Rothschild, Mazzini sponsored the Mafia in Italy. He then directed the members of his "Young Italy" movement to infiltrate the United States by way of the channels established by Albert Pike, a prominent member of the Scottish Rite of Freemasonry.

Through these criminal networks, opium and other drugs were trafficked into the United States. "Not coincidentally, the first large-scale importing of opium into the United States coincided with the coolie trade," which was sponsored by HSBC, *Dope, In*c. reports.

The Russian Revolution was another blood-letting sponsored and coordinated by the syndicate. As evidence of this, Simon Wolf, B'nai B'rith's representative in Washington, DC, led international efforts to tar the Russian czar as "anti-Semitic" before Wall Street mobilized funding to topple the regime. "American Jewish organizations, led from behind the scenes by the B'nai B'rith, began funneling guns to the anti-Czarist insurrectionists," the *EIR* reports. "B'nai B'rith, the Warburg family of Kuhn, Loeb and Company (went on to) fund (Russian Revolutionaries) (Vladimir) Lenin and Leon Trotsky; and father and son Bolshevik agents Julius and Armand Hammer, who helped found the U.S. Communist Party, (to) actively spread the Bolshevik cause in America and spent a decade in the Soviet Union following the 1917 revolution."

Overthrowing the Czar and installing the puppet Stalin regime served long-term British imperial and geopolitical designs, but at what cost to humanity? The Rothschilds concluded that a Eurasian alliance among France, Germany, Russia, Japan, and China for economic cooperation, buttressed by a "transnational railroad system," threatened to overtake Britain's maritime trade, thereby casting a shadow over the dynasty's aspirations to global commercial dominance. To sabotage the coalition, the syndicate launched and coordinated the Russian Revolution, resulting in the murder of millions of Russians and the fall and assassination of the Romanov Czar.

The B'nai B'rith "quietly steered other Jewish-American groups to smuggle arms into Russia on the eve of the Bolshevik Revolution (while) the ADL ran the Jewish underground from behind the scenes," *EIR* reports. Edgar Bronfman, the ADL's "friend in Moscow," was granted a concession for his company, Seagram's, to distribute booze to East Germany's Communist Party. By overthrowing governments and installing puppet regimes, the syndicate could ensure exclusive, controlled markets for compliant, politically-connected businesses who buttressed puppet regimes, which, in turn, defended and bankrolled the businesses.

EIR reports that the ADL and its "leading collaborator," the American-Israel Public Affairs Committee (AIPAC), have poured money into political campaigns, incentivizing employees within the federal government, to tow the line.

The Syndicate Takes Over China

Few could have anticipated the good fortune that would befall Cornelius Vander Starr. Born in 1892 to struggling European immigrants, Vander Starr was unremarkable by any measure. He was raised on the Pomo Indian reservation in Mendocino County, California where a military post, Ft. Bragg, had been established to keep settlers at bay while elites extracted the resources. Resident lumber mills processed trees and shipped the wood to local ports and rail lines. His father worked as an engineer on the California Western Railroads alongside Chinese coolies.

Against all odds, Starr rose from obscurity to preside over one of the largest, most profitable insurance companies in the world. He was an overnight sensation. "Some men leave an indelible mark on their colleagues without planning to do so," the Starr Foundation reminisced. "Yet, so content are they on living and working and doing that they find neither the time nor the patience for keeping any records of what they have accomplished or how they lived. Starr was such a man whose brilliance and remarkable energy were matched only by a passion for anonymity that amounted to almost shyness. But where the mark of a man has been left, it can be found."

Before his career took flight, Starr's mother opened the family house to boarders while the young Starr swept the halls of the local branch of the Odd Fellows, an international fraternity founded in England in 1066 and which counted Scottish freemason Alfred Pike, the author of Morals and Dogma, *as a member. Odd Fellows recruited men from the trades and lower classes to help them establish businesses, provide for their welfare, and collaborate with each other to dominate local markets, propelling many to success that they could not have realized on their own.*

With influential figures supporting him from the shadows, Starr enlisted in the U.S. Army, but never deployed. Instead he went to work for the Pacific Mail Steamship, a New York joint stock company that established mail routes and back channels through San Francisco, Hong Kong, Yokohama, and Shanghai. Henry Morton, the Steamship's captain, managed several hotels in Shanghai, including the famous Astor House, the Chinese affiliate of the eponymous luxury hotel established in New York City by John Jacob Astor who had made his fortune selling opium, the drug that financed the British Empire.

Starr would soon be headed to Shanghai.

The Pacific Mail Steamship was the property of William Averell Harriman, the son of a railroad baron who attended Groton School and Yale University – and would partner years later with George H.W. Bush to establish the National Security State within the United States.

With powerful contacts in hand, Starr relocated to China, where extra-territoriality granted him special rights reserved for foreigners to establish a business under the law of their home country. During the Second World War, Starr quickly rose to prominence by assisting the Allies through back channel communications and intelligence sharing.

In his new home, Starr was inspired by the vast untapped markets of China which promised to make him exceeding rich through insurance sales. "The providential and family loving Chinese would naturally be attracted to the principle of life insurance, though which they could pass on the fulfillment of their own hopes to their families," the Starr Foundation affirmed.

After Starr established American Asiatic Underwriters, Inc., he insured risks for high value clients, including a baseball team and Jewish refugees fleeing from Vladivostok, Russia to mainland Europe on a Czech ship. Starr became an overnight sensation.

At 27 years of age, he had managed to create the largest insurance company in the world. With money bursting from his pockets, he acquired the Shanghai Evening Post, *which reported news of interest to the Shanghai business community. As publisher, he cultivated Henry Luce, the China-born publisher of* Fortune, Sports Illustrated, *and* Time *magazine, and recruited such luminaries as Randall Gould, a correspondent for* Time, United Press International, *and the* Christian Science Monitor; *and John Ahlers, a correspondent for the* Economist, *an international news magazine owned by the Rothschild-backed Economist Group.*

Starr published his newspapers a few blocks away from his insurance headquarters so that his Shanghai offices could communicate with each other through chit coolie. As Starr discovered, insurance underwriting granted him access to sources and information that otherwise would have eluded him and his news gathering operation.

As the World Wars raged through Europe, President Franklin D. Roosevelt set up an informal intelligence apparatus called the Office of Strategic Services, through which elites passed along vital information drawn from their international networks. Starr was encouraged to insure the property of U.S. Service men, the Germans, Nazis, and Japanese as part of OSS intelligence gathering efforts. Journalists and insurance agents were perceived as valuable intelligence assets for the war effort given their ability to penetrate difficult to reach places, cultivate sources, and acquire vital information outsiders would not have been privy to. "Newspapers everywhere are expected to stick their noses in everybody's business (and provide) almost indestructible *cover for the collection of information," a former OSS officer told reporters.*

Thanks to the OSS, the Allies could identify "which factories to burn, which bridges to blow up, (and) which cargo ships could be sunk in good conscience," The Los Angeles Times *reports. "They ultimately brought down Adolf Hitler's Third Reich." The Insurance Intelligence Unit, a component of the Office of Strategic Services and its elite counterintelligence branch, gathered intelligence on the enemy's insurance industry, blueprints for bomb plants, timetables of tide changes, among others details about Nazi targets. Led by Starr, the OSS insurance unit enabled the Allies to cripple Hitler's industrial base and undermine the morale of the German people by incinerating their cities.*

Prior to the creation of the OSS, the executive branch had conducted American intelligence gathering loosely and on an ad hoc basis. Once the United States was drawn into the Second World War, British intelligence convinced the U.S. federal government to recruit a Republican lawyer by the name of William "Wild Bill" Donovan to establish an informal intelligence gathering service based upon the British Secret Intelligence Service (MI6) and Special Operations Executive.

By accommodating Britain, "America (was propelled) permanently onto the world stage," former CIA Director Stanfield Turner said. "Roosevelt did not know at the time that he had just paved the way for Donovan to enter his inner circle of advisers and that doing so would lead to the creation of America's first fully fledged intelligence service."

A lieutenant colonel who invested with the Rockefeller-controlled National City Bank, Donovan would eventually become one of the most decorated men in U.S. history. The OSS recruited individuals from elite families, many of whom owed their allegiance and affluence to their service and ties to the British Crown and its affiliated corporate allies. Among its recruits was Vincent Astor of the prominent Astor family, who made a fortune smuggling opium, the drug that financed the British Empire. Astor acquired Newsweek *and gathered intelligence through a secret society called The Room in which elites were plied with alcohol, the original truth serum, and invited to divulge their most closely guarded secrets. The OSS placed its people in position of power around the world, expanding the Rothschild intelligence network and back channels.*

During the war, the OSS trained Germans and Austrians for missions inside Germany – and recruiting exiled communists and Socialist party members, labor activists, anti-Nazi prisoners-of-war, Nazi scientists, German and Jewish refugees, Chinese, Arabs, French, all of whom became interwoven within the fabric of the American Deep State, which secretly wielded influence on the American federal government on behalf of powerful private interests. Through the OSS, communists were able to move into positions of power within the federal government, helping the British Crown and its agents weaken the country from within.

The OSS operated within the shadows of society, engaging in subversive, and at times, illegal activities while somehow remaining above the law.

The federal government initially resisted the network's covert operations, which involved "making things happen without allowing it to be known that the United States was the instigator." The agents were trouble makers who excelled at old world strategies of espionage, propaganda, sabotage, false flag events, smear campaigns, psychological warfare, subversion, assassinations, political manipulation, dirty tricks, guerrilla attacks, spontaneous riots, and other unconventional warfare strategies designed to influence public opinion, subvert society, and advance elite policy goals, changing America within a span of decades from a moral nation into an ethical cesspool.

Before the group was dismantled, the OSS set up operations in Istanbul, Turkey to host spy networks for both the Axis and Allies powers, reflecting elite involvement in both sides of the war through which they stood to profit. The railroads, which connected central Asia with Europe, placed Turkey at "the crossroads of intelligence gathering." Through Turkey, the OSS sought to infiltrate the Ottoman and Austro-Hungarian Empires. By the end of World War II, the OSS was running a private intelligence service out of an office in Wall Street, "using some of the biggest names in American business."

While working in intelligence gathering, Starr reportedly recruited an OSS Captain by the name of Duncan Lee to serve as general counsel for AIG. While Mao Zedong led the People's Liberation Army through Shanghai in 1949, Starr relocated AIG headquarters from China to New York City.

The CIA, a civilian foreign intelligence agency, was established in 1947 to succeed the OSS.

In 1974, Vice President Nelson Rockefeller led the President's Commission on CIA Activities within the United States, otherwise known as the Rockefeller Commission, after the New York Times *reported that the CIA had engaged in illegal activities against U.S. citizens, including opening mail, domestic surveillance, and experimenting with mind control through LSD and MK Ultra.*

The Commission reaffirmed that the Constitution protected U.S. citizens from unnecessary government intrusion and that "violent change, or forcing a change of government by the stealthily action of enemies, foreign or domestic, is contrary to our Constitutional system." Reflecting a pre-September 11, 2001 mindset, the Commission concluded that "the mere invocation of national security does not grant unlimited power to the government....(and) the preservation of individual liberties within the United States requires limitations or restrictions on intelligence."

However, Rockefeller was quick to assert that the "drawing of reasonable lines – where legitimate intelligence needs end and erosion of Constitutional government begins – is difficult."

The Commission argued for increased surveillance within the United States on grounds that "intelligence is information gathered for policymakers in government which illuminates the range of choices available to them and enables them to exercise judgment." Yet, that information was available principally to elites and their networks which sought to have the government serve them and their business interests, providing them access to information to which duly elected officials, including the President, were not even privy.

The Commission estimated that over 500,000 intelligence forces worldwide were working on behalf of Communists and that the number of Communists working within the federal government had tripled since 1960. As would later become clear, the same corporate interests that had warned the United States about encroaching Communism were financing or otherwise aiding and abetting its rise; they were also transferring technology to enemies of the United States that would later be used to subvert American interests and violate the rights of the U.S. citizens, tactics that increased the power of elites and enriched them further through government contracts.

By the end of his illustrious career, Starr, a humble man who grew up on an Indian reservation, controlled nearly 150 owned and affiliated insurance and insurance agency companies in over 100 countries. The *company he built would go on to write close to $700,000,000 in premiums each year and cover many billions of dollars in underwriting exposures. "You have to have worries, but you're better off having them in a Cadillac than in a rickshaw," Starr said. At its peak, AIG obtained a market capitalization of $180,000,000,000, making it "the largest insurance and financial services company in history."*

As head of AIG, the Starr Foundation reports, Starr "surrounded himself with promising youngsters whose bounce helped him feel alive. They were invited to visit his estate in Brewster, New York and many were given personal scholarships to help them in the world. Starr used to call this form of philanthropy 'corrupting.' He enjoyed overwhelming the minds and hearts of young people with opportunity. One of his protégés said, 'It was such a luxurious corruption that no young person of limited means would ever think of refusing. Many other people wished they were included in his life of corrupted minds'."

In the years that followed, AIG created a strategic advisory venture team with Kissinger Associates and the Blackstone Group, a private equity firm, "to provide financial advisory services to corporations seeking high level independent strategic advice." Blackstone acted as an adviser to AIG during the 2007-2008 financial crisis, helping the federal government support the notion that AIG was "too big to fail."

Yale in China

The British East India Company helped project the British Crown's influence into the United States political establishment through Yale, a university established by Eli Yale, who acquired his fortune through the opium trade. Among the recipients of opium money was Yale University, which attracted the children of elites, many of whom were connected to the East India Company. By and large, these were not the children of the professional classes or of the church communities but the children of mercenaries, pirates, and societal parasites, a self-perpetuating elite who sought to reinforce its privilege and amass greater wealth through public plunder, crony capitalism, and income redistribution schemes they devised to raid the public purse.

As elites positioned themselves to exploit the Chinese market, the Yale campus newspaper revealed that Yale University and Skull & Bones created Communist China. The university had also educated, trained, and sponsored Mao Zedong, the Communist agitator who led the Chinese Cultural Revolution. The People's Republic of China centralized control in the country so that international bankers and corporations could acquire the resources and opportunities they needed to develop China through government fiat and public money. Through China, the elites aspired to rule the world.

Under Mao's leadership, millions of innocent people lost their lives, just as they had done in the Soviet Union. The OSS was on hand to train Mao's Red Army, with Donovan personally briefing Operational Group members in Bethesda, Maryland before their departure to China in 1945. The OSS established bases around the world from East Asia to training camps in Catoctin Mountain Park, the location of Camp David.

Yale in China was founded by Yale Divinity School. In 1919, Mao was introduced to Communist theory in a Marxist Study Group in Shanghai; the Yale Student Union invited him to create a Yale campus in China. Under the advisement of his mentors, Mao promoted "Thought Reorientation" as editor of their journal. "Without Yale, support of Mao Zedong may never have risen from obscurity to command China," Yale Professor Jonathan Spence said.

Through his association with the university, Mao was able to establish a Chinese branch of the Communist Party. Since he had neither the funds nor real estate to achieve this task, "Yale stepped in by (renting) him three rooms (in) the Cultural Book Store" through which Mao published such titles as An Introduction to Marx's Capital, A Study of the New Russia, *and* The Soviet System in China. *"Maos's reputation grew," the newspaper reports. From this base he was able to organize several branch stores."*

The profits were reinvested in a Socialist Youth Corps and the Communist Party. Congress of the Chinese Communist Party, which financed the Socialist Youth Corps and the Communist Party, providing him a platform for the launch of the Communist Movement in China.

As Yale's hospitals, intelligence networks, and agents infiltrated China on behalf of the Anglo-American establishment, the university collaborated with the OSS at the direction of Reuben Holder. A loyal member of Skull & Bones, Holder installed Maoists into power; they, in turn, became the largest opium producers. At the same time, the secret society and its affiliated networks gave financial aid to Communists within the Soviet Union with the view to bankrupting and breaking the back of Russia and its satellite states to prevent free enterprise from flourishing there so that state-sponsored corporations created by and for the Anglo-American establishment could dominate those markets, reap the profits, and control their governments.

Back channel networks affiliated with the OSS and Skull & Bones worked with the Chinese to defeat the Soviets and Japanese during the Second World War.

Instead of being perceived as a threat by Western corporate elites, Mao was heartily welcomed. Writing for Henry Luce's Time magazine, for example, David Rockefeller, the Chairman of the Board of Chase Manhattan Bank, paid homage to "the real and pervasive dedication of Chairman Mao to Marxist principles," conceding that "whatever the price of the Chinese Revolution, it has obviously succeeded in producing more dedicated administration...and community of purpose."

After traveling to China with the Chase group, Rockefeller praised "the enormous social advantages of China," which he attributed to "the singleness of ideology and purpose....We, on our part, are faced with the realization that we have largely ignored a country with ¼ of the world's population....The social experiment in China under Chairman Mao's leadership is one of the most important and successful in human history."

Wall Street Bankrolls the Russian Revolution

The United States had invested billions of dollars building up the military industrial complex to challenge the Soviet threat. Then, as if by divine intervention, the Soviet Union collapsed in a puff of smoke. An economist from Stanford University's Hoover Institute, Anthony Sutton, who authored Wall Street and the Bolshevik Revolution, The Bolshevik Revolution *and* FDR, Wall Street, and the Rise of Hitler, *observed that the Communist threat had been manufactured and hyped by Wall Street from the beginning.*

Corporations have been playing one country off another to drive lucrative government contracts to themselves, enhance profit margins, and establish monopolies. They used the opportunity of war, he writes, to seize natural resources, install puppet governments, rescind civil liberties, loot the public purse, and secure opportunities around the world funded by taxpayers.

Sutton observed that Yale's secret society, Skull & Bones, promoted the Communist movement in China, gave aid to Soviet Communist revolutionaries – and then played the Chinese and Soviet threats against each other and against the United States in order to drum up profits for Wall Street.

In National Suicide: Military Aid to the Soviet Union, *Sutton argues that the Cold War was "not fought to restrain Communism" since the United States was financing the Soviet Union and either directly or indirectly arming both sides in Korea and Vietnam in order to generate multi-billion contracts for corporations.*

Through the World Wars, the Cold War, and War on Terrorism, corporate America has demonstrably pitted countries and ideologies against each other to generate profits for itself while weakening the United States and other countries and their citizens through debt, cultural subversion, and an erosion of civil liberties, all for the purpose of consolidating the world's wealth and power into the hands of the few.

While public funds were diverted from pensions, critical infrastructure projects, education, health care, and support for the people, these interests were fleecing taxpayers, lining their own pockets, decreasing quality of life standards, driving up prices through inflation, creating societal disruptions, and undermining the integrity of the nation's institutions. Every aspect of society was being rearranged and undermined to serve the power lust and greed of unprincipled political leaders and corporate parasites.

Sutton observed that Wall Street had financed the Bolshevik Revolution to undermine Russia as an economic competitor to U.S. corporations so that the country would be a "captive market and a technical colony to be exploited by a few high-powered American financiers and the corporations under their control." These were the very corporate interests that had financed the rise of Adolf Hitler and President Franklin Delano Roosevelt. They promoted "corporate socialism" as part of a "long range program of nurturing collectivism" to guarantee "a monopoly on the acquisition of wealth."

If the "free" West had created the Soviet Union, the USSR could be destroyed just as fast, and then transformed it into whatever the shadow elite wanted it to be.

The corporations behind the Bolshevik Revolution, Sutton writes, maintained offices at the Equitable Life building at 120 Broadway, in Manhattan, New York - the hub of corporate-banker coordination which funded Communist revolutionary and Fascist activity. One such company, American International Corporation (AIC) was an investment trust established by Federal Reserve founder Frank Vanderlip.

While attempting to corner markets in Russia and China, AIC's board and stockholders included a who's who of American financiers and industrialists, Sutton writes. For example, the cashier of the Berlin Equitable Life office was William Schacht, the father of H.H.G. Schacht, who was Hitler's financial advisor. Schacht's co-director was Emil Wittenberg, a director of the first Soviet international bank, Ruskombank; the other co-director was Max May of the Guaranty Trust in which JP Morgan held a controlling interest.

In correspondence to the U.S. Embassy in London dated June 1, 1920, Guaranty was identified as the Soviet government's "fiscal agent in the United States for all Soviet operations;" it served the purpose of establishing a "complete link of Soviet fortunes with American financial interests."

The very interests that controlled the Guaranty Trust and JP Morgan and which funded the Communist revolutions wielded vast influence with the Federal Reserve Bank of New York and the AIC, Sutton writes.

The corporations behind the Communist revolutions, moreover, were controlled through interlocking boards of directors. For example, C.A. Stone, who was President of the AIC, was director of the Federal Reserve. (The founder of J.P. Morgan was J. Pierport Morgan, a financier and strategic partner of Rockefeller's Standard Oil; Junius Spencer Morgan, the founding patriarch of the Morgan banking dynasty, was a merchant banker in London; the House of Rothschild dominated the British (and American) banking sectors.) William Straight, AIC's Vice President, was romantically linked to the sister of Averill Harriman and had worked for J.P. Morgan before joining the Chinese Maritime Customers Service, a Chinese governmental tax collection agency; he also was correspondent for the Rothschild-backed Reuters news agency during the Russo-Japanese War.

Reflecting that the apple doesn't fall far from the tree, Straight's son, Michael Whitney Straight, who published the New Republic, worked *as a KGB spy before joining President Franklin Delano Roosevelt as speech writer. The younger Straight belonged to Cambridge Apostles, a secret society at Cambridge University whose membership included Bertrand Russell, a socialist philosopher who trained Communist Chinese revolutionary leader Mao Tse-tung before that Rothschild bloodline staged the Communist Revolution in China, with ample material support provided by Yale University and Wall Street.*

Other tenants of 120 Broadway involved in the Bolshevik Revolution and its aftermath in 1917 include the Federal Reserve for the New York district; Weinberg & Posner Vice President Ludwig Martens, the first Soviet-appointed ambassador to represent Bolshevik interests before the U.S. federal government; Rockefeller Philanthropy Advisors; and Westinghouse director Charles Hill, who negotiated with Sun Yat-sen while Westinghouse in Russia was involved in the Russian Revolution, Sutton writes.

A Wall Street syndicate that financed Sun Yat-sen's revolution in China "is today hailed by the Chinese Communists as the precursor of Mao's revolution in China," Sutton writes, concluding that "activity on behalf of the Bolsheviks originated in large part from this single address," which also houses the Office of War Information through which war intelligence and propaganda were coordinated.

Sutton alleges that President Woodrow Wilson was aware that U.S. corporations were behind the Russian Revolution which sacrificed tens of millions of Russian lives in the interests of profits and market share for Wall Street. Sutton cites as evidence a letter dated October 17, 1918 in which William Lawrence Saunders, an AIC director and deputy chairman of the Federal Reserve Bank of New York, advised Wilson that "I am in sympathy with the Soviet form of government as that best suited for the Russian people."

Many documents and correspondence among political and corporate leaders reflect an "enthusiastic alliance of Wall Street and Marxist socialism," he writes.

Wilson was not just a passive observer of Wall Street's promotion of the interests of the Rothschild crime syndicate, but a facilitator of it. As Sutton and others have observed, Russian revolutionary leader Leon Trotsky, who was bankrolled by Wall Street, was able to enter Russia with a U.S. passport to continue the savage, blood-thirsty revolution that ended tens of millions of lives in the most harrowing and inhuman of circumstances. The logistics and strategies for Trotsky's passport were discussed in British and American diplomatic cables.

With taxpayer funding, treasonous leaders within the U.S. federal government created the Soviet Union, which posed an existential threat to the United States, with the expectation that they would be rewarded with prestige, power, and wealth, a dynamic they employed repeatedly before targeting their next mark. They didn't just create a shadow threat – they launched the Communist menace which threatened to destroy the United States and eradicate freedom and opportunity worldwide.

On the surface, Communism and free enterprise appeared to be diametrically opposed. Upon closer inspection, it becomes clear that they complement each other. "Both systems require monopolistic control of society," Sutton writes. "While monopolistic control of industries was once the objective of J. P. Morgan and J. D. Rockefeller, by the late nineteenth century, the inner sanctums of Wall Street understood that the most efficient way to gain an unchallenged monopoly was to go political and make society go to work for the monopolists — under the name of the public good and the public interest."

Rumors Sutton uncovered of Russian "monarchists working with the Bolsheviks" reflect Rothschild's influence within the Czarist Romanov family by way of Princess Alix, a granddaughter of Queen Victoria and an illegitimate Rothschild Royal bastard heir, who married Nicholas, the Russian Czar slain during the Bolshevik Revolution.

Federal Reserve Bank Director William Thompson, "was active in promoting Bolshevik interests," financing Bolshevik operations and speeches, and organizing a Morgan partner to influence British Prime Minister Lloyd George on policy, Sutton writes, identifying "a pattern of assistance by capitalist bankers for the Soviet Union. Some of these were American bankers; some were Czarist bankers who were exiled and living in Europe; and some were European bankers. Their common objective was profit, not ideology."

While American troops were losing their lives fighting Nazis and Communists at the cost of American treasure and standing in the world, U.S. corporations and political leaders were secretly working with the enemy. This conflict of interest, betrayal of the public trust, and treason against the country "can be explained by apolitical greed to simply, profit motive," Sutton writes, advising that the individuals who were working with the imperialists in London, led by Rothschild, were motivated by a desire to acquire access to the "largest, untapped market in the world."

That these same individuals spread propaganda to American citizen to terrorize them into panic over the Red scare, reflects a level of psychopathy and "moral depravity" that is inconceivable to most, he writes.

Among the propagandists who sold the Red Scare to the "gullible American public" in the 1920s, was Ivy Lee, a public relations executive for Rockefeller's Standard Oil and the Harriman family's rail interests. Reflecting the psychopathy of the robber barons, Lee was enlisted to burnish the Rockefeller image after the Rockefellers ordered the genocide of miners in the Ludlow Massacre. Lee convinced the U.S. Chamber of Commerce – corporate America's voice on Capitol Hill – to forge closer political and economic relations between the United States and the Soviet Union which was massacring people by the millions.

Revolutionaries, like Trotsky, were "internationalists" who promoted "world revolution" for the purposes of establishing "world dictatorship" and a global monopoly on wealth and power, Sutton writes. "The Bolsheviks and bankers (are both dedicated to) internationalism. (Revolution) and international finance are not at all inconsistent if the result of revolution is to establish more centralized authority. International finance prefers to deal with central governments."

The last thing the banking community wants is "laissez-faire economy and decentralized power because these would disperse power," Sutton writes. "This, therefore, is an explanation that fits the evidence. This handful of bankers and promoters was not Bolshevik, or Communist, or socialist, or Democrat, or even American. Above all else, these men wanted markets, preferably captive international markets — and a monopoly of the captive world market as the ultimate goal. They wanted markets that could be exploited monopolistically without fear of competition from Russians, Germans, or anyone else — including American businessmen outside the charmed circle."

IV.
Inside the Central Banks

*"Government is instituted for the common good;
for the protection, safety, prosperity, and happiness of the people;
and not for profit, honor, or private interest of any one many,
family, or class of men; therefore the people alone have
an incontestable, unalienable, and indefeasible right to institute
government; and to reform, alter, or totally change the same
when their protection, safety, prosperity, and happiness require it."*

President John Adams
American Founding Father

"From the 1950's onward, one of the primary goals of the World Bank was institution building," writes Dr. Eric Toussaint, Spokesman for the Committee for the Abolition of Illegitimate Debt. "This most often meant setting up para-governmental agencies based in the World Bank's client countries. Such agencies were expressly founded as relatively financially independent entities with respect to their own governments and outside the control of local political institutions, including national parliaments."

Both the IMF and World Bank have advanced "financial Neo-colonialism and the imposition of austerity policies in the name of debt repayment," writes Toussaint.

The Saudis were key institutional partners of the World Bank from the very beginning. As evidence of this, the Saudis were familiar with the families who controlled the Federal Reserve. In unguarded moments, the Saudi Royals identified the controllers of the New York Federal Reserve, the most powerful bank within the Federal Reserve system.

These exchanges revealed that eight families own eighty percent of the New York Bank; these families have all married and bred into each other's families, creating a monolith of financial power. The families include Goldman Sachs, Rockefeller, Lehmans and Kuhn Loebs of New York; the Rothschilds of Paris and London; the Warburgs of Hamburg; the Lazards of Paris; and the Israel Moses Seifs of Rome.

Another source, Thomas D. Schauf, reveals that ten banking interests control all 12 Federal Reserve branches. These include N.M.

Rothschild of London, Rothschild Bank of Berlin, Warburg Bank of Hamburg, Warburg Bank of Amsterdam, Lehman Brothers of New York, Lazard, Brothers of Paris, Kuhn Loeb Bank of New York, Israel Moses Seif Bank of Italy, Goldman Sachs of New York and JP Morgan Chase Bank of New York.

There were also tie-ins with the central banks and the joint-stock companies that preceded them. While much attention has been given to the East India Company (EIC), fewer are aware of the Dutch East India Company (DEIC), which was established in 1602.

The DEIC engaged in the same sort of tactics and trades as the EIC – that is gunboat diplomacy in pursuit of monopolies. The networks around the DEIC and the EIC, pirates both, merged to form a powerful financial clique formed a powerful monied class. To this end, they established systems in which the wealth of nations was harvested and redistributed to themselves.

The Bank of Amsterdam was established as a basis for a central bank. This, in turn, became the inspiration for the Bank of England, which became the inspiration for the Federal Reserve System, which became the inspiration for the European Central Bank...By the 21st century, just about every country in the world had its own central bank, including the Saudis.

The Saudi Central Bank

For a time, the Dutch East India Company (DEIC) eclipsed the East India Company (EIC) in wealth and reach after it secured a monopoly on trade in the lucrative Asian markets. Access to the Asian market would only have been possible through an alliance with the Vatican and Black Nobility, the veritable gatekeepers who had forged relationships with rulers and kingdoms within Asia spanning centuries. The Vatican was able to capture Eastern markets on behalf of the Venetians and other powerful Italian merchant families, with Khazars, Turks, and Mongolian serving as mercenaries.

The Dutch East Indies, a colony of the Netherlands, was developed as a DEIC trading post. Indigenous people were massacred by the hundreds of thousands in these territories as the Dutch merchants staked claim. During the Napoleonic Wars, which were being financed and coordinated on all sides by the Rothschilds, French Emperor

Napoleon Bonaparte installed his brother, Louis, to the Dutch throne while Great Britain, which was simultaneously being targeted for conquest by Napoleon, moved in to occupy the Dutch Indies. The Dutch provinces were eventually incorporated into the French Empire, which had fallen to Rothschild.

As previously discussed, the Rockefellers coerced Britain into relinquishing control of Saudi oil. Based upon a Pact between Nations signed in 1921, gold seized from nations and their citizens during World War I was distributed to Indonesia (formerly, the Dutch East Indies), a Dutch colony; and the Philippines, a U.S. colony; while the Rothschilds controlled the gold exchanges out of the City of London, with a view to establishing a global monopoly on gold.

In 1926, the Saudi Hollandi Bank, which provided financial services to the DEI, was established on behalf of the Netherlands Trading Society (BTS) to hold the gold reserves and oil revenues of the Saudi government. Established in 1824 at the Hague, BTS pursue international commerce, trade, agriculture and banking operations. In time, BTS would evolve into a financial entity that became ABN AMRO.

Once the Rockefellers convinced the United States to fight alongside Britain in World War II against the Nazis, Prince Bernhard of the Netherlands, an avowed Nazi himself, negotiated the "surrender" of the German forces within the Netherlands. Bernard became an important strategic ally to Prince Philip, the consort of Queen Elizabeth II while his mother-in-law, Queen Wilhemina became the world's first female billionaire.

In 1952, Saudi King Abdulaziz Al-Saud established the Saudi Arabian Monetary Authority (SAMA), a Saudi central bank to manage the wealth from oil. "U.S. government officials on a financial mission to Saudi Arabia advised King Abdulaziz that it was crucial for the state to have monetary and banking regulations, as well as its own central bank," writes Dr. Khalid Alsweilem, the former Chief Counselor and Director General of Investment at SAMA.

That same year, the Saudi sovereign fund, was established and the Saudi gold sovereign was adopted as the official currency of the Kingdom. SAMA – the central bank of Saudi Arabia – the Saudi central bank – managed the Saudi fund, which was controlled ultimately by the Saudi Monarch, the public face of the international syndicate.

In 1954, as Saudi Arabia was linked into the global financial system, Prince Bernhard launched the Bilderberg Group to integrate Europe and North America into the new global system.

In 1957, the World Bank became Saudi Arabia's official development partner, helping global planners acquire the capital it need to develop the Third World on behalf of corporations.

Since the World Bank determined the price of oil within global markets, it could establish the terms and impositions of loans for third world development in coordination with central banks around the world.

In 1959, SAMA was granted the exclusive right to print and mint a gold-backed Saudi currency – just like the Federal Reserve. Vizor, a company from Dublin, Ireland provides the technology for the regulatory infrastructure of SAMA – and for the Bank of England and the Bank of Canada, reflecting a confluence of interests among these central banks. Vizor has also provided software for the tax authority of the Bahamas, a tax haven where Khashoggi had casino interests. Former Trump Atlaantic City executive Jim Allen who would later preside over Seminole Gaming, opened a casino there.

In 1971, the Saudis established another government-owned investment vehicle, the Public Investment Fund, to develop the Saudi economy. SAMA managed the sovereign wealth fund that would eventually be tapped by the shadow elite to acquire key strategic assets around the world.

In 1974, Saudi Arabia formalized a technical, collaborative relationship with the World Bank, which opened an office in Riyadh.

As its influence expanded, SAMA forged relationships with the IMF, Group of 20 (G-20), Bank of International Settlements, Financial Stability Board, Financial Action Task Force, Middle East and North Africa Financial Action Task Force, International Association of Insurance Supervisors, Islamic Financial Services Board, Accounting and Auditing Organization for Islamic Financial Institutions, Gulf Monetary Fund, Islamic Development Bank Group, and the International Association of Deposit Insurers.

All currency notes issued by SAMA are fully backed by gold. The Saudi Central Bank controls SAMA Foreign Holdings and the sovereign wealth fund of Saudi Arabia.

Sovereign wealth funds maximize long-term returns and help nations acquire strategic control over specific industries or companies.

The wealth of sovereign wealth funds has grown exponentially through investments in stocks, bonds, real estate, private equity, hedge funds, and institutional real estate.

Despite having been established with a mandate to combat global poverty, poverty has only proliferated through global planning – an outcome that is not surprising considering that the goal is not to address deprivation, but to consolidate wealth and power into the hands of the elite.

V.
Launching the Petrodollar

"There is danger from all men. The only maxim of a free government ought to be to trust no man living with power to endanger the public liberty."

President John Adams
American Founding Father

In 1968. large pools of oil were discovered in Prudhoe Bay, Alaska at the shores of the Arctic Ocean – oil fields at least as large as those of Saudi Arabia. Before the oil could be tapped, the issue of land title needed to be resolved, and so Congress passed the Alaska Native Claims Settlement Act (ANCSA) that disbursed nearly $1 billion in compensation from the federal government to the Eskimos residing on the land. Most of that money disappeared into private hands, never reaching the Eskimos. The remaining funds provided seed money to launch Alaska Native Corporations (ANCs), which Donald Rumsfeld and Dick Cheney established through the Nixon Administration's Office of Economic Opportunity.

Once the issue of land title was resolved, Kissinger blocked development of Alaska's oil fields, with a view to elevating Saudi Arabia as the global producer of oil. Going forward, the United States would be dependent upon foreign oil and undermined from within. Having outlived its usefulness, the United States was set on a downward trajectory while global planners set their sights on tapping new markets in Saudi Arabia, China, and elsewhere.

In lieu of tapping its oil reserves to the benefit of the American people U.S. oil was being shipping overseas. For example, in 2017, AP reports that Alaska embarked upon "a major step toward realizing a long-sought pipeline to move natural gas from the North Slope to Asia, siding with interests from China after major oil companies stepped back from the project."

While Kissinger was planning the petrodollar, he invited the Saudis to visit the oil fields of Alaska. As American oil producers salivated over a ready supply of oil that would drive the economy and prosperity of the nation, a marketing campaign was unleashed against oil development to turn the American public against oil production.

In 1967, the SS Torrey Canyon, an American oil supertanker with a cargo capacity of 118,285 long, hit a reef between Cornwall, England, and the Isles of Scilly, spilling an estimated 25-36 million gallons of crude oil into the English Channel. This, in turn, created one of the largest oil spills in history.

The following year, another environmental disaster occurred – this one off the coast of Santa Barbara, California. This catastrophe spilled 3.4 million gallons of crude oil into the Santa Barbara Channel, devastating marine life, birds, and the coastline.

The outrage over the environmental damage to wildlife and natural environment spurred the public's outrage against oil, resulting in the establishment of new federal agencies, like the Environmental Protection Agency. While the American people were led to believe that such agencies would serve the public interest as faithful steward of the environment, they facilitated government overreach, allowing global planners to block – or green light –development in service of private interests, but under the cover of environmentalism and virtue signaling.

Around the same time, oil production peaked in the United States. Efforts were underway to lock the United States into a series of interdependencies, thereby enabling global planners to pull the strings through their institutions, regulatory agencies, and banks.

Global planners were interested in using other people's money to build their private empires, and so they engaged in indiscriminate spending, conceiving every project imaginable in which to unleash the spigot of federal dollars. Due to the federal government's profligate spending, gold could no longer sustain the dollar. If all dollars were redeemed in gold, there wouldn't be enough gold to go around. Saudi oil was seen as a substitute for gold so that the federal government could continue its unrestrained spending. Kissinger ensured that all oil transactions were conducted in dollars, the world's reserve currency.

The federal government promised the Saudis "protection" if they purchased weapons from the federal government. The United States subsidized the contractors – and then the contractors sold the finished products to foreign countries, enabling them to profit again. Planners managed players on a global chessboard, prompting their puppet leaders to use the weapons in strategic ways – to topple governments and install puppet regimes, seize resources, and consolidate more of the world – and markets under their own control.

The Saudis were encouraged to buy gold while the Rothschilds controlled the price of gold in London through gold exchanges. While U.S. currency was decoupled from gold, Saudi Arabia's was gold-backed.

Among the organizations through which federal dollars were laundered was the United States Agency for International Development (USAID), which was granted an initial budget of over $50 billion. The USAID accounts for more than half of all U.S. foreign assistance, the highest in the world. The Foreign Assistance Act authored the USAID to fund the development of over 100 countries in Africa, Asia, Latin America, the Middle East, and Eastern Europe, with the public's money. In turn, politically-connected corporations exploited those opportunities to corner markets.

President John F. Kennedy had created USAID through Executive Order 10973, which specifically provided "for the assistance in the development of Latin America and in the reconstruction of Chile."

Once Rothschild staked its claim on a territory, a coup was staged, followed by a dictatorial government led by a Rothschild puppet ruler who corralled his/her nation's resources under his/her own control, and established monopolies. Once power and wealth was consolidated, stability was restored, with global planners in control. The so-called dictator enjoyed the spoils, often living a lavish lifestyle at the expense of the impoverished people.

Meanwhile, the United States bankrolled and armed these tyrannical regimes who were then weaponized against their own people. In 1973, Augusto Pinochet staged a military junta in Chile and then declared himself President of the "Republic," or military dictator the following year. If U.S. support had led to this, how could the United States justify interference in other nations or aid in the interests of spreading freedom and democracy when its resources wound up in the hands of dictators who extinguished freedoms and brutalized their nations, in the process, betraying everything the United States stood for?

USAID also poured money into the Philippines at which point, Ferdinand and Imelda Marcos formed a dictatorship, seized state industries, placed them under the control of the state, and established monopolies. In addition to helping themselves to state assets, the couple reportedly purloined America's gold supply in cave and committed human rights abuses while filling their homes with treasures. They too lived like Royalty at the expense of the American taxpayer.

Kissinger required the Saudis to purchase arms from the United States and then tapped Adnan Khashoggi, Prince Bernard, and others to bribe foreign governments into contracting with Lockheed Martin and other contractors. The weaponry was used to terrorize and fleece other nations. The fact is, there would be no wars, without the material support, approval, and direction of global planners.

The syndicate tapped the wealth and resources of the United States to fund Communist revolutions around the world and then built up the U.S. military – the *de facto* arms dealer of the world – to fight the "Communists," while arming and financing both sides.

Saudi arms dealer Adnan Khashoggi not only helped move money around the world, but his influence peddling tactics involved taking people of influence into international waters to compromise them.

During the Nixon Administration, an international pedophile compromise operation ebbed towards the surface – a disgusting practice that gathered international headlines during the Jimmy Saville and Jeffrey Epstein scandals decades later. New York Det. "Jimmy Boots" Rothstein reports that as many as 70 percent of the nation's top government leaders within the federal government have been compromised by pedophilia and sex trafficking, one of many strategies employed by the syndicate to degrade the morals of America's leaders while compromising them to ensure their compliance to the global agenda.

In addition to entertaining five heads of state including kings, Arab princes, Third World leaders, and European and American businessmen on his yachts, Khashoggi poured money into American political campaigns, despite not even being an American. He donated generously to Nixon's presidential campaign and gifted the President's daughter with a $60,000 bracelet while forging intelligence networks around the world with Secretary of State Henry Kissinger. While Saudi Arabia and the World Bank collaborated under the pretext of ending world poverty, Khashoggi lived on $250,000 a day.

Khashoggi played a crucial role in the evolution of the U.S.-Saudi relationship. "Our father understood the art of bringing people together better than anyone," Khashoggi's children told reporters.

To this, the *Independent* opined, "How crass it would be to mention that the weapons he helped sell perfected the art of blowing people apart. (Khashoggi) helped sell enough of these weapons to become one of the world's wealthiest men: a fortune once estimated at £2.4

billion, friendships with Saudi and Hollywood royalties, homes all over the world, a superyacht later sold to Donald Trump (for approximately $30 million), and a personal bodyguard nicknamed Mr Kill."

During his lifetime, Khashoggi acquired 12 homes, including a property on Fifth Avenue – the street associated with the crown jewel of Jared Kushner's real estate empire – 666 Fifth Avenue, owned by Kushner Companies – and other elite holdings.

By 1979, the Saudis had invested $27 billion in U.S. contracts and $30 billion in U.S. real estate, government security, and stock options. As the hand of globalism tightened around America's neck, the Saudis acquired interests in Rupert Murdoch's News Corp., Apple, Yahoo, TWA, Hewlett Packard, eBay, Amazon, Microsoft, Twitter, and Planet Hollywood.

Since acquiring petrodollars, the Saudis have poured money into American political campaigns and nonprofits, helping them shape American foreign policy. "The Saudi petrodollars that have flooded into the United States during the last 30 years have affected American business, politics, and society," Gerald Posner writes in *Secrets of the Kingdom: The Inside Story of the Saudi-U.S. Connection*. "The money had bought the House of Saud a coveted seat at the table with American corporate and political elites, and the Saudis have assiduously courted the access that results from such enormous infusions of cash."

For example, after presiding over the World Bank, John McCloy was retained as lobbyist for Aramco, the Saudi oil company. During one influence peddling campaign, McCloy hand delivered a letter from the Chairmen of Exxon, Mobil, Texaco, and Standard Oil to President Richard Nixon, recommending that he limit his support of Israel on grounds that the Jewish state was the source of all the instability in the Middle East.

Deeply suspicious of Israel, the House of Saud attempted to warn the United States that the Zionist state was secretly controlled by Russian Communists, perhaps not realizing that Wall Street had bankrolled these very Communists, with support from the federal government which professed to be fighting them.

As part of a strategy, Aramco's executives paid lip service to opposing Israel while the U.S. Treasury Department treated royalty payments to the Saudis as taxes; this reduced its federal tax liability from $50,000,000 to $6,000,000.

Meanwhile, members of the CIA were recruited to join Aramco's PR and Government Relations team to influence policy. Upon discovering that the Saudis liked little boys, the CIA procured children for the Saudi Royals; Aramco even lobbied for exemption from New York's anti-discrimination laws in 1959 to force applicants to disclose their religious affiliation, to ensure they didn't accidentally hiring a Jew.

While helping Arab countries extract oil, Kissinger advanced the 1975 Memorandum of Understanding, which guaranteed Israel's oil needs in the event of a future crisis; at the same time, Kissinger prevented the United States from tapping its own reserves in Alaska, rendering the United States vulnerable to political upheavals within the Middle East that elites were fomenting by playing both sides against the middle. In turn, the United States was reduced to a patsy which subsidized foreign countries and sustained the losses to advance agendas on behalf of global planners.

After Kissinger opened up channels for transferring U.S. technology to Israel, Israel passed the technology to Communist China. Amir Bohot and Yaakov Katz's book, *The Weapon Wizards: How Israel Became a High-Tech Military Superpower,* reveals that a delegation of high ranking Israelis traveled to meet a Chinese delegation in 1979. "Until that winter day," the authors write, "Israeli defense officials had never been to China. The two countries did not have diplomatic ties, and nobody on the Israeli side—except for the members of the delegation, the prime minister, the defense minister, and a handful of others—knew about the trip. If word got out, Israel knew that the Americans would be furious."

By 1979, the IDF Talpiot program was launched to support an Israeli-Chinese relationship, which transferred U.S. technology to China via-à-vis Israel, establishing the basis for what would later become the Belt and Road Initiative. In the decades that followed, China emerged as a credible threat to the United States economically, strategically, and militarily. The syndicate had planned this outcome at the end of World War II. Israel and China's treacherous leaders were just as complicit as America's, having sold out their own people and national interests in a quest for wealth, power, and status conferred through admission into the so-called elite.

Kissinger's philosophy of linkages also applied to people. The more people could be compromised and rendered dependent upon the power structure, the less likely they were to act independently. The elites therefore nurtured dependency among the people and among leaders for the purposes of consolidating power.

Israel, whose origins trace to the Rothschilds and the Balfour Declaration, served as a proxy state for Rothschild. Speaking presciently, Ben Gurion, the first Prime Minister of Israel, announced in 1930 that he was a Bolshevik and that Israeli citizens viewed the USSR as "our homeland."

The Soviet Union was at the center of the Israeli identity, Ben Gurion said, conceding that China is "weak, but a great world power in the future." The Yalta conference, where the British, American, and Russian leaders negotiated the terms for world peace, made allowances for the rise of China.

In the Middle East, elites were playing both sides against the middle. Chase Manhattan Bank, for example, served as trustee of an Israeli bond issue while encouraging Nixon to strengthen U.S. financial relationships with the Arabs. As its Chair, David Rockefeller said, "in international banking, you often get involved in this way."

Saudi Arabia kept one sandal in the world of radical Islam and another in the West while exporting Wahhabism throughout the world through radicals armed with technology and weaponry provided and funded by the U.S. government. The Saudis were largely compliant to the demands of Western oil companies until Libyan dictator Muammar Gaddafi broke rank and demanded higher royalty payments from American oil firms. Faced with the rise of nationalism, the oil companies quickly made concessions to Libya, emboldening other oil Middle Eastern countries to demand higher payments for their oil as well.

In 1972, the major oil companies formed a cartel, the Organization of Petroleum Exporting Countries (OPEC), to gain leverage against Western oil companies who were attempting to form their own cartel within Indian Country. By 1972, Western oil companies conceded to OPEC's demands and agreed to more favorable terms in which to extract oil from Arab lands.

While Qaddafi won a small victory, standing up for Libyan interests placed a target on his back. Not only had he challenged the oil consortium, but he refused to decouple the Libyan currency from gold, preventing global planners from manipulating the value of its currency and forcing his country into debt.

One of the most in-demand commodities in the world was oil whose price was denominated in dollars and set by the World Bank. After Nixon removed the dollar from the gold standard, the Saudis were told to purchase oil in dollars. In return, the Saudis received American taxpayer supported protection against their enemies. The rest of the world was forced to hold a high amount of dollars in their reserves to purchase U.S. debt, placing the dollar at the center of the global financial and economic system, one backed by the petrodollar.

According to the Strategic Culture Foundation, an online platform that provides commentary on Eurasian and global affairs, "As long as the U.S. continues to maintain its dominance of the global financial and economic system, thanks to the dollar, its supremacy as a world superpower is hardly questioned. To maintain this influence on the currency markets, the pricing of oil in U.S. dollars is crucial."

As the Saudis nationalized their oil wells, Standard Oil damaged them on the way out the door, placing the petrodollar on unsure footing for the long-term....

Sabotaging the Saudi Oil Fields

"With its oil output soaring and prices rising, Saudi Arabia enjoyed a once-in-a-millennium revenue windfall," Matthew Simmons writes in *Twilight in the Desert: The Coming Saudi Oil Shock and the World Economy.* When oil was capped in the United States, the Saudis "had to step into the vacuum created by the unexpected peaking of us oil production. (This) rapid production surge was not without some unfortunate hidden costs. The rush to produce as much oil as the world demanded strained the physical limits of the reservoirs and pressures in various part of Saudi Arabia three great fields began to drop."

In turn, the "overproduced" Saudi oil fields were damaged, thereby ensuring that the syndicate could no longer tap an unlimited supply of cheap oil from which to develop the world.

That this happened was noted in technical reports circulated throughout the oil industry – and in an article investigative journalist Seymour Hersch wrote for the *New York Times*, entitled "Saudi Oil Capacity Questioned" in March of 1979. According to this article, from 1970 to 1973, Saudi oilfields were overproduced over fears from senior managers of Chevron, Texaco, Mobil, and Exxon that Saudi nationalization was imminent. As a result, shareholders "wanted to extract as much wealth from these fields as fast as the oil could be produced," Simmons writes.

In closed Senate hearings that followed the 1973 oil shock, investigative journalist Jack Anderson reported under sworn testimony, that in 1972, Aramco's owners realized that "high production was causing some damage to these fields, but since they would soon lose their ownership, a conscious decision was made to 'milk these fields for every salable drop of oil and put back as little investment as possible'," Simmons writes.

When deposed before Congress, "Saudi Aramco management calmly testified that the only way Saudi Arabia was able to meet the 1970 to 1974 oil demand surge was by opening the valves of its prolific wells so each could produce at much faster rates," he writes.

By 1973, it became clear "to the most knowledgeable Aramco technicians that these wells would soon need to rest – that is, reduce the oil each was producing (or) else the water entering the well flows would soon threaten to kill the goose laying the golden egg."

Aramco's U.S.-based management team repeatedly assured the Saudis that "nothing was amiss," he writes. The report was ignored in the wake of the Watergate scandal – which, according to New York Det. "Jimmy Boots" Rothstein, was really about recovering a book of pedophiles, implicating politicians and other so-called elites.

Overproducing the wells rendered them vulnerable to damage. "As high reservoir pressure dissipates, water begins to commingle with the oil," Simmons writes. "Gas bubbles to the top of the reservoir where it forms a gas cap, and soon the oil remaining underground becomes inert and ceases to flow. It can then be pumped out, but the pumping process also brings out far more water and gas that crowd out the oil. The faster a high pressured oil field is produced, the faster the advantages of this high pressure are lost," resulting in "serious damage to the wells."

A 1978 report from the General Accounting Office highlighted the unique position that the Saudis occupied in the global oil markets as "the world's biggest producer and dominant global oil exporter," he writes, conceding that the United States "for years to come would have to come to terms with increasing dependence on foreign oil imports to sustain its economy."

However, the truth was, the United States had more than enough oil to meet its own production needs. At the same time, the Saudis, who were growing increasingly wealthy and influential through oil, were "firmly committed (to) the role they were playing on the world stage as the sole stabilizer of world oil markets," Simmons writes.

However, by 1985, the damage inflicted upon the Saudi oil fields had significantly slowed Saudi oil production, leading the nation's senior leadership to "decide that enough was enough," he writes. "By the late 1990's almost all OPEC producers other than Saudis were starting to bump against peak sustainability production rates."

By this point, oil production in every Middle East OPEC country was still coming from a handful large oilfields.

Few outside technical groups and key insiders were informed of the problem, that the world had reached "peak oil."

"When Saudi Arabia and its OPEC cohorts abandoned data transparency, they had no idea of the disruptive consequences that would follow," Simmons writes. "In the end, their actions left even the financial viability of their national economies at the mercy of oil traders and hedge funds that now vigorously bet on the future direction of oil prices. These speculators, of course, have little solid basis for the bets they make, but its precisely the lack of good information that turns the oil markets into a high stakes game in which the speculators can be the players. Thus, loss of control of the markets and their own economic fates became the greatest and most painful aftermath of the data storm that resulted from OPEC's policy of secrecy."

The only "meaningful non-OPEC oil additions" from 1977 to 2003 emanated from the former USSR, he writes. "And these surprising and anticipated gains were mainly the result of reworking existing fields in which faulty water-flooding had bypassed massive amounts of oil," Simmons writes. "Many oil observers were optimistic about Russia's continued ability to grow its oil wells. By mid-2004, the Russia oil miracle was beginning to fray. (Concerns) were also being raised in some circles that most publicly traded Russian oil companies right now (were) overproducing these fields to maximize profits."

By this point, the syndicate was back in power at Kremlin. Thus, quick, easy profits and rapacious greed took priority over common sense and the public interest.

In 1991, Georgetown University Associate Professor of Governor, Thane Gustafson "describes in amazingly accurate detail how the Soviets were overproducing their great West Siberian oil fields," Simmons writes. "Gustafson's key insight was to recognize that the USSR production surge (coincided with) a crash effort to skim dramatic one-time gains from the giant Western Siberian oil fields."

As Simmons explains: "Following the demise of the USSR, the previously state-run oil system was privatized. A group of energetic opportunists gained control of most of the newly privatized companies. Their goal was to maximize profits by boosting outputs, regardless of whether high production rates were sustainable."

In 1977, something had gone awry. As Export-Import counsel Peter Beter conceded, Rockefeller-controlled foundations raised concerns that the "program for world domination had jumped the tracks."

During the Spring of 1976, the Rockefeller-Soviet alliance had dissolved; what followed was a "mutual double cross," he said.

The Rockefellers panicked when the Communist Christians reclaimed control of the Kremlin as they feared retribution for supporting the genocide of the Russian people and destroying the Russian oil wells in the interests of power and profit, Beter said.

According to Beter, Kissinger advised to fill the American political establishment from top to bottom with Bolsheviks as who better to counter the Russians than the Bolsheviks themselves? Unlike the Bolsheviks who were internationalists, the spiritual Russian communists were nationalists.

While the syndicate devised strategies on how they could restore power within the Soviet Union, a Bolshevik Revolution was planned for the United States. Hundreds of thousands of Bolsheviks arrived from the Soviet Union and were placed in positions of power. The Soviet agents the Rockefellers had placed within the federal government were removed as the original agents had taken orders from Moscow, which was now under the control of Rockefeller's sworn enemies, Beter said.

The new Bolshevik agents were not only enlisted against Russia, but "against you and me," Beter warns in his audio letters. After power was consolidated within the Soviet Union, criminal elites attempted to consolidate power. "They want Bolshevik dictatorship here in the United States," Peter said. "Rule or ruin is their credo."

While acknowledging their "Satanic frenzy for power," Beter said that the Bolsheviks "seek personal gain no matter at what cost."

One lessons from the Russian Revolution that the syndicate took to heart is that "revolution is best carried out with the full power of the national government," Beter said, conceding that the Bolsheviks answer directly to the Rothschilds.

"Soviet Russia was controlled by a ruthless gang of criminals, moral and ethical lepers, who pose as philanthropists and champions of the masses," Beter said. "They were bent on conquering, looting, and raping the world, and will not stop until either they have accomplished it or themselves have been destroyed. Any dealings with them as a government merely gives them the advantage of the delays and aids implied in international amenities, that they scorn but use to full advantage."

The Carlyle Group and Crony Capitalism

In 1987, the Carlyle Group was established after David Rubenstein learned about a tax loophole forged by Sen. Ted Stevens that enabled Alaska Native Corporations to "leverage (tribal) losses by selling them to profitable companies looking for a break on their taxes," Dan Briody writes in The Iron Triangle: Inside the Secret World of the Carlyle Group. *"Before long, they were flying Eskimos into Washington, DC, buttering them up, and brokering deals between them and profitable American companies. (They) couldn't get enough free money, (and so) a cottage industry (was) born. (They) recognized the ongoing potential of the business and decided to incorporate. With a crew in place, liabilities limited, and money coming in the door, (they) decided to (establish) a company on a scheme that denied the federal government close to $1,000,000,000 in taxes. (Everybody's) happy, but the taxpayers."*

The ANCs created "endless subsidiaries so that the parent firms could have indefinite access to contracts," the Washington Monthly *reports.*

The Carlyle Group contracts with QinetiQ, a British defense contractor in which the British Monarchy holds the "golden (controlling) share." Reflecting the relationship between Carlyle, QinetiQ, intelligence operations, and the syndicate, QinetiQ appointed CIA Director George Tenet as a non-executive director. Tenet had promoted the false narrative advanced by Ahmed Chalabi and the Iraqi National Congress – that Iraqi leader Saddam Hussein was harboring weapons of mass destruction. This was used as a pretext for invading Iraq after the terrorist attacks of September 11, 2001.

QinetiQ has established military devices, including trace-and-trace devices which are then sold on the markets for civilian uses.

In the years that followed Carlyle's establishment, government contractors, like Lockheed Martin and Halliburton, exploited loopholes in the Small Business Administration's minority preference rules to use ANCs as front groups to acquire lucrative, noncompete government contracts intended to provide poor Natives some equal footing in government contracting. The elites from London worked through the federal government to set up an unlimited number of public-funded enterprises and corporations to enrich themselves.

Twelve corporations were created through the Alaska Native Claims Settlement Act, which resolved the issue of land title after oil was discovered at Prudhoe Bay.

The thirteenth was established in Seattle, Washington, the headquarters of Boeing and Microsoft. By 2013, the thirteenth corporation was "involuntarily dissolved." According to reports, "from early to mid/latter 2000's, total gross cumulative revenue of just over $82,000,000 was booked." (13thregion.info).

The 13th corporation followed a familiar pattern. Originally seeded with $52 million, half was distributed to shareholders. The 13th corporation then couldn't "say exactly what happened to the remaining $27 million of land claims the corporation kept," **Juneau Empire** *reports. "Lawyers looked into the corporate books. They determined that there may have been enough evidence of dubious activity to pursue lawsuits, but proceeding with litigation would have cost more than would be recouped."*

A sovereign funds (The Alaska Permanent Fund, or AFP), was established in 1976; it grew to a reported $64 billion, thanks to Alaska oil and mining opportunities. Its purpose is to provide a basic income, or Permanent Fund Dividend, to Alaskans.

This fund was established after oil from Alaska North Slope was transported through the Trans-Alaska Pipeline System to provide for future generations who would no longer have oil as a resource in Alaska. The fund has awarded the state hundreds of millions of dollars in bonuses. In a similar vein, tribal casinos have forged revenue-share arrangements with perpetually cash-strapped governments that reap the financial benefits while tribal members and ordinary people languish in poverty.

As could be expected, the AFP is a member of the International Forum of Sovereign Wealth Funds, which collectively represents 80 percent of the assets managed by sovereign funds globally – or a reported $5.5 trillion. The IFSWF works in partnership with the International Monetary Fund.

In turn, the public's wealth is stealthily being absorbed by a shadow elite and mysteriously being parked in real estate across the world, driving up the cost of homes, rendering them unaffordable to locals. Ordinary taxpayers are being relegated to a permanent renter class, in line with the sentiments of World Economic Forum founder Klaus Schwab, who informs the public that they will "own nothing and be happy."

Within Carlyle, a nexus of powerful, politically connected liberals and neoconservatives intertwined like a double helix. "Carlyle would never have gotten to the level that it is at today had it not been for this premeditated commingling of business and politics," Briody writes. The firm aggressively recruited former high ranking government officials while investing in companies and interests regulated by the former agencies that employed them. George Soros, a billionaire financier who has endowed the Native American Rights Fund and the National Congress of American Indians, invested $100,000,000 in Carlyle Partners II, one of the largest and most successful Carlyle funds.

The firm also employed George W. Bush before he became governor and invested $10,000,000 in the firm. For a while, Secretary of Defense Donald Rumsfeld was Chairman while his former assistant from the Office of Economic Opportunity, Dick Cheney, presided over Halliburton, an oil company that acquired federal contracts through ANCs during the War on Iraq when Bush was President and Rumsfeld was Secretary of Defense. Former President George H.W. Bush got in on the game too, as adviser to Carlyle while his son was President.

Carlyle now manages accounts valued at over $157,000,000,000, making it the ninth largest Pentagon contractor between 1998 and 2003. By 2011, Carlyle's founder, David Rubenstein boasted a net worth of $2,800,000,000, earning him the rank of the 138th richest person in the

United States. His wife, Alice Rogoff Rubenstein, who had worked for Washington Post *publisher Donald Graham and served as CFO for the* U.S. News and World Report, *became publisher of the AlaskaDispatch.com, an influential online news magazine which shapes political discourse in Alaska.*

"(Alice) now wields even more political influence over Alaskan, American and global politics," the Anchorage Press *reports. "She has enough power and money to win over candidates from pretty much every persuasion."*

Between 1997 and 2005, ANCs received a reported $4,400,000,000 in contracts. The Wars on Iraq and Afghanistan, which had depleted the national treasury of $2,400,000,000,000 by 2017, spurred a bonanza of taxpayer-supported contracts for the ANCs. One ANC subsidiary, Nana Pacific, for example, received a $70,000,000 contract with the Department of Defense to rebuild an Iraqi port. Over $225,000,000 in military construction contracts were awarded to Olgoonik Corporation, a Native village corporation based in a small village of Wainwright, Alaska, which assigned the work to Halliburton.

The Chugach Alaska Corporation generated revenues of $700,000,000 for work ranging from monitoring seismic activity from a base in Korea to running military bases – and another $2,500,000,000 operating the Ronald Reagan Ballistic Missile Defense Test Site. Among the defense contractors that contracted through the ANCs were Bechtel and Lockheed Martin.

Despite being the greatest recipients of federal funds, tribal members remain among the poorest in the nation. "Reservation poverty is so pronounced, it can be clearly seen on national maps, with hot spots of poverty in the northern plains, eastern Arizona, southeastern Utah, and western New Mexico, which overlap directly with Indian reservations," a spokesman for the National Congress of American Indians said. "The billions spent in Indian Country have hardly made a dent in the well being of Indians."

Where was all the money going? The federal government ensured that tribal organizations do not have to account for how their money is spent. They could hide behind the impenetrable walls of tribal sovereignty and ignore FOIA requests. What is clear is that the intended beneficiaries are not the Indians. As Alaska Sen. Dennis DeConcini told the Senate Indian Affairs Committee in 1989, "A majority of companies who represented themselves as legitimate Indian contractors are, in fact, secretly backed or controlled by nonIndian firms. These so-called Indian companies that include the largest construction firms active on Indian lands, receive Indian preference from the Department of Housing and Urban Development, the Bureau of Indian Affairs, and the Small Business Administration, which were approved by the Bureau of Indian Affairs as legitimate contractors."

British Prime Minister John Major became the head of the European branch of the Carlyle Group. Serena Dunn Rothschild, the wife of Jacob Rothschild, the patriarch of the Rothschild crime family, served as the chief financier and de facto owner of the Tory Party who selected its leaders. Carlyle contracts with QinetiQ, a British defense contractor in which the British Monarch, who answers to Rothschild, holds the golden, controlling share.

A Native-American OPEC

As President Richard Nixon appreciated, the nation's "federally recognized Indian tribes" – that is, federally recognized by Rothschild's color-of-law federal government, provided the perfect smokescreen behind which government energy and defense contractors could amass a fortune under the pretext of improving the lives of Indians. In the decades that followed, the federal government worked hand-in-glove with the Indian tribes to drive national defense and energy policy while kicking government contracts to politically connected firms.

The lure of easy money through government contracting became intrinsically linked with a hawkish foreign policy and the pursuit of empire, all in the name of helping improve the financial lot of Indians who somehow continued to languish in poverty despite the barrels of money rolling onto their reservations. The federal government was vested in the welfare of Indians ,and yet the chief beneficiaries of tribal policies were government contractors.

Navajo Chairman Peter MacDonald, who served on Nixon's Committee to Re-elect the President (CREEP), established the Council of Energy Resource Tribes (CERT) to spearhead energy development on tribal lands to counter OPEC, which had launched an oil embargo.

The energy crisis signaled the increasing exposure of the United States to the vagaries of the global oil markets at a time when the country faced growing demands for oil at home. Political momentum was building within the country for energy independence.

Up to this point, oil companies had exploited resources on tribal lands without restraint, with the Bureau of Indian Affairs negotiating leases favoring private corporations – a development that is not surprising considering that Standard Oil founder John D. Rockefeller had established the federally recognized tribes as offshore jurisdictions on American soil through which European social democracy could be projected into the United States.

Tribal members served as mere window dressing within the game of oil politics and received only a fraction of the royalties in which they would otherwise have been due. For example, the Navajo Nation received $2.7 million for coal which Peabody Energy, the largest private sector coal company in the world, sold for $141 million on the market.

Prior to the oil shock of 1973, the Seven Sisters controlled about 85 percent of the world's petroleum reserves, but their position was challenged by the OPEC cartel, which was formed in 1960 to combat the dominance of the Seven Sisters in the global oil market.

Tribal oil interests, led by Rockefeller, attempted to counter OPEC's power with an Indian OPEC. A Native Chief by the name of Peter MacDonald led the way.

Born in 1928, MacDonald was a Navajo Code Talker who transmitted intelligence to the U.S. military through his native Navajo language.

After World War II, MacDonald studied engineering at the University of Oklahoma. He then joined Hughes Aircraft where he worked on the Polaris nuclear project and learned how to write proposals for defense contracts, a skill that would serve him well as chairman of an energy-rich tribe.

Throughout his career, MacDonald remained a fierce advocate of tribal sovereignty. He boasted of his ability to obstruct the will of the American people by mobilizing members of his tribe to establish voting blocks for local, state, and federal candidates who curried his support and campaign contributions.

In 1982, **Mother Jones** *published a scathing critique of MacDonald's leadership: "For although he remains a Navajo, proud and loyal, it is by virtue of his Anglo acculturation, which began the moment* *he set foot in a (Bureau of Indian Affairs) school, that Peter MacDonald has made it.*

"(Employing) principles and political machinery adapted from the white man's world, he has become the consummate American power figure – famous and increasingly insulated. And in the process of rising to such unparalleled prominence, he has become a total mystery to his own people. (MacDonald) has achieved nearly unbreakable control over the Navajo destiny, dispensing patronage and punishment at will.

"He has set the reservation's economy on a course that many economists, environmentalists, and anthropologists predict will destroy Navajo culture and livelihood by the end of the century."

MacDonald was celebrated as an energy baron by presiding over the Navajo reservation that controlled billions of dollars worth of uranium and coal. While he became a millionaire who mingled with corporate and political elites, ordinary tribal members under his charge languished in poverty. As **Mother Jones** *reports, in the 1980s, the Navajo reservation was exporting enough energy resources "to meet the needs of the whole state of Arizona for 32 years, and yet the Navajo people remain some of the poorest on the continent."*

During the Great Society, MacDonald administered federal anti-poverty programs as Director of the Office of Navajo Economic Opportunity (ONEO).

MacDonald cultivated a cult of personality similar to that of leaders of the former Soviet Union. "His portrait hung in the waiting rooms of ONEO offices across the reservation," **Mother Jones** *reports. "Like antipoverty administrators in so many American ghettos, MacDonald was able to parlay control of welfare into an awesome political base. (He) was a radical. (He'd) come into Council chambers and deliver fiery speeches against the white man, the Bureau of Indian Affairs, the energy companies. (In) one campaign, MacDonald promised a new era of Navajo self-sufficiency based upon prudent and profitable exploitation of the reservation's bountiful energy resources. And even while holding up the U.S. government as a straw man, MacDonald promised Navajos he would find more federal goodies during his reign, like the ones he had given them as director of the ONEO".*

While MacDonald promised to preserve the tribe's mineral resources for future generations, his intensive coal and uranium development depleted them. His counsel throughout this ordeal was

George Vlassis, an attorney from White & Case, a firm whose founders established the Federal Reserve and represented the Bankers Trust Company.

"To mend the tribe's shattered pastoral economy, (MacDonald) has done little besides create a sprawling, voracious bureaucracy over which he has almost complete control," Mother Jones *reports. "(His) brand of development has created a classic Third World colony look on the reservation: visible signs of wealth and status in bureaucratic Window Rock surrounding by a sea of rural poverty and helplessness. (The) Chairman controls everything, the Council, the courts, the committees, the police. (His) Administration responded (to opposition) by firing critics, cutting off funds to local chapters, and commencing a series of crude political manipulations that have increased the power of his office."*

***

In 1974, MacDonald established the Council of Energy Resource Tribes and hired as his adviser, Iran's oil minister, Dr. Ahmed Kooros, whose investment strategies led the Saginaw Chippewa Indian Tribe of Michigan to achieve $1 billion portfolio status. "I was involved because of my connection to OPEC," Kooros said. "When I came here, I was actually the Minister of Oil and Development of Iran, and I was representative of Iran at OPEC in those days."

A former Vice President of Economic Affairs for the Central Bank of Iran, Kooros worked as Deputy Minister in charge of Economic Affairs and Oil in the Ministry of Economic Affairs and Finance before joining CERT. "The American Indians are in a position comparable to the one the OPEC countries were in in 1968," Kooros told reporters at the time. "They have a similar level of underdevelopment and the resources to do something about it. What they should get should be more commensurate with the real price of energy."

Kooros negotiated a right-of-way contract between the Navajos and Atlantic Richfield Company (ARCO), one of the eastern companies of the Standard Oil Trust. "When I look at the ARCO-Navajo case, I went to see what it is, what does this pipeline do," he said. "The tribe is a sovereign entity. It can give, grant, or deny a right-of-way contract. We negotiated very strongly, I mean the Tribal committee, with people representing ARCO for quite a bit. Finally, ARCO accepted the principle, the application of the principle of the opportunity cost, and alternative routes. (These) were the most beautiful moments of my life to see that sovereignty became the rule. (The) relationship with this company and the Tribes became extremely friendly."

ARCO sponsors the Spirit Award Dinner, which "brings in all the companies active on Indian reservations (so) that sums of money would be mobilized, collected, and used for education," Kooros said.

Much of that education was devoted to preparing tribal members for careers in the energy and defense sectors, strengthening the interrelationship between these industries and the tribes, and improving the capacity of tribes to serve these industries more effectively. "The programs actually contributed to the education of a good number of Indian students," Kooros said.

"American energy executives were put on notice that they would be dealing with an OPEC-type cartel right away within their own borders," Mother Jones reports. "And yet, the cartel was operating within the Indian tribes. CERT was taken seriously, with MacDonald called Shah of the Navajo. CERT officials traveled to OPEC countries to learn bargaining techniques and cartel economics. It was soon clear to the Department of Energy analysts that MacDonald could really give them trouble. So they responded by funding CERT."

The threat MacDonald posed was largely overblown. However much tribal leaders speak of tribal sovereignty, federally recognized Indian tribes exist at the pleasure of the federal government and are largely dependent upon public funds for their existence. Had the federal government considered him a genuine threat, they would have removed and replaced him with a more compliant leader.

CERT went on to develop and exploit energy resources on tribal lands with generous financial support from the federal government. The organization retains close relationships with leading oil companies, including ARCO, Exxon, Gulf Oil, among others. Through the association, the Navajos Four Corners Generating Station became one of the largest in the world.

President Ronald Reagan tapped MacDonald to serve on his Energy Task Force. The Reagan Administration's "new federalism" rolled back federal oversight of tribes, essentially freeing them to spend *more of the taxpayers' money at will so they could pursue private enterprise with limited government interference.*

In 1982, Reagan signed the Indian Mineral Development Act, which allowed tribes to enter into joint ventures with private businesses. He also transferred the White House liaison for tribes from the Office of Public Liaison to the Office of Intergovernmental Affairs to restore tribal governments to "their rightful place among the government nations."

Reagan signed the Indian Self-Governance Act through which tribes became eligible for block grants from the Department of Interior for the purposes of self-determination. He then spearheaded a BIA Guaranteed Loan Program which provided a federal guarantee for collateral private lenders, increasing the ceiling on guaranteed loans for Indian businesses under the Indian Financing Act.

The Indian Mineral Act, which Nixon supported, was signed into law during the Reagan Administration, transferring authority of tribal lands (and their oil and mineral rights) to tribes that were privately controlled by major corporations and the nation's leading oil companies.

Reagan's Assistant Secretary of Indian Affairs, Ross Swimmer, was tapped to advance tribal entrepreneurship. Swimmer's own tribe, the Cherokee Nation, was by then already grossing $24 million annually to produce military components.

In the end, MacDonald was forced to resign after Barry Goldwater directed the General Accounting office to audit him in response to his campaign against Nixon over the Administration's decision concerning a land issue with the Hopi tribe. Federal authorities discovered a kickback scheme that led to the indictment of three men who had misappropriated $13.3 million the federal government had earmarked for the Navajo Housing Authority.

By some estimates, CERT affiliated tribes control five percent of the nation's oil, 10 percent of the gas, 30 percent of the coal, 30 percent of the low sulfur coal reserves, and 40 percent of the nation's mineable uranium. CERT tribes also offer lucrative markets for solar, wind, and geothermal energy, worth well into the billions of dollars.

By some accounts, over $100 billion worth of oil can be tapped on tribal lands through fracking. While asserting its desire to "secure the energy future for all Americans," CERT demands that "tribes (and by extension, the corporations that control them) have absolute control of their own resources."

CERT identifies as a Native League of Nations, modeled after the United Nations and its predecessor organization, the League of Nations. Its Executive Director, David Lester, has advocated the "convergence of Indian policy with the national consensus on major national energy policy goals."

CERT is also committed to combating climate change. "Efforts will be made to ensure that Indian tribes may participate in whatever carbon regime is put in place, and, just as important, retain the ability to develop their economies and provide economic opportunities for their members," CERT announced in a statement.

The Bush Administration invested more than $44 billion in climate change and energy security programs, including more than $22 billion for technology, research, and development. President George W. Bush signed legislation providing more than $67 billion in loans and guarantees to support innovative energy projects that reduce greenhouse gases and air pollution. Many of these contracts were granted to energy-rich tribes affiliated with CERT..

One member of the Cheyenne River Sioux Tribe joined the Army Corps of Engineers to contract with the Rio Tinto Group, a British multinational and mining corporation headquartered in London which is linked to the Rothschilds. Rio Tinto's rise follows the typical monopolistic pattern of the nation's leading industrialists. In 1968, Rio Tinto acquired U.S. Borax, which controls the world's largest deposits of the industrial mineral. In 1989, Rio Tinto bought British Petroleum's failing mining unit for $4,300,000,000. Most recently, Rio Tinto has made inroads into China.

Another Navajo tribal member, Steve Grey, worked for the Department of Energy's Lawrence Livermore National Lab's American Indian Program, where scientists allegedly doctored their own research and technology to create a climate of fear in order to generate sales, said Michael Crichton, author of Jurrassic Park *and* State of Fear.

Many of the energy-rich tribes have become fabulously wealthy through casinos and government contracting while the taxpayers have subsidized them. The tribes are generating enough wealth to be self-sufficient, and yet they continue approach the federal government with tin cup in hand. "When the Navajo Nation gets to a million population, the taxpayers, they're not going to afford us," a Navajo Indian said. "They're having a hard time right now. They're the government. They're the ones that's giving us money to live. They cannot afford us no more with more Native American population growth. They're saying right now at the Hill, you go to the Hill, this is what I hear: 'Man, I can't even afford my own kids. I can't even take them to college anymore, and yet my tax is going out.' They complain about the war. They complain about the fuel costs. They complain about us. 'When are these Native Americans going to get on their feet? We've been putting money all my life in there. Still today, we're still putting money in it.' It's talk out there right now. Believe it."

President Donald Trump tapped Swimmer to serve as Co-chair of his Native-American Coalition, which has affirmed that the Administration will "ease energy regulations, allowing Native-Americans to harness their own energy resources."

Trump's tribal counsel, Greenberg Traurig, whose Colorado office is the correspondence address for CERT, reported record profits for 10 consecutive years, with a reported annual revenue of $2.3 billion in 2023 after having opened an office in Riyadh the previous year.

Filipino Kleptocrats Get in on the Game

Philippine President Ferdinand Marcos was billed as "the most decorated war hero in the Philippines." As NPR reports, "He and Imelda were quite a glamorous couple. They were likened to John and Jackie Kennedy. They liked to promote themselves as the Philippine Camelot. (They) were a good looking couple, and they sort of represented the new Philippines. (Together) they crafted a careful image of themselves as the strong man and the beauty, capable and charming, stern but loving. (If) you look especially at the foreign coverage at that time, they were seen as, like, these new leaders who were coming forward to lead this country and bring about, you know, the promise of Philippine progress and democracy."

Marcos ran on a platform of making the Philippines great again. "They came at a time when people wanted to believe that the Philippines was a rising star of the Asian region and that it had a bright future ahead of it and that democracies were going to lead them to that future," NPR reports.

Right after the petrodollar was launched, and USAID shoveled dollars into the Philippines,\ and then Marcos declared martial law.

  Ferdinand Marcos was accused of stealing billions of dollars from state coffers. He then faced charges that he had violated the rights of the Philippine people.
  As President, he pursued infrastructure projects that generated lucrative contracts for corporations funded by the International Monetary Fund (IMF) and World Bank – institutions created after World War II in 1944 to provide loans and subsidies to foreign governments.
  In the 1970's, Marcos led a military government of "uncommon brutality, disbanding Congress, silencing the media, and using the army to torture and kill thousands of citizens," Bloomberg *reports. "(Through) all of this, Marcos and his wife, Imelda, had become exceedingly wealthy. They amassed dozens of luxury homes whose walls they decorated with pieces, by Cézanne, Manet, Picasso, and Van Gogh, from a museum-worthy art collection. Imelda filled her closets with designer footwear and flaunted extravagant pieces of jewelry, including a 70-carat light-blue diamond worth $5.5 million, at least 400 times her husband's official annual salary, which never exceeded $13,500. (Ordinary) Filipinos struggled to find work in a country with an unemployment rate that had spiked to an estimated 23 percent when the recession hit in 1984; import restrictions made basic products, such as ballpoint pens and razor blades, elusive. Finally fed up, they surrounded the presidential palace to demand that Marcos cede power."*
  The Guinness World Records *characterized Marcos' plunder as "the greatest robbery of a government."*
  Decades later, Imelda Marcos was convicted of laundering $231 million, revenue she acquired by raiding the treasury, collecting kickbacks, absconding with earnings from secretly owned private corporations, and laundering money, The South China Morning Post *reports. Rather tellingly, after learning that a Philippine court had sentenced her to 77 years in jail for corruption, Imelda reportedly "shrugged off the verdict" and "went partying."*
  The indictment reflects that since 1972, Ferdinand and Imelda Marcos, aided by five others including the California Overseas Bank, embezzled, stole, purloined, and diverted "to their personal use – and the use of others –certain Philippine government funds."
  The California Overseas Bank was controlled by Marcos and his partner, Roberto S. Benedicto, a kleptocrat in his own right as a taxpayer-subsidized media mogul and corporate tycoon whose empire

consisted of 85 corporations, 106 sugar farms, 14 haciendas and other agricultural lands, 17 radio stations, 16 television stations, two telecommunications, seven buildings, 10 vessels, and five aircraft. Benedicto also owned 13.5 billion shares of Oriental Petroleum.

Marcos appointed Benedicto Ambassador to Japan from 1972 to 1978 – and placed him in charge of the Philippine National Bank. In this capacity, the mogul secured more than $550 million in World War II reparations and then used the post to promote his own private interests, including lucrative joint ventures between Japanese corporations and his own – while Marcos and his associates reportedly received commissions of 10 to 15 percent of Overseas Economic Cooperation Fund loans from 50 Japanese contractors.

Japan had reportedly smuggled stolen gold on behalf of the syndicate into the Philippines, where it was allegedly hidden in caves.

Ferdinand and Imelda Marcos accepted millions in bribes, kickbacks, and gratuities in the form of cash payments and corporate stocks which were deposited in Swiss accounts at Credit Suisse with Benedicto's assistance, according to an indictment.

The Bilderberg Group, which was established by Prince Bernard, is among the representative shareholders of Credit Suisse, the credit side of the Swiss Banking Industry.

The man who moved Marcos' money around the world, Saudi arms dealer Adnan Khashoggi, was later implicated in the Lockheed Martin bribery scandal with Prince Bernard. By the time, the Saudis launched their sovereign fund, they were heavily investing in Credit Suisse as part of a broader plan to diversify their portfolio.

While Marcos ruled as dictator and siphoned public funds, Benedicto acquired a monopoly on the Philippine sugar industry, beginning in 1974. After Marcos established martial law, Benedicto seized control of the Philippine Exchange Company, which monopolized local haciendas (sugar barons) and international trade, enabling him to buy cheap sugar from local producers and sell it overseas at top dollar.

By the time Ferdinand and Imelda Marcos left office, they were reported to be worth anywhere between $5 billion and $13 billion, with some speculating that they might have stolen as much as $30 billion – assets acquired by diverting foreign aid and U.S. military aid to themselves while collecting kickbacks from contracts.

According to reports, before pouring American funds into the Philippines, Ferdinand Marcos and Nixon met at the White House in 1969 when a number of prominent leaders attended the funeral of President Dwight Eisenhower, who launched the military-industrial complex within the United States – one that set the United States on a path to converge with the Soviet Union.

In Waltzing with a Dictator: The Marcoses and the Making of American Policy, *Raymond Bonner reports that Nixon had phoned Marcos days before the Philippine leader had instituted martial law. Bonner writes that both Nixon and the CIA had been briefed on the plan for dictatorship – and communicated that they were agreeable to it as long as the new government served U.S. interests (and by extension, the interests of the City of London) in the region.*

By agreeing to the dictatorship, Nixon supported Philippine efforts to control the media and courts, arrest opponents, and violate civil liberties. The Nixon Administration was unconcerned that the Marcoses were misdirecting U.S. funds, a strategy of theft of public assets established and encouraged by Henry Kissinger. Marcos contributed $250,000 to Nixon's political campaign.

According to the Panama Papers, Marcos was among the first to exploit secret jurisdictions and hidden ownership of companies to launder and steal wealth from public coffers. As the Guardian *reports, Ferdinand Marcos' career "starts with a cynicism that now seems familiar – manipulating electorates, using money to buy power and power to make money. But he went one big step further in merging politics and finance, converting the instruments of government into one vast cash machine. Ultimately, he emerges as a laboratory specimen from the early stages of a contemporary epidemic: the global contagion of corruption that has since spread through Africa and South America, the Middle East, and parts of Asia. Marcos was a model of the politician as thief."*

As Marcos wrote in his diary, "The legitimate use of force on chosen targets is the incontestable secret of the reform movement," the Guardian *reports, conceding that some 34,000 trade unionists, student leaders, writers, and politicians were tortured with electric shocks, heated irons, and rape in the Philippines; 3,240 men and women were dumped dead in public places; and 398 others simply disappeared. Yet, somehow despite having committed such atrocities, Marcos inspired the fawning praise and adoration of America's leaders, within Rothschild's federal government in the United States, celebrating the couple's strength and commitment to "democratic values."*

While America was "fighting Communism," its leaders were propping up regimes that acted as brutally as the very Communists they were fighting. "With total power over politics, (President Marcos) closed in on the country's wealth," The Guardian *reports. "This was no longer just about kickbacks. Marcos started to steal whole companies, using the crude tactics of a gangster. He wanted the nation's electricity company, Meralco, owned by Eugenio Lopez, patriarch of one of the families who had run the country for centuries. He had Lopez's son charged with plotting to assassinate him, which carried the death penalty. The old oligarch handed over his company for $220 (It was worth $400 million.). To have gunmen is a gangster's requirement; to have gunmen in uniforms, with all the power of the state behind them, is a gangster's dream."*

Marcos stole money from USAID, gold from the Central Bank, loans from international banks, and military aid from the United States, The Guardian *reports, conceding that "he decreed that more than a million impoverished coconut farmers must pay a levy, supposedly to improve the industry, amounting to $216 million. He had already issued decrees to gift most of the coconut trade to his own companies; now he stole great chunks of the levy fund, all the while taking kickbacks on government contracts. All the Marcoses had to do was turn on the taps anywhere in the world and cash would come pouring out."*

Imelda Marcos hosted parties at a townhouse on East 66th Street in New York – the location of Founder's Hall, the first major "philanthropic" foundation created by John D. Rockefeller, Jr., an heir to the Standard Oil fortune who launched the ecumenical movement within the United States which projected Communist thinking from the church pews and enlisted Christian congregations to serve the interests of the corporate boards.

Ferdinand Marcos had fabricated his war record – his true histories bore little resemblance to the history that was sold to the public. Just when the world thought it had rid itself of this parasitic family, Ferdinand Marcos, Jr., the son of the dictator – called "Bongbong" – was sworn in as President of the Philippines in 2023.

Vice President Kamala Harris' husband, Douglas Emhoff personally handed Bongbong an invitation from President Joe Biden to visit Washington, DC. Astonishingly, Harris reaffirmed that the U.S.-Philippine alliance is based upon "deep cultural ties and our shared democratic values" and a commitment to "our economic and investment relationship," which includes promoting clean energy, addressing climate change, inclusive growth, and combating human trafficking.

Since 2020, USAID, the Department of Defense, and the State Department have "invested" $22.6 million in the Philippines for the coronavirus pandemic, in addition to "many of USAID's ongoing development projects valued at more than $100 million a year across the health, economic development, governance, education, and environment sectors." Over the past 20 years, the United States, the world's largest provider of bilateral assistance in health, has invested $582 million in the Philippine health sector, and has provided nearly $4.5 billion in total assistance to advance the country's development goals.

In 2022, Saudi Arabia's Public Investment Fund made a $1.5 billion investment in Credit Suisse and then connected Credit Suisse to the Saudi National Bank, making it the largest shareholder with less than 10 percent ownership.

VI.
The Decade of Greed

"We have no Constitution which functions in the absence of a moral people."

President John Adams
American Founding Father

The 1980s was a decade of unspeakable greed. Far from protecting the nation's cherished and hard fought freedoms, the conservative movement embraced liberty – that is, license to do what thou wilt, particularly with regards to the pursuit of profits. Freedom, an envisioned by the nation's founders, could only be sustained by a moral, law-abiding citizenry governed by a representative government retrained by a system of checks and balances whose leaders truly served the interests of the people. The new breed of conservatives identified the problem as government, but government wasn't intrinsically evil. Rather, evil was working through the government under color of law. Instead of focusing their efforts on exposing and correcting the reasons behind government overreach, they promoted a false antidote, one of moral license, rapaciousness, and callous predation to enrich themselves at the public's expense.

Among the poster boys of the religious right were Jack Abramoff, an Orthodox Jew; and his sidekick, Ralph Reed, an evangelical Christian whom Time christened "the right hand of God." The syndicate worked through these and other front men willing to serve the interests of the City of London. Abramoff became powerful, influential, and ultimately infamous as a well-connected Rothschild agent. By following his career and activities, the crime syndicate's networks are revealed. Jack Abramoff could have mistaken for Leonard Zelig or Forrest Gump. Somehow he wound up at critical points of history, playing whatever role he was assigned in order to advance the agenda.

Revolutionaries of the Right

Jack Abramoff could have been great leader, accomplished actor, or remarkable businessman under different circumstances. He was smart, hard working, intellectual, wonderful with people, but born into a crime family. What would be considered treasonous activities by some was, for Abramoff, just a clever way to make money, or perhaps, just business as usual.

Within the world of Rothschild, he could have followed one of two dialectics – as rabid Communist revolutionary or a warrior of the religious right "defending" freedom. Both sides were controlled by the Rothschild crime syndicate to advance the global agenda. Abramoff hated hippies and determined that his talents were better served on the right, particularly as the Communist Christians had reclaimed power at the Kremlin.

Abramoff was born in Atlantic City where his father, Frank Abramoff; and uncle, Bernard, were involved in real estate ventures. The Abramoff anticipated that casinos would dramatically increase the value of property within the city. Soon Bernard Abramoff was managing five million dollars worth of real estate in Atlantic City on behalf of Angelo Pucci, a Toronto-based real estate developer with ties to organized crimes.

Among Pucci's mob contacts was Paul Volpe, a member of the Cosa Nostra, a powerful Italian-American branch of organized crime aligned with the ADL and various secret societies. Through Bernard, young Abramoff acquired contracts with the criminals running the Soviet Union. As Antonio Nicaso and Lee Lamothe write in *Global Mafia,* "In Toronto, Soviet Gangs practiced organized extortion, gambling loan-sharking, and drug trafficking (in) conjunction with the Paul Volpe group. (During) the 1970's and 1980's, various police investigations turned up Soviets, many of whom said they were Jews who had immigrated from Israel."

Russian gangs were behind many criminal activities within the ethnic communities that partnered with the New York La Cosa Nostra. Volpe's contacts were reportedly investing millions in Atlantic City on behalf of the mafia, whose crime was so organized that it had its own Commission – a governing body that regulates mafia activity in the United States and settles mafia turf battles. Founded by Charles "Lucky" Luciano, the Mafia Commission is presided over by a Board of Directors comprised of representatives of major mafia families. The mafia never would have gained a toehold in the United States, much less been celebrated by Hollywood, had the Rothschild-controlled federal government and its agents of propaganda in the media not created it and supported its rise every step of the way.

Mafia gang groups were state-sanctioned criminals. The federal government worked with them and advance their interests. There was even a code name for the federal government's secret alliance with Jewish and Italian-American crime families: Operation Underworld. It was through Operation Underwood that the federal government gathered intelligence and advanced shadow interests by way of organized crime.

In 1983, Volpe was discovered in the trunk of a car in a Toronto airport, after having been shot dead, but by then, Abramoff was on to bigger and better things. The future lobbyist parlayed his ties to secret societies, Ronald Reagan's inner circle, and organized crime into the Chairmanship of the College Republicans in 1981.

He became known, even celebrated, for his roguishness – that of defying rules and expectations. He wasn't independently minded in so much as he had powerful forces backing him who led him to believe he was accountable to no one; he acted as though he were a law unto himself.

As senior executive for the Diner's Club, Frank Abramoff was able to open doors for his criminally-minded son. The Diner's Club was owned by Alfred Bloomingdale, a member of the Knights of Malta who enjoyed "global access" on Reagan's Foreign Intelligence Advisory Board. The FBI had investigated Bloomingdale over his connections to organized crime.

Through Bloomingdale, Abramoff was connected to Roy Cohn, who had perfected the art of the compromising the nation's politicians to advance the interests of the syndicate. Cohn provided counsel to the leading mafia families and advised Sen. Joe McCarthy whose accusations of Communist infiltration were so indiscriminate and extreme that they discredited and doused any legitimate concerns about Communist activity within the federal government. McCarthy's activities proved to be distraction and misdirection, just as the hidden hand had intended. As Senator, McCarthy could grandstand all he liked, but he was still an employee within the Rothschild corporation dba as the federal government and so he advanced the syndicate's interests in the theater of politics. "All the world's a stage, and each actor plays his part," British bard William Shakespeare once quipped.

As Chair of the College Republicans, Abramoff wrote to Cohn, requesting the use of a secret fundraising list for the Republican Party. "Alfred Bloomingdale, a close personal friend of my family, told me to contact you immediately," Abramoff wrote. "Although we (College Republicans) are an arm of the (Republican National Committee), we must become financially self-sufficient. (Because) of his close association with the President, Mr. Bloomingdale was able to free up the RNC contributor list for our use. Within the next couple of weeks, we must raise $50,000 in order to mail and phone bank these lists. I have no doubt that we will pyramid that $50,000, to over $1 million within the first year."

Cohn had been connected to Donald Trump – and the future president's strategists, Roger Stone and Paul Manafort during the Nixon Administration. Through Cohn, Stone met a major mobster, "Fat Tony" Solerno to whom Cohn had reportedly confided that everything in the government is "fixed" and "can be handled," including the U.S. Supreme Court, which "costs a few more dollars," *The Weekly Standard* reports.

Stone, Abramoff, Manafort, and Trump were among the willing who served the syndicate in exchange for professional and financial advantages. Even if they were ultimately prosecuted over alleged crimes they may have committed on behalf of the syndicate, the shadow hand controlled all layers of power, ensuring that they were never truly at risk of any real or damning consequences. In the meantime, they stood to become extraordinarily wealthy, powerful, and influential – far more than their talents would otherwise have delivered. Their paths would intersect and intertwine in the decades that followed.

After presiding over the College Republicans, Abramoff cut his teeth at regime change in South Africa, this time partnering with the George Soros-backed National Endowment for Democracy (NED).

NED's London-based sister organization, the Westminster Foundation, was bankrolled by the British Government, "reflecting wider British imperialistic designs – which began as part of a British covert action between the Reagan Administration and NED leaders on behalf of the South African apartheid regime," *Executive Intelligence Review* (*EIR*) reports. Abramoff's team was involved in "assassinations, white supremacist propaganda, and a spying apparatus."

For the express purpose of spreading freedom around the world, Abramoff established an office for the International Freedom Foundation (IFF) in Washington, DC as "a front for the South African regime's secret policy and military intelligence," *EIR* writes. Other offices were opened in London, Hamburg, Brussels (capitol of the European Union), Rome, and Johannesburg.

He then created Citizens for America, "an Anglo-American imperialist faction within the Reagan-Bush Administration, led by the Heritage Foundation, which was steered by the Fabian Society's Stuart Butler," *EIR* reports. "Abramoff's group was enmeshed within a global network of mercenaries, illegal arms dealers, drug traffickers, money launderers, terrorists, and private spies.

Abramoff; his lieutenant, Grover Norquist, who later presided over Americans for Tax Reform; and the South Africa National Student Foundation ran a summit conference in 1985 "for rightist guerrilla movements, African diamond smugglers, heroin-trafficking Afghan mujaheddin, and Oliver North's cocaine-smuggling Nicaraguan-Contras," the *EIR* reports. Jack Abramoff's IFF financed South African aparteid. Citizens for America, which was reportedly backed by the CIA, bankrolled Ollie North.

The IFF's center in Johannesburg was run by Craig Williamson, who has been described as a "South African spy, police informant, and assassin." Williamson reportedly confessed to having participated in state-sponsored murders as part of a larger South African military intelligence initiative to undermine the anti-apartheid movement led by Nelson Mandela. Both the left and right were controlled by different factions of the same syndicate to advance wider global designs. Meanwhile, Soros, who would reconnect with Abramoff in Russia, was cozying up to the African government to establish "imperial plantations" and mining operations.

NED toppled South African governments and replaced them with puppet regimes aligned with the Anglo-American corporate-political establishment which then opened up opportunities for the syndicate to loot and establish monopolies. According to the *EIR*, the South Africans provided funding to Jack Abramoff during and after his 1981 take-over of the College Republicans while Craig Williamson, the assassin, personally trained Abramoff in the art of dirty tricks.

The "gang of right-wing con men (around Abramoff eventually) destroyed Washington and made a killing," *Harpers* reports.

The new conservative ethos advanced by Abramoff celebrated "confrontation," according to *Harpers,* which reported on his constant references to *The Godfather*, his penchant for dressing as a mafioso in a black trench coat and fedora, his Meyer Lansky memorabilia, and a "murderer argot."

Abramoff was a conservative version of a revolutionary. "War was the order of the day, from President Reagan's fight with the air-traffic controllers right down to the college campus, where Abramoff became famous for his declaration: 'It is not our job to seek peaceful coexistence with the Left. Our job is to remove them from power permanently'," *Harpers* reports. "Abramoff liked to describe (his Conservative Republicans) as 'the sword and shield of the Reagan Revolution,' and in 1984, the young firebrand used his moment at the rostrum of the G.O.P. convention in Dallas to lecture the assembled small-business types on revolutionary theory."

Abramoff organized what *Harpers* describes as "one of the strangest spectacles in American political history, a media event designed to cement conservatism's identification with revolution."

At this revolutionary gathering, guerrillas appeared in place of rock bands, *Harpers* reports, adding: "Every kind of freedom fighter was there, joining hands in territory liberated by arms from a Soviet client regime. There were Nicaraguan Contras, some Afghan mujahideen, an American tycoon. (As) freedom's embodiment, Abramoff had chosen a terrorist: Jonas Savimbi, the leader of an armed cult."

And then there was Iran-Contra. "The outlines of the Iran-Contra story are well known," *Harpers* writes. "President Reagan's CIA was waging a 'secret' war against the Sandinista government of Nicaragua; the Democratic Congress understandably objected, as we were technically at peace with that nation, and, in 1983, cut off funds to the CIA-backed Contras. Over at the National Security Council, however, Marine Lieutenant-Colonel Oliver North came up with a scheme to get money to the Contras anyway, using a network of private donors, weapons sales to Iran, and private supply operations. He also organized behind-the-scenes efforts to lobby Congress to change its mind."

In a notebook entry from 1985, North named Abramoff as a person who could influence the Contra-aid vote in Congress. That same day, Abramoff reportedly telephoned North to advise him that the votes could be available in exchange for favors. "We do not ordinarily remember Iran-Contra for the business opportunities it generated, but in the long, winding history of conservatism-as-industry it remains a particularly instructive chapter," *Harpers* reports. "None of this put much money into the pockets of the Contras, though."

In one instance, the conservatives took "customary profiteering to dizzy entrepreneurial heights" by giving only $2.7 million of $12 million raised to the Contras, *Harpers* reports. "Funds were passed around to lovers, friends, and middlemen. Iran-Contra was the scandal with the Midas touch, and it continued to rain money on the faithful even after the whole rotten operation had been rolled up."

The IFF sold copies of a videotape of North testifying before Congress. "Oliver North videotapes eventually became something of an industry unto themselves, but the one made by Abramoff, entitled *Telling It Like It Is*, is almost certainly the only bit of filmed entertainment ever to be dedicated 'to the memory of William J. Casey,' the CIA director made famous by his unabashed contempt for Congress," *Harpers* reports.

(Chillingly, Casey has been quoted as saying: "We'll know our disinformation campaign is complete when everything the American public believes is false.")

Reflecting the syndicate's hand in Iran-Contra, *EIR* recounts how Swedish Prime Minister Olof Palme was assassinated by a lone gunman on the streets of Stockholm in 1986 while in the process of curtailing Swedish arms dealers who were trafficking arms to the Contras and to Iran. "The Iran-Contra scandal had not yet broken publicly, and Palme's probe threatened to blow the lid on the entire covert program," *EIR* reports. "Curiously, many of the guns being sold by the Swedes—with the collusion of Oliver North, CIA chief William Casey, and the Israelis—were coming from East Germany and other Soviet bloc states."

At the same time, the conservative profiteers made a mockery out of their traditional conservative Christian base. "The trade in Ollie-mania boomed for years, as the persecuted patriot was indicted for his crimes and came to require a legal-defense fund (and also, apparently, a host of fake legal-defense funds)," *Harpers* reports. "Jerry Falwell compared Ollie to Jesus Christ. There were Oliver North key chains and pocketknives and T-shirts and eventually even a TV show in which Ollie told America the secrets of war.

"There was (also) the usual round of plunder, as funds raised to help Ollie stayed with the fund-raisers instead. And inevitably there was 'Ollie, Inc.,' as the man himself went into the nonprofit direct-mail business.

"By 1994, when he ran for a Senate seat in Virginia, Oliver North had become the most successful political fund-raiser in the land, bringing in some $20 million over the course of his campaign."

The Iran-Contra investigation revealed how private money was being raised through the sale of government property and favors – to fund private armies and overseas operations. In other words, the City of London, led by Rothschild, was once again harvesting the assets of a nation – this time, the United States – to enrich itself and its cronies while advancing its agenda throughout the world at the expense of the American people.

Casey, whom Abramoff eulogized, had established what *Harpers* describes as "the construction of a foreign-policy instrument (free) from the meddling of Congress, financed by sales of weapons and another precious commodity that government had in abundance but had hitherto been reluctant to market—access."

In the years that followed, the government would be privatized, with services delegated to private contractors, like Erik Prince, who were accountable to no one and whose companies would be hauled before Congress over allegations they had murdered innocent civilians in cold blood. In the meantime, countries were being looted and destroyed and their governments stripped of any ability to restrain the metastasizing crime syndicate.

Iran-Contra, Marc Rich, and the Oligarchs

The Iran-Contra scandal was finessed through the Reagan Administration to secure the release of hostages by selling arms to Iran. Lest the people catch on the fact that their government was being run and managed by criminals and operating under color-of-law, the syndicate relied upon drugs, arms sales, and human trafficking to fund their operations. Money from the sale of arms to Iran was redirected to the Contra-rebels in Nicaragua. The Contras, an invention of the theater that was the Cold War, were fighting the "Marxist" Sandinistas, whilst committing human rights atrocities, like rape and torture.

The middleman between Oliver North and Iran was Adnan Khashoggi, the Saudi arms dealer who moved money around the world for the Filipino dictators Ferdinand and Imelda Marcos, partnered with Bilderberger Group founder Prince Bernhard, and trafficked young women to political and Hollywood elites. After North was caught and prosecuted for his role in Iran-Contra, he went on to preside over the National Rifle Association which was implicated during the Trump Administration in a scheme to assist criminal Russian oligarch with their money laundering.

Another actor in the Iran-Contra saga was Marc Rich, who has been described as "the most notorious swindler in America," but even this description fails to do this con-man justice.

In 1983, the federal government went through the motions of prosecuting Rich. He was sentenced up to 325 years in prison over charges of racketeering, mail and wire fraud, failing to report $100 million in taxable income, and "trading with the enemy." Rich managed to flee before the law caught up with him.

As a naturalized, unextraditable Swiss citizen, Rich held Spanish and Israeli passports. He would go on to mentor the Russian oligarchs on the strategies they employed to loot Russia after Abramoff, helped secure their election of reformers who facilitated the looting.

The syndicate treated the nations and people of the world as marks to be fleeced and exploited for pleasure, power, and profit. In 1983, while Rich was cultivating the oligarchs, Reagan was busy promoting the Strategic Defense Initiative (Star Wars) to shoot down any projectiles launched against the United States from the Soviet Union while the syndicate managed both sides of the Cold War.

The federal government "invested" over $30 billion in this contrived war, with little to show for it. Who would prosecute those misappropriating the wealth? After all, they were faithfully executing the agenda of the corporation which held the power to prosecute them. Perhaps this dynamic accounts for why politicians and public figures so often succumb to fits of uncontrollable laughter. They can't believe they are getting away with scams like this and becoming unspeakably rich in the process.

In 1983, to create a little drama to render the Cold War credible, the Soviets shot down Korean Airlines Flight 007 over the Sea of Japan, prompting NATO to deploy missiles all over Europe; this, in turn, generated more money for contractors while spreading conflict and mayhem around the world. Of course, the plane was a 747 made by Boeing which was headquartered in Seattle, a city advancing globalism.

By this point, the Communist Christians had reclaimed power of the Soviet Union and were hardly a threat to anyone but the hidden hand. As evidence of this, in place of the blood-thirsty savagery and psychopathy of the Stalinist era, *Forbes* journalist Paul Klebnikov describes them in this way:

"Business in Russia for Western companies was relatively straight forward. It was important to have the right contacts and introductions, but basically Soviet government officials overseeing the trade deals acted according to precise economic principles. Typically the officials were informed by the central planners at Gosplan that the USSR needed a particular quantity of a particular type of good; then the only question was which Western firm offered the best deal in terms of price, quality, and delivery schedules.

"The Soviet Union had an excellent reputation as a commercial partner: The Soviet trading establishment was an honest counter party, did not engage in bait-and-switch shenanigans, and did not try to renege on the bill. In the late 1980's, once the central government began losing its authority and more business was handled by semi-independent commercial organizations, the market became corrupted-an inside deal among cronies."

By this point the hidden hand was angling on reestablishing control over the Soviet Union/Russia. In 1985, Mikhail Gorbachev was appointed General Secretary of the Communist Party. Reagan declared the Cold War won shortly after thundering, "Mr. Gorbachev, tear down this wall," referring to the symbolic Berlin Wall, which separated the free West from the oppressed, Communist East.

Right after Rich managed to evade the feds in 1983, he was on the ground in the Soviet Union, figuring out how he could leverage his contacts and criminal networks to fleece this country. As the Soviet Union collapsed, he would go on to become wealthier, stealing Russian assets and selling them around the world at high mark ups. More on this later.

By his 50s, Rich was a billionaire. The Russian press accused Rich, "based on information leaked from the government authorities, of bribery, illegal export of raw materials, aiding in capital flight, even laundering drug dollars," Klevnikov writes.

By the 1980's, it was clear that the Soviet Union has changed. This was no longer Stalin's USSR. "As far back as the late 1980's, it had become apparent that the nascent Russian market economy operated according to one simple principle: Commercial success depended upon political influence," Klevnikov writes. "If you had good political connections, you could become fabulously wealthy. If you did not, you would most certainly fail." The new right endeavored to shore up its power at the Kremlin so that Russia's wealth would be theirs.

There were clear linkages between Rich, Iran-Contra, Rothschild, and the syndicate, the *Executive Intelligence Review* reports. Rich sold 20th Century Fox to News Corp CEO Rupert Murdoch, an alleged Mossad asset who went on to partner with Jacob Rothschild and World Bank economist Larry Summers, a key strategist who helped shore up wealth for the Russian oligarchs. Reflecting the network in place, Rich had ties to Georgian-Israeli Grigori Loutchansky, a Russian mafioso who was involved with the Lucchese, Gambino, and Colombo crime families.

In 1987, a member of the Colombo crime family allegedly ordered a mob hit against a federal prosecutor William Aronwald for the crime of "disrespecting" the Cosa Nostra, an influential Italian-mafia terrorist organization, reflecting the crossover among the Italian and Jewish mafias while Rothschild wielded financial and political control over the Vatican and Crown.

Meanwhile, Paul Marcinkus, who was implicated in a Vatican Bank scandal with Rich, "was linked to Michele Sindona, a powerful Italian banker and member of Italian branch of Freemasonry, the Propaganda Due, who managed heroin profits for the Gambino crime family and laundered money from his personal banks through the Vatican and into Swiss banks." Marcinkus was implicated in the collapse of the Banco Ambrosiano in which the Institute for the Works of Religion (Vatican Bank) was the main shareholder and which was accused to laundering money to the Contras during the Reagan Administration.

Yet, when all was said and done, nobody did money laundering like the Filipino dictators.

Kleptocrats in the Philippines

In 1980, Roger Stone, Paul Manafort, Charles Black, and Peter Kelly established a firm, Black Manafort Stone and Kelly (BMSK) for their political lobbying and consulting activities. Trump retained the firm to defend his casino interests in Atlantic City.

Ferdinand Marcos was re-elected President of the Philippines in 1981. By the time Ronald Reagan was President of the United States, the kleptocratic impulses of this couple was in full swing. While Stone and Manafort were forging relationships with the regime, Imelda Marcos was photographed with Trump and his second wife, Marla Marples.

An associate who joined Manafort on the Philippines account once remarked that working at the firm was "like playing one big game of *Stratego*: building armies and scheming to take over the world; at times, that is exactly what was going on," *Politico* reports.

BMSK "helped the dictator move and invest the billions that he plundered from the public, with some of the so-called Marcos cronies becoming quite wealthy themselves," *Politico* reports.

While Imelda and Ferdinand Marcos lived lives of unrestrained luxury, ordinary Filipinos languished in poverty – until, in 1986, a People Power Revolution forced Marcos from power. Yet, "it wasn't an overthrow of Marcos by the people of the Philippines," reports Bill Cooper, the author of *Behold a Pale Horse*. "It was organized, instigated, and carried out by the CIA and the KGB," reflecting the syndicate's controls of both sides of wars and revolutions.

In 1988, Ferdinand and Imelda Marcos were indicted in a racketeering scheme in which they stood accused of embezzling public funds to purchase four buildings in New York for $103 million while "defrauding U.S. financial institutions of $165 million." Reagan expressed his deepest sympathies for the misfortune of the Marcoses, whom he characterized as good friends, Reagan spokesman Marlin Fitzwater said.

In 1969, during a state visit to Manila, Ronald Reagan, as Governor of California, was photographed dancing with Imelda Marcos while President Marcos danced with Nancy, Reagan's wife. Marcos had reportedly made illegal contributions to the political campaigns of Jimmy Carter and Ronald Reagan and retained close, affectionate relationships with these and other political leaders.

Later on, Stone and Manafort separated from BMSK and forged their own political consulting firms. BMSK became BKSH, a firm which the Bush Administration retained to market the false intelligence reports that led the United States to war against Iraq on trumped up charges circulated by Ahmed Chalabi and the Iraqi National Congress. BSKH was acquired by the powerful PR firm, Burson-Marsteller, which had emerged on the stage as a powerful PR firm in 1983 over its skills in "managing perception."

Among its hires was Susan Eisenhower, the daughter of President Dwight Eisenhower who laid the foundations for the planned convergence of the USSR and the United States in the 1950's. In 1985, the firm forged an alliance with Xinhua News Agency and established China Global Public Relations Company, the first local PR company in China. A subsidiary of the Xinhua News Agency provided public relations support for foreign firms in China and for Chinese firms forging business abroad.

Burson-Marsteller is agent for the Saudi Basic Industries Corporation (SABIC) at the Helmsley Building at 230 Park Ave., South in New York, New York.

Burson-Marsteller's parent PR company, Wire and Plastic Products (WPP), owns such powerful PR firms as Hill & Knowlton, which expanded its operations to China in 1984 and represented BCCI during its money laundering crisis. Hill & Knowlton played a prominent role in marketing neoconservative designs for war during the Administration of President George W. Bush.

A Rothschild-affiliated company, WPP crafted the highly successful and profitable ad campaign, "A Diamond is Forever" for De Beers, the diamond company founded by Cecil Rhodes; financing for the campaign came from the London-based N.M. Rothschild & Sons.

WPP has gone on to represent major oil companies while running advertising campaigns to "greenwash" these companies – that is, provide misleading information to portray their environmentally unfriendly policies as environmentally friendly. Berkshire Hathaway – the company of billionaire Warren Buffett, a close sponsor and friend of Microsoft founder Bill Gates – attempted unsuccessfully to acquire WPP in 2012.

Once Abramoff joined Microsoft's lobbying firm in 1993, he was retained by Marcos to help the dynasty retain power in the Philippines.

NarcoDollars, Junk Bonds, and Casinos

In *Red Cocaine: The Drugging of America and the West,* Joseph Douglass writes that in the 1980's, Cuba worked with Colombia's Medellin drug cartel to smuggle cocaine into the United States. A key facilitator was Gen. Raul Castro, the Minister of Defense and Fidel Castro's brother. "Several defectors had previously reported strong ties between Cuba and the cartels," he writes. Cuba is the main sponsor of Colombia's M-19 guerrilla revolutionaries and the military/terrorist arm of Colombia's Communist Party, the Revolutionary Armed Forces of Colombia (FARC), both of which are also heavily involved in narcotics production and trafficking.

In 1988, Kenneth Bialkin left Willkie, Farr for Skadden Arps Slate Meagher and Flom represented insider trader, Michael Milken. By this point, Milken was "laundering drug money through his junk bond schemes" as the nation began the process of deregulating the banking system and financial markets.

Bialkin had reportedly engineered the consolidation of the mafia brokerage houses while "narco-dollars, or money being laundered through drugs, were flooding into the United States," *EIR* writes. The attorney "apparently recognized that if he could create a large enough and diversified enough financial structure to accommodate the hot cash, the rewards would be nearly endless," *EIR* reports. "In rapid succession, he executed the absorption of Lehman Brothers into Kuhn, Loeb and Company. Shearson Hayden Stone bought out Loeb Rhodes. And, by 1984, all of those houses had been in turn bought out by American Express Company, which changed its name to Shearson Lehman American Express," with Bialkin, a close associate of Henry Kissinger, serving on the Board.

Meanwhile, Edmund Safra's Republic National Bank of New York reportedly served as a money laundering hub for both the Medellin Cartel and the Syrian-Lebanese Mafia.

In 1991, Harvard Law attorney Alan Dershowitz was Milken's attorney after the junk bond king faced felony charges for violating U.S. securities laws. As part of his defense, Dershowitz reportedly purchased an advertisement in the *New York Times* to denounce a book critical on Milken as anti-Semitic. Written by James B. Stewart, the front-page editor of the *Wall Street Journal*, *Den of Thieves* exposed the alleged criminality surrounding Milken's operation at Drexel Burnham. "In his book, Stewart cut through the myth of Milken as a financial genius, showing instead that much of his success was due to illegal acts which preyed upon both those who invested their money with Drexel's brokers, and on the U.S. economy as a whole," *EIR* reports.

"The petro-dollars of the seventies paved the way for the narco-dollar invasion of the 1980s," *EIR* reports. Milken's junk bonds provided "an ideal way to repatriate drug money and other illicit drugs. From his promotion of junk bonds in the mid-1970s, Milken built up a network of corporate raiders around him, many of whom had organized crime connections. They had excess dollars, money which they used initially to buy real estate, restaurants, casinos, and other cash-based businesses ideally suited for washing money. However, as the drug trade flourished, these traditional means of laundering money became inadequate. They needed bigger, more expensive targets."

Milken convinced Drexel Burnham's CEO to use junk bonds to fund corporate takeovers, a modern day version of piracy. "The same raiders who had been purchasing junk bonds could use their money to take over large corporations, especially corporations with a large cash flow, such as food, beverage, and tobacco companies," *EIR* reports.

In the 1980s over $1.5 trillion was invested in corporate takeovers and leveraged buyouts. Of this amount, more than $60 billion "went directly into the pockets of the investment bankers, the deal makers (i.e., the corporate raiders) and their attorneys," *EIR* writes. (A leveraged buyout refers one company's acquisition of another company using a significant amount of borrowed money to meet the cost of acquisition. The assets of both the company being acquired and the acquiring company are often used as collateral for the loans.)

One of the leading deal makers, Henry Kravis "exploited his ADL ties to raise money for the takeover of his firm, Kohlberg Kravis & Roberts (KKR), with Milken and his allies financing the raid. Once Drexel Burnham decided to use junk bonds to finance takeovers, the Kravis-Milken connection was a natural."

In 1990, firm borrowed $58 billion from banks, Savings and Loans, insurance companies and pension funds, to raid more than 35 companies. Kravis is now worth a reported $500 million while the firms he raided are strapped with debt, thereby threatening the soundness of pension funds. In this way, the syndicate continued to gobble up American assets through collaborations with the Rothschilds corporation dba as the federal government, which instead of protecting the interests of the American people, betrayed them in no small measure.

To pay debt from corporate raids, companies were asset-stripped and forced to close down factories, rendering hundreds of thousands of people unemployed. Many corporate raids bankrupted the targeted company, forcing the federal government – and by extension, taxpayers, to cover the debt. In some instances, the debt was covered by borrowing from a federally insured bank – or looting pension funds.

While working with organized crime figures to loot corporate America, Milken poured money into the ADL's coffers. "Behind Milken's business model was a "$6.25 trillion—the gross profits of the international dope trade from 1978-1990," *EIR* reports.

By 1989, cocaine had become an epidemic. Cuba "assisted the smugglers to move drugs into the United States and, as part of the same operation, provided arms to terrorists and revolutionaries" in Latin America, Douglass writes. "The three activities - drug-trafficking, terrorism, and organized crime – provided complementary functions; and the Soviet Bloc activities in all three areas were managed by the strategic intelligence sections in the KGB and GRU intelligence services. These strategic intelligence sections perform only special tasks of strategic importance, the most important of which (are) strategic espionage, drugs and narcotics, terrorism, deception and sabotage on behalf of the syndicate."

Two firms, officials of which were identified in Senate hearings as having assisted in money-laundering operations, were Merrill Lynch and E. F. Hutton.

Of note: E.F. Hutton was the sole and underwriter and exclusive agent for Digital World, a shell company that merged with Trump's Truth Social, a social media platform owned by Trump Media & Technology Group. Merrill Lynch was the financial advisor of the Seminole Tribe of Florida, a tribe with deep connections to Meyer Lansky, Adnan Khashoggi, Trump, Abramoff, Marcos, and the Crown.

The Tribal Connection

The Seminole Tribe of Florida was the first federally recognized tribe in the United States to acquire a casino. The federally recognized Indian tribes were established by the energy companies, principally the Rockefellers, who also laid the foundations for them to acquire settlements for historic grievances that were used as seed capital for casinos.

The first tribe in the nation to acquire a casino was the Seminole Tribal of Florida whose nascent casino operation was bankrolled by

Meyer Lansky, the founder of Murder Inc. and the National Crime Syndicate.

Lansky's crime syndicate reportedly coordinated criminal elements between the United States and Israeli intelligence – and, in turn, established an international drug running operation from Southeast Asia through the CIA-linked Corsican Mafia in the Mediterranean. Drug running, casinos, and human and arms trafficking generated tremendous cash flow for the syndicate which then moved the money around the world to fund their operations and lavish lifestyles – at the expense of the United States, the moral fabric and stability of its society, and welfare of its people. Through these connections, crime and drugs proliferated around the United States.

Lansky's lieutenant, James Weisman ran the Seminole Management Association (SMA), which ran the tribe's Hollywood casino.

The Murder, Inc. founder has been credited with convincing Seminole Chief James Billie to pursue gambling. In 1979, Lansky told Billie that the tribe could generate as much as $3 million in six months, *The Miami New Times* reports.

As narco-dollars poured into the financial system – and as the prospects for casinos and lucrative public-private partnerships and government contracts for the hundreds of Alaska Native Corporations and federally recognized Indian tribes loomed on the horizon, two major investment banks, Goldman Sachs and Morgan Stanley (whose antecedent was JP Morgan) simultaneously decided to go public in 1986.

After issuing its IPO, Goldman Sachs transformed into a "trading powerhouse, one that was acting as its own investment banker," Lisa Endlich writes in *Goldman Sachs: The Culture of Success*. "The instinct of the organization was that, without knowing how we could get that capital, there was a leap of faith, that we could achieve our goals. I think it was instinctive, not a studied decision. In 1986, the plans for international expansion were mostly just talk. The firm had a few foreign offices, one each in Switzerland, Tokyo, London, and Hong Kong. (The) goal of the firm was to build the premier investment banking firm that would dominate every aspect of business. It would be an astonishing feat, one that no firm had achieved before. In 1986, there were many investment banks in contention for the top spot, and the outcome of the race was far from assured."

With a client roster that included six of the seven sister (Rockefeller) oil companies, and General Motors, Morgan Stanley also decided to break with tradition and go public. "Prior to 1986, Morgan Stanley partners could expect to become respectably rich in a respectable way, but not hugely – even excessively – rich," Patricia Beard writes in *Blue Blood and Mutiny*. "As the risk-reward equation was heightened, Wall Street attracted people who were less interested in first class business than in the promise of mega-paydays."

Never before had these investment banks accepted outside equity – but once they decided to do it, their profits increased exponentially, enabling them to outpace the competition and establish monopolies. The outside capital funded the mergers and acquisitions departments of both banks, creating entities that were "too big to fail," meaning that their reach was so deeply embedded within the federal government, that the Rothschild corporation dba as the U.S. republic would bail them out as needed, courtesy of U.S. taxpayers.

The outside capital for for both banks arrived circuitously by way of Sumitomo Bank in Japan, with McKinsey and Co. advising, the authors wrote.

Sumitomo, incidentally, was among the first Japanese companies to gain a toehold in Saudi Arabia. Sumitomo Chemical joined Saudi Aramco to build a petro chemical complex in Saudi Arabia in 2009, *Nikkei Business Daily* reports. The Japanese company has since opened offices in Alkhobar, Riyadh, and Jeddah. Sumitomo Mitsui Banking Corporation (SMBC) is a core member of Sumitomo Mitsui Financial Group (SMFG), a Tokyo-based bank holding company that is ranked among the largest 25 banks globally by assets under management. SMBC Group has offices in 19 cities across Europe, the Middle East and Africa (EMEA) including its regional headquarters in London. SMBC Bank International is headquartered in the City of London. Sumitomo was also on hand to assist with Amarco's IPO.

In 1987, Trump acquired a 93 percent stake in Resorts International, a casino *Europe Reloaded* characterized as a "CIA/Mossad front." Among is principal investors were Tibor Rosenbaum, David Rockefeller, and Baron Edmond de Rothschild. A Hungarian-born Swiss rabbi, Rosenbaum worked with the Rothschilds to establish the Bank of International Settlements and the Frankfurt-based Banque de Credit International Geneve. Rosenbaum also worked closely with the Mossad and Lansky, whose networks overlapped with "Lucky" Luciano – a founder of the National Crime Syndicate in New Jersey.

Lansky reportedly coordinated intelligence between the Mossad and CIA. The Brooklyn-based National Crime Syndicate consisted of 14 criminal organizations, including Italian-American, Jewish, African-American, and Polish-American mobsters. Since its creation, the group has been implicated in alleged murder, racketeering, rum running, extortion, bribery, drug trafficking, illegal gambling, prostitution, robbery, fraud, money laundering, loan, sharking, pimping, among other vices and criminal activities. Mafia legends, like Al Capone, Bugsy Siegel, Frank Costello, and prominent members of the Gambino crime family, were among its members.

After its Initial Public Offering (IPO), Morgan Stanley booked $82 million income in 1989 while "some firms were reporting gigantic losses," Beard writes.

In 1990, Trump opened the Trump Taj Mahal in Atlantic City, New Jersey which he reportedly financed with $675 million in junk bonds at 14 percent interest before struggling to make the bond payments. As Taj Mahal teetered towards bankruptcy, a Rothschild bankruptcy banker by the name of Wilbur Ross represented the bondholders. Through a Ross-brokered deal with billionaire corporate raider Carl Icahn, Trump was allowed to retain a 50 percent stake in the business while Ross remained by his side to help build a profitable brand around Trump, who became an investor in the Seminole's gaming operations.

Billie and Trump would both acquire yachts previously owned by Marcos while the syndicate moved quickly to evangelize the West into Christianity, but a form that was bastardized and intended to indoctrinate (and fleece) the flock.

Christianity as a Trojan Horse for Globalism

The Reagan Administration established diplomatic relations with the Vatican, a development that inspired discomfort among Americans who were concerned with the Holy See's imperialistic designs on the United States. The Vatican, just like the Crown, had been under the control of Rothschild since the Napoleonic Wars. Yet, for centuries, the Vatican had pursued a policy of *unam sanctum*, in which it sought to establish itself as God's temporal authority over the world, claiming the world's assets – and souls, as its possessions.

While complaining about anti-Semitism, whenever its ambitions were frustrated, to guilt Christian nations into abandoning Christian oaths for office and opening the doors of power to the syndicate's criminal operatives, the Rothschilds understood that politics and religion were deeply intertwined, that, indeed, for millennia, the Protestant Monarchs professed the "divine right to rule," by way of authority granted through Jesus; the Vatican asserted its right to serve as God's temporal authority over humanity through St. Peter while the Chinese Emperors professed a "mandate from Heaven" to rule that traced to Noah.

Since establishing its color-of-law authority over the United States during the Civil War, the syndicate attempted to undermine the religious substance and morals of the nation and its people. Judaeo-Christianity was diametrically opposed to the ethos of the syndicate. The syndicate's power plays were always the same. It governed from the top down, establishing a local, regional, national, and then supranational authorities above peoples, nations and regions – and claimed to speak on behalf of everyone else, without even consulting those of whose behalf they claimed to speak. Once an organization outlived its usefulness or fell out of favor, the syndicate would discard it and erect another in its place.

Upon assuming authority by appointing themselves at the pinnacle of power, they dictated their values and agenda from above and acted as if they represented – and could therefore speak on behalf of everyone else. Agendas were communicated top-down to pastors, rabbis, and imams who sung from the same playbook, citing supportive religious texts, reinterpreted to fit the agenda. Followers would then be enlisted to lobby the government to enact that change while media praised their efforts and castigated their detractors, creating the illusion of consensus for the new moral code.

During the Reagan Administration, the shadow elite advanced efforts to realign Christianity to support Communist ideals so that the Soviet Union and United States could be seamlessly merged under a global Communist structure that promoted materialism. Christianity moved away from the gospel of salvation to embrace "New Age" principles and even a "prosperity gospel," that promoted greed.

The syndicate advanced the ecumenical movement to merge the religions and disparate denominations under one umbrella, to advance the political agenda of the shadow elite. The leaders of these groups claimed to speak for millions of followers who had never been consulted as they attempted to impose their values and belief systems upon others.

One prominent conservative evangelist, Edgar C. Bundy, concluded that ecumenicists were a destructive force in the United States. "Many of the largest missionary societies in the United States and throughout the world did not wish to be represented by the Federal Council of the Churches of Christ in America, and they never became part of that organization," Bundy writes in *Collectivism in the Churches.*

The Federal Council of Churches was established in 1908 and renamed the National Council of Churches. The NCC answered to the World Council of Churches, a global organization that promoted the material unity of churches and nations throughout the world, providing a stark contrast to Christian spiritual unity under the leadership of Jesus Christ. These churches were not interested in promoting the true Gospel of Christ. Rather they intended to reshape values within Christian societies so that congregants would gradually become indoctrinated in the Communist ethos.

"The truth is that Jesus Christ was not interested in lobbying before Pilate, Agrippa, or Caesar's government for the betterment of social, economic, or political conditions," Bundy writes. "His Gospel was the Gospel of personal salvation and to the Herodians. He said: 'Render therefore unto Caesar the things which are Caesar's, and unto God the things that are of God'.... Neither Jesus Christ nor the Apostles ever called upon the temporal rulers of their day to address their conferences, nor did they ever call upon governments to advance the cause of the church."

Two years after the Federal Council was established, representatives from Protestant denominations and missionary societies, principally from North America and Northern Europe, convened at the United Free Church in Edinburgh, Scotland, for the World Missionary Conference, which was chaired and organized by John Mott, a Methodist layman and community organizer and close friend and confidante of John D. Rockefeller Jr., who bankrolled the ecumenical movement in the United States.

After Mott was appointed first honorary president of the World Council of Churches, Rockefeller, a philanthropist and heir to the Standard Oil fortune, donated $1 million to the Friends of the World Council of Churches, which then established a Commission on

International Relations whose stated purpose was to "stimulate the churches of all nations to a more vigorous expression of the demand of the Christian conscience in relation to the political policies of governments."

Mott laid down "marching orders" intended for "members of every Protestant church around the world in an effort to expand Christianity." He also courted the financial elite. As an "apostle of unity," Mott convinced Protestant denominations to set aside doctrinal differences in the interests of advancing "a vision of worldwide Christianity based on concepts they believed Christians around the world could agree on and work together to implement."

The movement was modeled and streamline in the organizational mold of Rockefeller's Standard Oil. The ecumenical movement endeavored to unite the churches under a global bureaucracy just as the United Nations sought to unite the nations under global government. Religion was then subtly altered to mold public consciousness into accepting a global Communist system.

"The League of Churches was to become a union of all churches on faith and order as the final purpose of the League of Nations," writes Willem Adolph Visser T. Hooft, a Dutch theologian who was later appointed Secretary General of the World Council of Churches. "The dream dreamt by so many philosophers, the dream of international order, based on law and justice, seemed at last to become a political reality."

During the Eisenhower Administration, the KGB-controlled Russian Orthodox Church joined the World Council of Churches, the global body over the NCC. Godless Communists then entered the church hierarchy and advanced the social justice doctrine through the church ranks.

As Protestant denominations were establishing their own central authorities, Rabbi Isaac Mayer Wise agitated for a synod to serve as a central authority for American Judaism. The sick End of Times doctrine was promulgated by the shadow elite – that the world would be destroyed (at their hands), with the blessing of Christians, who were indoctrinated to accept the destruction of their divinely ordered word and the rejection of Christian values, with the belief that Jesus would return to save them. So-called Christian generals even promoted nuclear confrontation with the Soviets, with the hope this would led to an Armageddon to prompt the return of Jesus.

While the Bible spoke to a spiritual unity of God's people, the Scofield Bible, which was written by Cryus Scofield, promulgated the idea that the Jews would be granted a material kingdom for a presided over by an anti-Christ, a major worldly figure around whom all the worlds religions would unite.

The Rothschilds planned to install a so-called descendant of King David, or a Jesus bloodline sometime after 2015, when their 200-year contract with the British Monarchy expired. Their chosen Messiah was to be a Rothschild, which had bred into the Jesus bloodline, starting with the Rothschild Monarch, Queen Victoria.

Whether or not such lineage exists, the notion of a Jesus bloodline – which has historically conferred a "divine right (rite) to rule," had been advanced by Rothschilds through the Priory of Scion and its own potential candidates – consisting of either Rothschild bloodlines or Rothschild puppet figures. In this way, the Rothschilds aspired to rule over the world in perpetuity, with the world's blessings and tacit acceptance. After all, this outcome had been prophesied by their own Bibles, as altered by the syndicate.

Scofield, incidentally was a member of the Lotos Club, an exclusive literary society founded by Samuel Untermeyer, an attorney behind the Federal Reserve Act. What was the great literary work that warranted Scofield's membership in this exclusive club? His reinterpretation of the Bible to advance the Rothschild's wider agenda to established its seat of global power in Israel, a country established and owned by Rothschild, where the dynasty planned to be celebrated as the undisputed world leaders, as ordained by God, if not celebrated as Gods themselves.

In 1911, Untermeyer addressed concerns that the United States had fallen into the grips of a "Money Trust." Untermeyer assumed leadership in the matter – and promoted the House Committee on Banking and Currency to look into it. Given that the federal government was by then a Rothschild corporation, Congress would not have investigated the matter had the Rothschilds not allowed it.

Untermeyer was tapped to cross-examine J.P. Morgan, a key financial figure (and witness) most knowledgeable about the power and agenda behind the Money Trust whose influence was gripping, and indeed, fleecing the nation.

Untermeyer proposed a solution – the establishment of the Federal Reserve System, which solidified the trust's control over the U.S. economy, with Untermeyer playing an important role in crafting the legislation.

He also played a key role in the Clayton Anti-Trust Act, which the public celebrated as a means to prevent corporations from engaging in anti-competitive, monopolistic behavior. While appearing to defend free trade, the federal government was unleashed to block the monopolies who rivaled the syndicate for make share while the syndicate went on to dominate the markets.

If the public grew outraged over the syndicate's monopolies, such as Standard Oil, anti-trust action could be pursued, generating the perception that anti-trust action has solve the problem. The dominant company might then reappear under a different name or break up, with the original company controlling the spin-offs. Corporations were controlled through interlocking boards of directors, speaking in unison to advance a common agenda on behalf of "corporate America." Yet, they weren't speaking for everyone – or even most, just the handful of players rigging the system and operating on behalf of the syndicate.

In the years leading up to 2015, books, like Dan Brown('s *Da Vinci Code* gained vast popularity speculating about a possible Jesus bloodline - that Jesus may have actually married Mary Magdalene and sired a child. Various so-called Jesus bloodlines were ready to come forth to play the role of the Messiah. The rise of the Messiah would coincide with the establishment of a Third Temple in Israel, marking Rothschild's dominion over humanity, with the blessing of all of Christendom.

Opening the Gates of Hell

KGB defector Anatoliy Golitsyn warned the West that Communism had not been defeated, but had rather gone underground as international Communists prepared for a final, devastating assault against the free world. The agenda was documented in Golitsyn's books, *New Lies for Old* and *The Perestroika Deception*.

The long-term plan among Communist elites, he writes, was to weaken the United States so that it would merge with Russia with the United States under a Communist New World Order. The plan for convergence started in 1958 – after the Soviet Union and China ironed out their differences and devised a strategy to export Communism throughout the world.

Golitsyn remarked on the "jubilation" he observed among American and West European conservatives who celebrated Mikhail Gorbachev's *perestroika* (restructuring) and *glasnost* (openness), a strategy that was intended to bring about the political, cultural, and economic demise of the United States. The strategy was based upon Vladimir Lenin's New Economic Policy (NEP). Gorbachev had simply rebranded Leninism.

After the savage butchery, looting, and torture of millions of Russian citizens at the hands of Bolsheviks, Communism had acquired a bad reputation, such that no one wanted to be associated with it, anymore, including the Wall Street financiers who had bankrolled the movement.

Between 1921 and 1928, Lenin promoted NEP as a temporary retreat so that Communists could regroup and centralize power before advancing again. They would emerge as a kinder, gentler version of themselves. Gorbachev was not interested in opening up to the West but rather, in conquering the West on behalf of the shadow foreign interests who controlled him. Since the West was controlled by the same hand, both sides played along with the narrative, with the public none the wiser.

The Soviet strategy involved indoctrinating the American people, through the dishonest use of language. Through *perestroika*, the Communists aspired to mark "a clean break from the past," so that the West would be lulled into a false sense of security.

In interviews, Gorbachev described the Cold War as a "joint victory" between the Americans and Soviets, stating with unbridled glee, "We all won."

By "we," he did not mean the Russian and American people, but the elites controlling both nations.

The United States was then enlisted to finance its own demise. Public funds were poured into Russia and its former Soviet satellite states while the Soviet command structure remained intact.

Reagan never should have accepted *perestroika*, Golitsyn writes. "The moral grounds for a reversal of the American response and for a rejection of the Soviet strategy of 'perestroika' are very simple. A system which has killed 20 million of its own people (50 million if those killed under Communism in China are included), has raped its intellectuals, and brought suffering and misery to the peoples of the Soviet Empire, does not deserve to be renewed. The American people are under no moral obligation to help with the reconstruction of such a system."

Secretary of State Henry Kissinger, who provided strategic guidance for the West's demise, had even remarked that the United States knew nothing about the new generation of Soviet leaders. The syndicate kept the American people in the dark.

A number of insiders had acknowledged that the shadow hand had planned the end of the Cold War years, if not decades, in advance. The Berlin Wall was scheduled to fall, reuniting East and West Germany. Once this happened, the barrier that kept the criminal Communists out of the free West would be broken. From there, the syndicate would march onward, unimpeded, exploiting the openness and trust of the free world for its own advantage.

The strategy involved eliminating the Communist Christians from power in the Soviet Union so that the criminally-minded Bolsheviks the Christians had ousted, could return to power. The syndicate would then spread throughout the power structure of the former Soviet Union and United States and loot both while the criminals consolidated power and spread their networks around the world.

Forbes reporter Paul Klebnikov, who authored *Godfather of the Kremlin,* observed that the looting of Russia began taking place under *perestroika* and glasnost. To cite an example, in the 1980s, the Soviet Union held around 1,300 tons of gold. Between 1989 and 1991, most of this gold was sold. "At the same time, the Soviet Union's foreign exchange reserves had fallen from $15 billion at the start of Gorbachev's rule to a paltry $1 billion in 1991," Klevnikov writes. "Though the true picture of the U.S.S.R.'s balance of payments at this time is almost impossible to ascertain, it was clear that the Soviet Union lost about $20 billion in capital flight in 1990-91."

Gorbachev's liberal reforms "gave free rein to Russia's gangsters," Klevnikov writes. "Along with the political prisoners released from the gulags, thousands of professional criminals were freed as well. More importantly, Russia's main gangster-business empires were established under Gorbachev. Unbeknownst to the Soviet leader, many of them were sponsored by such pillars of the Soviet establishment as the KGB and the Central Committee of the Communist Party."

The Communist Party abandoned "its official monopoly on power and allowed popular elections in the nation's parliaments," he writes. "Once the controls of the central government were relaxed, provincial political bosses and enterprise directors did as they pleased. Their first impulse was to enrich themselves."

The syndicate then ran its own candidates in those elections and coordinated the victories. Once in power, the syndicate unleashed the tap of public funds and proceeded to loot.

At the end of the Cold War, the economist Alan Greenspan (and future Chairman of the Federal Reserve) rushed over to Moscow to meet Gorbachev and other Soviet leaders. The central banker, who coordinated policy with the central bankers of London, then "spoke of the necessity of privatization as a means of … cutting the Soviet budget deficit," reflecting the influence of the Crown.

Control of Soviet industry was seized from the hands of the Communist Christians and placed into the hands of the criminal Bolsheviks, with the Soviet and U.S. governments bankrolling and facilitating these efforts. Worse, the new Russian leaders wanted the American taxpayers to bail them out. "Gorbachev and his colleagues turned to the West," he writes. "They wanted to borrow $30 billion to buy Western consumer goods and resell them to Soviet consumers at ten times the cost. This, they argued, would take care of the excess cash of the population and stabilize the ruble, allowing market reforms to proceed."

The European Union signed the Schengen Agreement in 1985, providing visa-free movement throughout Rothschild's European common market. Once the Cold War was over and restrictions lifted, criminals spread throughout Europe and the world, including the Japanese yakuza, the Chinese, the Colombian Medellin cartel, the Italian mafia, the Jewish mafia, the Russian mafia. These groups then linked up and joined forces for the criminal looting of the world.

Perhaps this had been the plan all along. While the globalists harped endlessly about the need for open borders, those borders were like the walls of healthy cell that protected an organism from infection; or a fortress around a castle that warded off invading hordes, or even the lock on a front door that kept out the thief of the right. Rothschild created common markets in which people could move freely – in the so-called interest of pursuing work, opportunities, and welfare benefits while leveling the world for corporations to expand their fields of exploitation. At the same time, these criminal groups were the creations of the Rothschild crime syndicate.

The desperately poor, opportunistic, and criminally minded were invited to invade the West, with the red carpet rolled out for them. The newcomers were encouraged to take advantage of those opportunities and allowed to circulate and force their host country to accommodate them rather than apart to the new society. Anyone who dared protest this state of affairs, was called a racist, with the law inevitably siding the newcomers. The United Nations, Rothschild's nascent global government, was on hand to defend the right of people to migrate wherever they wanted in their pursuit of opportunities and benefits.

The City of London Does Banking with the Bolsheviks

Throughout the Reagan era, the KGB established banks and commercial enterprises offshore – and then transferred billions of dollars to these institutions through VEB (Vnesheconombank), a Soviet foreign trade bank," or the Russian State Development Corporation and Investment Company.

In its previous incarnation, Vneshtorgbank (and before that, Roskombank), the Soviet Union's first international bank, was established in 1922 by Olog Aschberg, a Swedish banker of Russian-Jewish descent who had presided over the Stockholm Bank, the first bank of Sweden for Trade Unions and Cooperatives.

The Stockhold Bank contributed funds to help support the Bolshevik Revolution. As a reward for his service, Aschberg was invited to do business in the Soviet Union during Lenin's New Economic Policy, an effort to restore normalcy and productive relations with foreign nations while burying its savage extermination of millions of innocent Russians.

From 1945 to 1990, the Soviet Union was managed by Victor Rothschild, the father of Jacob Rothschild. Victor Rothschild, 3rd Baron Rothschild "worked remotely" from London and reportedly helped stage manage the Cold War – through which Zionists generated an absolute fortune playing the Communist and free West against each other at the expense of lives, nations, and fortunes.

Meanwhile, the dynasty used the opportunity of the Cold War to extend its intelligence networks around the world and install puppet regimes.

In addition to serving as a British intelligence officer and spy for the Soviet Union and serving as advisor on intelligence to both Conservative and Labour Governments, Victor Rothschild frequently visited Chequers, the country residence of Prime Minister Edward Heath, who has been widely accused and investigated for child molestation, allegations the cantankerous Heath flatly denied..

In the 1980s, the KGB set up fake banks and commercial enterprises offshore, especially in Greece, Cyprus, Italy, and Portugal. Billions of dollars were transferred to these institutions through VEB, the Soviet foreign trade bank.

Victor Rothschild was a member of the Knights of Malta and the Order of St. John, a Royal order established in 1888 by Queen Victoria, the first Rothschild Monarch. The order was dedicated to St. John the Baptist, the patron saint of the freemasons.

Despite being a British member of the Rothschild family and Soviet spy – or, perhaps, because of these attributes, Victor Rothschild received the Legion of Merit, a military award of the U.S. Armed Forces given for exemplary service awarded to military and political figures of foreign governments.

The syndicate's hand in VEB was evident in sentiments Viktor Gerahchenko expressed in 1992. The bank, he said, "does not have a central banking license. It does not need it, since it does not conduct any commercial operations." The bank, which supported the government programs and structural reforms of Russia as the syndicate consolidated its power in the Kremlin, is the only Russian Bank "the central bank does not check," he said.

The son of a leading Soviet banker who ran the Financial Department of the Foreign Office, Gerashchenko had served as chairman of the Soviet State bank and Governor of of the Russian Central Bank during Perestroika and afterwards.

In October of 1919, the White Army launched an assault on Petrograd and came close to capturing the city for the Christian Czar. This is the point at which Moscow Narody Bank (MNB), opened a branch in London in partnership with the London Branch of Mosnarkbank, an offshoot of the Bank of Russia.

After receiving an apparent jolt of funding form London, in November of 1919, the Red Army overtook the White Army, securing a win for the Bolsheviks.

In 2002, Gerashchenko became Chairman of Yukos, a major Russian oil company controlled by Jacob Rothschild.

In 2008, Rothschild's proxy, Russian President Vladimir Putin, was appointed Chairman of VEB's supervisory board.

The following year the bank quadrupled its assets to two trillion rubles, or $65 billion.

VII.
The Syndicate Goes Global

"Those who trade liberty for security, have neither."

President John Adams
American Founding Father

The Reagan Administration was building bridges with the Soviets while professing to be fighting them. That it could or would do otherwise was not even in the cards, given that the federal government, as a Rothschild corporation, was principally concerned with advancing the City of London's interests.

In 1983, the Reagan Administration launched the Strategic Defense Initiative (SDI), otherwise known as "Star Wars," a fanciful scheme to protect the United States from a Soviet nuclear attack. With the launch of Star Wars, the money disappeared into thin air. Worse, while building a pseudo-defense against the Soviets, at great cost to the taxpayer, the federal government was giving the Soviets $9.8 billion in international aid. No aid had been provided to the USSR the previous years. So, on the one hand, billions of the taxpayers' money was being invested to protect the U.S. from a Soviet existential threat. On the other, the U.S. was feeding the existential threat. For good reason, conservative commentator William F. Buckley complained that the United States was being "satellized" by the Soviet Union.

Reagan's vice president, George H.W. Bush, was among the most outspoken champions of the New World Order. Bush's father was trading with the Nazis while the United States was fighting them. As President, Bush continued to pour money into the former Soviet Union. In 1989, he signed the Support for Eastern European Democracy (SEED) Act to inject capital into the former Soviet satellite states to support politically-connected businesses under the pretext of "spreading democracy." Bush also opened the doors for politically-connected corporations to enter the coveted Chinese market, starting with Bill Gates, who established five year plans with the Chinese government and military to ensure they moved in lockstep with the agenda laid out by global planners.

Bush committed the American people to financing "the development of the Russian private sector" through the Freedom for Russian and Emerging Eurasian Democracies and Open Market Support (FREEDOM) Act, which created American Business Centers under the U.S. Commercial Service to develop markets in Russia and former Soviet satellite states for the purposes of stimulating economic growth, with additional support provided by the IMF and World Bank.

The Clinton Administration built upon SEED to establish the Defense Enterprise Fund, which privatized the Russian defense industry – that is, transferred its control from the state and into the private sector, which was controlled by the syndicate, which had created the Soviet monster in the first place. After the Christians purged the Bolsheviks and restored normalcy to their institutions, Rothschild corporation, dba the U.S. federal government, placed Russia back in the hands of international criminals to the great detriment of Americans, Russians, and the world.

Over $400 million was granted to Russia and neighboring countries through USAID. Through agencies like RAEF, the Bolshevik government could tapping U.S. taxpayers not to benefit American citizens or even to provide a wider public or societal good. Instead the funds were used to bankroll the private interests of a small, charmed, criminal clique.

RAEF was described as an "investing company" whose purpose was to secure a "reasonable return over time through (public) investment, after expenses." To this end, RAEF "recruited from the business community" and reported, not to the Russian leadership, but to a "Board of (American and Russian) private citizens." The group endeavored to "stimulate private sector development in Russia," the sworn enemy of the United States, "with a particularly interest in the Russian Far East," which RAEF described as "a region of enormous vitality and potential."

RAEF's *Annual Report* stipulated that the organization was "building a private business sector and a financial infrastructure" to increase "the availability of consumer goods." American taxpayers were tapped to capitalize the businesses to produce products that could then be sold within Russia or overseas at a high market up so that politically-connected individuals and their firms could exploit these opportunities for profit.

RAEF's *Annual Report* affirmed that Russia's 150 million consumers have "an appetite for high quality goods and services." To this end, the United States passed along U.S. patents by way of the technological networks Kissinger had established during the Nixon Administration. The patents had been developed in the United States and then promptly shared with a rival country.

Among those who led efforts for U.S. investment into Russia was Wilbur Ross, a advisor for Donald Trump and the Rothschilds. (*The Paradise Papers* revealed that Ross had acquired a multi-million dollar stake in a company that does business with a close associate of Vladimir Putin.)

President Bill Clinton appointed Ross to manage a U.S.-Russia Investment Fund (USRIF) to invest over $300 million in 44 Russian companies within a decade. The public's money was used while private investors were positioned to reap the benefits, leaving American citizens holding the debt. USRIF became a major shareholder in the European Bank of Reconstruction and Development – and partner of JP Morgan Chase, whose corporate antecedents had bankrolled the Bolshevik Revolution, exterminating tens of millions of innocent Russians for the purposes of capturing market share, stealing natural resources, establishing, and seizing control of the government.

The Clinton Administration poured public funds into such companies as DeltaBank, the first bank to sell credit cards and residential mortgages in Russia. (USRIF) built upon the $340 million Russian-American Enterprise Fund (RAEF) and the $100 million Fund for Large Enterprises (FLEER), which President George H.W. Bush had established and seeded with funding from the U.S. Agency for International Development (USAID).

RAEF was located at 17 State Street, the heart of the financial district of New York – and home of Wall Street and the New York Stock Exchange. The individuals who served on the Board of these Russian investment enterprises were a who's who of central bankers, private investors, and corporate executive:

RAEF's Chairman: Gerald Corrigan, former President of the Federal Reserve Bank of New York;

RAEF's President/CEO: Robert Towbin, Director of L.F. Rothschild.

RAEF's Board of Directors:

Victor Dmitriev, President of Russian Bank for Reconstruction and Development;

Richard Fisher, President and CEO of the Federal Reserve of Dallas; Brown Brother Harriman; Kissinger McLarty Associates;

Robert Brown III, President of First Russia Capital Corporation;

Sarah Carey, the President of Steptoe & Johnson, an attorney who advised on opening the Soviet Union to foreign investment by providing counsel to multinationals angling to do business there.

Steptoe & Johnson has employed key personnel in Rothschild's corporation dba as the federal government, including, for example, the Chairman of the U.S. International Trade Commission, U.S. Secretary of the Interior (Bruce Babbitt), General Counsel to the National Security Agency, U.S. District Court judges, prosecutors, counsel to Vice President Dick Cheney, the Governor of Puerto Rico (the location of the private IRS Trust (https://tabublog.com/2017/06/26/irs-is-a-privately-owned-puerto-rican-trust/), General Counsel of the Army, legal advisor to Henry Kissinger, General Counsel for the CIA, U.S. Ambassador to India....

In the 1980s, Carey served on the Board of Directors of Yukos Oil and opened up a law office in Moscow to facilitate deals with the Russians. While serving on the Board of the Defense Enterprise Fund, Carey led efforts to privatize the Russian defense industry. She also chaired the Eurasia Foundation, which distributed $400 million in grants to Russia and neighboring countries, with funded from USAID.

Another RAEF Board Member was Robert Hormats, Vice Chair of Goldman Sachs International (also: Kissinger & Associates)

While U.S. taxpayers were being fleeced, RAEF supported an "ambitious goal," endorsed by the Russian and U.S. governments, of "supporting the Russian private sector (and) earning a reasonable return on capital," the 1994 *Annual Report* reports.

The return for a public investment was not used to pay down the national debt or invest in infrastructure, affordable housing, affordable health care, or other benefits for American citizens; instead it was "invested" to generate a return to for individual aligned with Rothschild Inc. Essentially, they were spreading the public's money around to themselves. If this wasn't bad enough, check out what went down at Harvard University.

The Harvard Connection

Harvard University, another development partner of the World Bank, facilitated the looting of Russia, with economist Larry Summers leading the way. Summers had served on the Council of Economic Advisors from 1982 to 1983 when the Reagan Administration was launching SDI (Star Wars), pouring billions of dollars into a fanciful scheme to protect the United States from the Soviet Union, which was in the process of satellizing the United States. While terrorizing the public with prospective threats of nuclear war to justify the expenditure, the Reagan Administration was sending $9.8 billion in international aid to the Soviet Union, which was in the process of removing Communist Christians from power, re-installing the criminal class, and padding the syndicate's pockets with the public's money.

At Harvard, Summers became one of the university's youngest professors, an accomplishment obtained not by the quality of his intellect – as Harvard has a vast pool of talent from which draw. Summers distinguished himself through his knowledge and complicity in a treasonous agenda against the United States that resulted in doors magically opening before him with the assistance of the hidden hand.

Summers became Chief Economist of the World Bank which was then presided over by Lewis Thomas Preston, the Harvard-educated grandson of a partner in Rockefeller's Standard Oil. Preston worked for JP Morgan and its subsidiary, Morgan Guaranty Trust.

While working at the World Bank, Summers developed "shock therapy," a strategy was arguably not even his idea, though he promoted it. The doctrine created managed chaos from which a new order could emerge. The people Summers placed into power were Rothschild-connected individuals who proceeded to help themselves to public funds, loot Russian assets, and establish monopolies. This was done in the interests of greed, with little consideration given to the millions of Russian people harmed in the process, a people who had already endured the savagery of the Russian Revolution and were in the process of recovery. Summers returned like a proverbial boot in the face.

Summers' protégé at Harvard was Andrei Schleifer, a Russian-American Jew. Together the men worked on the Russian project. They were tasked with rescuing the Russian economy. "While Schleifer was being paid by U.S. taxpayers to advise the Russians on capital markets in the 1990s, his wife, Nancy Zimmerman, bought and traded Russian equities for a Boston hedge fund she ran," Nation reports. "They even used Schleifer's U.S. taxpayer-funded offices to run Zimmerman's Moscow-based hedge fund operations."

After working for the World Bank, Summers was appointed to the U.S. Department of Treasury under President Bill Clinton. In1993, Summers secured a no-bid contract, funded by USAID, to support Schleifer's efforts at Harvard University as the lead adviser to Russia's economic reform efforts.

The Clinton Administration removed the contract from competitive bidding, citing "foreign policy considerations," the *Los Angeles Times* reports. "The first stage of privatization, which received substantial input from U.S.-paid Harvard advisors, fostered the concentration of property within the hands of a few Russians and opened the door to widespread corruption."

"So Schleifer benefited from his relationship with Summers twice: first, by getting a choice contract as the U.S. government's man in Moscow in the 1990's when Summers was in power in the U.S. government, one that benefited his wife's hedge fund," *Nation* reports. "Then after Schleifer returned to Harvard to face a lawsuit, Summers, now President of Harvard, presided over a controversial settlement that all but let his protégé off the hook."

Summers shored up wealth and power for oligarchs, ruthlessly rapacious members of a transnational crime syndicate that was coalescing around the Kremlin. "The Russian oligarchy arose out of the mayhem of rapid privatization in the 1990s," Paul Klebnikov writes in *Godfather of the Kremlin*. "After the fall of the Soviet Union in 1991, Russian president Boris Yeltsin, a leader in the revolt against Communism, had to figure out how to transition from a command-and-control economy to a market one."

Yeltsin's advisors, including Russian economists Yegor Gaidar and Anatoly Chubais, collaborated with the team at Harvard University, led by Larry Summers.

And just like that, the Bolsheviks were back in power and poised to conquer the world. Klebnikov describes the new ethos at the Kremlin as one that "went back to the earliest days of Communism. Lenin and his heirs understood the gangster mentality, and their secret police had used gangster methods to intimidate or eliminate political opponents."

"It was in the Central Committee in the 1920s that Stalin emerged victorious and proceeded to have his rivals executed," Klebnikov writes. The reformers of the 1990s "seemed to care about the Russian people, (but) the people who guided Russia under the Yeltsin regime were both heartless and cruel. (They) were building capitalism using purely Bolshevik methods. A Bolshevik is a man for for whom the aim is important, but the means are not."

Yeltsin embarked upon "shock therapy," as devised by Summers, devastating the Russian people in the process. Under the Communist Christians, more than 100 million people had achieved basic material prosperity. Under shock therapy, Klebnikov writes, millions "were plunged (back) into poverty. School teachers, doctors, physicists, lab technicians, engineers, army officers, steelworkers, coal miners, carpenters, accountants, telephone receptionists, farmers – all had been wiped out. The crash liberalization of trade, meanwhile, allowed Russia's natural resources to be looted by insiders. The Russian state was deprived of its revenue source; consequently, it had no money for pensions, workers' salaries, law enforcement, the military, hospitals, education, and culture. (Shock) therapy set in motion a relentless decline - economic, social, and demographic - that would last until the end of Yeltsin era.

"From the beginning of (shock therapy), Russia's gross domestic product shrank by approximately 50 percent in just four years. Eventually, Russia would sink below the level of China, India, Indonesia, Brazil, and Mexico. On a per capita basis, Russia would become poorer than Peru. Decades of technological achievement were lost. Renowned scientific institutions fell apart. The Russian cultural establishment disintegrated. And the country's assets were sold off."

Between 1990 and 1994, male mortality rates rose 53 percent; female mortality rates, 27 percent. Male life expectancy plunged from an already low level of sixty-four years in 1990 to fifty-eight in 1994."

Summers' main contact in Russia was Anatoly Chubais, who oversaw Russia's privatization process in which "companies worth tens of billions of dollars were handed over to insiders for a fraction of their worth in blatantly rigged auctions," the *Nation* reports.

The auctions of state assets were also rigged. Foreigners were forbidden to buy shares, ensuring that politically-connected individuals surrounding the reformers acquired the assets. Prices were agreed ahead of the auctions, allowing the oligarchs to acquire industries for pennies on the dollar. Once the companies were acquired, the oligarchs proceeded to loot them. "These six industrial giants, the crown jewels of Russian industry, were valued by the Russian secondary market at least twenty times higher than the price at which they were sold in the voucher auctions," Klebnikov writes. "Privatization in Russia (went) through several stages. (The) first stage is the privatization of profits. The second is the privatization of property. The third is the privatization of debts. In other words, it was not necessary to buy an enterprise to control it. The company could remain in state hands. All one had to do was co-opt the management and then funnel the company's revenues through your own middlemen, thus privatizing the profits without spending time and money privatizing the enterprise itself. Almost all the big business empires of the early 1990s had been created in this way."

Summers characterized Chubais, who destroyed Russia, as a "demigod'" and the Russian reformers, who were looting the Russian economy, "a dream team."

Their legacy was such that by the end of the Clinton Administration, Russia's GDP had collapsed by more than 60 percent and "its population was suffering the worst death-to-birth ratio of any industrialized nation in the twentieth century," *Nation* reports. Meanwhile, Russian newspapers report that Chubais boasted that he had "swindled" the Western and U.S. institutions that bankrolled the reforms and made the oligarchs obscenely rich.

From 2001 to 2006, Summers presided over Harvard as the university's first Jewish President. The previous president, Neil Rudenstine, who held the position from 1991 to 2001, excelled as a fundraiser while Russia was being looted, raising more than $2.6 billion. Harvard's endowment grew from $4.7 billion in 1991 to more than $15 billion under Rudenstine.

During his tenure, Rudenstine launched the Science Coalition while oversaw the growth of federally sponsored research programs at Harvard from $200 in 1991 to $320 million in 2000 .

Established in 1994, the Science Coalition works with 50 of the nation's leading research universities, including Yale University, to sustain the federal government's investment in research in order to stimulate the economy and drive U.S. competitiveness.

As anyone can plainly see, America has lost its competitive edge, in no small part to the technological networks Henry Kissinger. American university, supported by taxpayers, developed the technologies which are promptly given to America's strategic competitors and multinationals in the interests of promoting globalism.

New technologies, including social media have been weaponized against the public, a Bolshevik clique known for spying and dictatorial tendencies have harvested personal information, contacts, private health records, intellectual property, the content of emails and Internet searches, for example, in order to build profiles that may ultimately contribute to a social credit score, of the sort already en force in China thanks to the efforts of Google CEO Eric Schmidt. The social credit score, in turn, could determine whether or not a citizen could participate in society, engage in commerce, or even access his own money.

The Russian reformers received the "enthusiastic support of the Clinton Administration and its key representative for economic assistance in Moscow, the Harvard Institute for International Development (HIID)," which designed the World Bank's Global Competitive Report Index in 1999 based upon a 1996 survey of managers sponsored by the World Economic Forum.

In 1996, the Russian oligarchs appeared at Davos, including, for example, Anatoly Chubais and businessmen like Mikhail Khodorkovsky, Klebnikov writes.

HIID became the umbrella organization for U.S. overseas and aid and development programs, like USAID. Harvard's Institute coordinated the funding, training, research, and training in Africa, Asia, Central and Eastern Europe, and Latin America, essentially helping politically-connected private industry dominate those markets, harvest resources, and redirect public assets to a charmed group of insiders.

While the funding was provided under the banner of helping to rebuild the Russian economy on a basis of "western concepts of ethics, democracy, and free markets," *Nation* reports that their efforts promoted international crime, subverted democracy, and facilitated crony capitalism.

Established by Summers, as Clinton's Deputy Secretary of the Treasury for International Affairs, HIID disbursed $300 million to Russia and was allowed to spend the money as it saw fit, with no oversight granted to the USAID. At the same time, Harvard had political access to the reformers in control of the Russian government who were redistributing Russia's industrial assets, wealth, and natural resources to the oligarchs.

Harvard apparently profited through this access to Russian power and American funds, a corrupt arrangement that ultimately contributed to Summers' dismissal as President of Harvard.

With the arrival of Mikhail Gorbachev – and his support among the religious right, the International Development of the Central Committee and the KGB "developed a strategy of transferring billions of dollars of Communist Party capital to captive companies in the Soviet private sector and abroad," Klebnikov writes. "In the landmark election of 1990, the first free elections for the national parliament as well as republic-level and regional parliaments, the KGB had fielded several thousand candidates."

The KGB created "the first non-Communist political party," led democratic reform efforts, and established "a network of captive banks and trading companies, both in Russia and abroad, to collect billions of dollars of government funds for the Communist elite," he writes.

Shock therapy gave rise to the hyper-inflation that ruined the livelihoods of ordinary Russians while Chubais oversaw mass privatization – taking industries controlled by the state, which had been reclaimed by the Communist Christians, and transferring them to the Rothschild crime syndicate. Klebnikov described the privatization as "the biggest transfer of state assets to private owners in world history."

No measures were put in place to protect the elderly, poor, and infirmed from hyperinflation. The result was a "dramatic decline" in Russian life expectancy, Klebnikov writes. Fewer mothers were having children. People were committing suicide. Others died of starvation.

"While price reform was wreaking havoc, other aspects of democratic reform were being ignored," he writes. "(The reformers) paid no attention to the other aspects of building a civilized society: creating an effective government, a workable constitution, enforcing the rule of law, creating a viable parliament. (In) other words, they completely failed to create a civil society to serve as the framework for economic activity. Even questions of economic policy that did not directly stem from the need to free prices were ignored: industrial policy, trade policy, de-monopolization, enforcing competition, rationalizing the tax system, establishing a viable banking sector, creating clear rules of the game."

Klebnikov describes the reformers as "primitive and destructive."

The reformers dismantled everything. By 1994, most of Russia's foreign trade was handled by private trading companies. "Foreign entrepreneurs, mostly crooked ones, arrived and taught (Russian) entrepreneurs how to do it," he writes. "The first to benefit from the new regime were the directors of the main export-oriented enterprises. They simply established trading companies abroad and sold them their produce for a fraction of the world price; the profit rarely returned to either the enterprise or the Russian state."

The privatization leveraged the syndicate. What followed was societal chaos, execution-style killings, and the spread of a global mafia. The young reformers "were supposed to clean up Russia, devise a proper legal system, and foster a market economy," he writes. "Instead, they presided over one of most corrupt regimes in history. The clique in power was not satisfied with stealing – it (wanted) everyone to see (them) stealing with complete impunity."

During the reform people, the police state was privatized. Telephones were tapped, and surveillance was dramatically increased. This, in turn, established a template for the privatization of security and prisons in the United States, accompanied by an erosion of civil liberties and focus on data harvesting for the purposes of citizen control. "Every large financial industrial group created its own mini-KGB, collecting information, eavesdropping on rivals, stealing documents," Klebnikov writes.

"Gangsters had been fighting and killing each other throughout the Gorbachev and Yeltsin years, but the bloodshed that was unleashed in 1993-94 was special," He writes. "(Dozens) of top gangster bosses had come out of prison after Communism fell, and they found the nation's prime economic assets up for grabs. Huge industrial companies, mines, and oil fields were being privatized. Anyone ruthless enough could attain unimaginable wealth almost overnight."

Russia had become a gangster-dominated economy, buttressed by political access to the Kremlin and Rothschild surrogates in the United States. A number of them went to Israel and obtained Israeli citizenship, claiming dual Russian-Israeli citizenship.

In 1995, 12 of Russia's most profitable businesses were auctioned off to the oligarchs. These oligarchs, in turn, ensured that Boris Yeltsin was re-elected. Yet the oligarchs were not savvy businessmen. Rather, they had received Russia's industries for pennies on the dollar. For example, Boris Berezovsky and Roman Abramovich acquired large stakes in an oil company, Sibneft for $200 million. In 2009, when Putin renationalized the company – thereby taking it back under the direct control of the Rothschild-controlled Kremlin, Russia paid $11.9 billion to recover it when it easily could have confiscated the asset.

The oligarchs donated millions of dollars to Yeltsin's re-election and hired the best political operatives they knew, including Jack Abramoff, a Microsoft lobbyist at Preston Gates. They "laundered government money with their banks, and fed it into the Yeltsin's campaign machine," Klebnikov writes. The oligarchs "blanketed the airwaves with pro-Yeltsin propaganda. Yeltsin, in turn, "conducted Russia's first American-style presidential campaign. Despite waving the banner of free markets and democracy, the reformers of the 1990's did much of their reforms undemocratically, often by presidential decrees that were hammered out through backroom deals with the rich and powerful."

Russia turned into a big money laundering racket. "Western intelligence agencies were aware of the KGB money laundering program, but they decided not to do anything, even when it became apparent that a large portion of the KGB money was being embezzled by freelance operatives, rogue businessmen, and gangsters," Klebnikov writes. "When the CIA received an indirect request from the Russian government in 1992 to help track down the missing billions, it decided against it, for fear of jeopardizing its own agent network."

USAID was directed to "hand over responsibility" for reshaping the Russian economy to HIID, which was established in 1974, right after the fiat currency was launched to "assist countries with social and economic reform." This was the year in which the Saudis signed a Technical Cooperation Program Agreement with the World Bank to serve the development partner.

Opportunities for that development were assigned to multinational corporations that owed no allegiance to any country or peoples and which had profit as its primary objective; government was their facilitator, and the United States was their mark. Somehow money was no object as public funds poured in their direction. The corporations and their executives profited in the extreme while ordinary people were strapped with debt.

Under the Clinton Administration, HIID was reportedly awarded $57.7 million, two-thirds of which was granted without competitive bidding – a waiver signed off on by five U.S. federal agencies, including the Treasury Department and the National Security Council, which were primarily responsible for overseeing U.S. aid policy towards Russia.

HIID coordinated $300 million in USAID grants to contractors, including the Big Six accounting firms and the PR giant, Burson-Marsteller.

In 1992, Chubais, with assistance from HIID, established the Moscow-based Russian Privatization Center (RPC) through which $300 million in aid and millions more in loans from international financial institutions passed. With HIID advising, Chubais circumvented normal governmental channels, thereby removing key layers of oversight that opened the doors for looting. Chubais was Chairman of the Board while Andrei Shleifer served on the Board of Directors alongside Ira Lieberman, a senior manager for the World Bank's private sector development department.

With HIID assisting, the RPC received $45 million from USAID – and millions more from the European Union, European governments, and Japan – in addition to $59 million in loans from the World Bank.

The organizations receiving aid spread like wildfire, creating more hungry mouths to feed, an objective served by the dissolution of the USSR, which somehow left the United States not only funneling "aid" into Russia, but into its satellite states. HIID created a number of regulatory institution in the former USSR, including a Federal Commission of Securities, established by decree and run by cronies.

The Law-Based Economy organization received $20 million from the World Bank and USAID to develop legal and regulatory frameworks for markets, ensuring politically connected individuals oversaw the business. An article written by Fritz Ermarth, a veteran CIA Russia operative and former chairman of the National Intelligence Council. Ermarth, spoke to the Clinton Administration's "disdain for analysis about the corruption of Russian politics and their Russian partners."

Ermarth attributes this attitude to the "warping of intelligence analysis to fit political agendas."

The First Russian Specialized Depository, which "holds the records and assets of mutual funds investors," was funded by a World Bank loan and established to enrich HIID insiders, *Nation* reports, adding that the participants reportedly lacked the capital and expertise for the enterprises they pursued. "Thus the very people who were supposed to be the trustees of the system not only undercut the aid program's stated goal of building independent institutions, but replicated the Soviet practice of skimming assets to benefit the *nomenklatura,"* Nation reports.

But the corruption goes even deeper. For example, during the controversial Russian loans-for-shares auctions, no foreign businessmen were allowed to participate in what were close auctions. As a result, oligarchs were free to acquire Russia's valuable assets at rock bottom prices. An exception was made for Harvard Management Company (HMC), which invests Harvard's endowment; and billionaire investor George Soros, who had worked with Microsoft lobbyists, like Jack Abramoff, to secure the election of the reformers in the Kremlin in the first place.

Through this participation, Soros became a major shareholder in Russia's second largest steel mill – and Sidanko oil. He also invested in a high-yielding IMF-subsidized bond market, *Nation* reports. "The U.S. assistance program in Russia was rife with conflicts of interest involving HIID advisers and their U.S.AID.-funded Chubais allies," *Nation* reports. "HMC managers, favored Russian bankers, and insider expatriates working in Russia's nascent markets."

The (Al) Gore-Chernomyrdin Commission facilitated the cooperation of U.S.-Russian oil deals through a Capital Market Forum chaired by insiders while a HIID advisor coordinated its subgroups. Among those serving on subgroups were HIID nepotism hires and CEOs of Salomon Brothers, Merrill Lynch, and other investment firms. "By unconditionally backing Chubais and his associates, the Harvard operatives, their U.S. government patrons, and Western donors reinforced the new post-Soviet oligarchical system," *Nation* reports.

Chubais was eventually "investigated" by the West for money laundering – an investigation that "ranged from suspect banking deals to bribery," *The Los Angeles Times* reports. Yet the Clinton Administration had no interest in holding the key players accountable. An audit performed by the Russian Chamber of Accountants acknowledged "serious misappropriation at the Russian Privatization Center," a private, nonprofit linked to Chubais and funded by the West, Klebnikov writes. "The Chamber of Accountants discovered that much of this money was distributed directly to cronies and to key political bosses in return for their support of market reforms."

In 1996, Chubais was on Harvard's payroll.

Within U.S. political circles, Chubais was celebrated after admitting he had "conned" the IMF of another $4.8 billion investment brokered by Summers in 1996. "As we now know, the IMF money disappeared in short order," *The Los Angeles Times* reports. As fits the pattern, whether with the Filipino dictators or any other West-funded tyrants, Chubais became chairman of Russia's electricity monopoly. In this role, he worked with IMF and World Bank officials, Summers, and other key officials within the Clinton Administration.

In 1998, Summers' name appeared on the pedophile Jeffrey Epstein's flight logs; the economist was by then soliciting donations from Epstein – a habit that continued through Summers' tenure as President of Harvard.

With the end of the Cold War, the crime syndicates linked together, as observed by investigative journalist Claire Sterling in *Thieves' World: The Threat of the New Global Network of Organized Crime*. "No one has benefited more from the political changes of the 1990s than international organized crime," she writes. "Within the space of just three or four years, the world's great crime syndicates have joined in a planet-wide criminal consortium unlike any in history. A Pax Mafiosa has emerged— an agreement to avoid conflict, devise common strategy, and exploit the planet peaceably together."

"Ironically, it was Mikhail Gorbachev's liberal reforms that gave free rein to Russia's gangsters," writes *Forbes* journalist Paul Klebnikov. "Along with political prisoners released from the gulags, thousands of professional criminals were freed as well. More important, Russia's main gangster-business empires were established under Gorbachev."

During the 1990s, Sterling writes, the syndicate, armed with a quarter of a trillion dollars of investment capital, penetrated worldwide money markets and spread blackmail and corruption throughout Western Europe and the United States. Its power centered around the Kremlin.

"The big syndicates of East and West were pooling services and personnel, rapidly colonizing Western Europe and the United States, running the drug traffic up to half a trillion dollars a year, laundering and reinvesting an estimated quarter of a trillion dollars a year in legitimate enterprise," Sterling writes. "Much of their phenomenal growth derived from the fact that they had the free run of a territory covering half the continent of Europe and a good part of Asia—a sixth of the earth's land mass, essentially ungoverned and unpoliced. The whole international underworld had moved in on post-communist Russia and the rest of the ex-Soviet bloc: raced in from the day the Berlin Wall fell. Where Western governments tended to see Russia as a basket case, the big syndicates saw it as a privileged sanctuary and bottomless source of instant wealth."

The syndicate worked as it always had. Its criminal members disliked having to compete in a free market, build a business from scratch, or earn an honest living. Rather, they preferred to have well placed contacts kick them government contracts, give them money, resources, and, if possible, billion-dollar businesses, just for the taking.

The government was their tool to finance and protect the enterprise of those within a charmed circles and then weaponized against everyone else, shoring up the world's wealth for a select group of insiders and their families for all perpetuity. The syndicate was Machiavellian to the core, completely bereft of morals, conscience, or empathy. They were pure savage, blood-thirsty barbarians, the descendants of mercenary armies who accompanied or were themselves pirates of the old Venetians, Lombards, and East India/Dutch companies.

If the market couldn't be rigged, they simply took up arms and felled the obstacle. "To be well connected, a foreign crook had only to hook up with a fellow crook in the Russian mafia or a corrupt Russian politician, both readily available," Sterling writes. "The foreign crook could then obtain a Russian bank account and a license to export, buy rubles for his dirty dollars at a huge discount, and pay in rubles for his raw material exports. So, he could not only launder his money but come out 400 percent or 500 percent ahead. Some were coming out 1,000 percent ahead."

Overnight, the former Soviet Union transformed into a massive money laundering machine, laundering money from arms trafficking, human trafficking, drug trafficking, casinos, corporate looting, government looting, looting of every imaginable sort. "Russia is where the big crime syndicates discovered how useful they could be to one another to capture and ransack a vast and prostrate country," Sterling writes. Narcodollars peddled by the syndicate flooded into legitimate businesses, corrupting the banking systems, stock markets, and commerce worldwide.

Before the privatization could proceed, "Boris Yeltsin needed to gain absolute power," Klebnikov writes. "In the first years after the fall of Communism, he was not yet the autocratic ruler he would later become."

Not only had the West interfered in Russia's elections to secure the appointment of candidates who would serve the interests of criminal kleptocrats, but it appears that the dissolution of the Soviet Union violated the Soviet constitution and required a national referendum, Klebnikov writes. If this were true, then, not only was Yeltsin's government of questionable legitimacy, but the United States, with Harvard's assistance, was funneling money into an illegitimate government.

The oligarchs bankrolled the political campaigns of the reformers, who then turned around and rewarded the oligarchs with state assets and money. The campaigns recycled government funds. At a time when schoolteachers, doctors, soldiers, and workers were going for months without pay, and millions of old people were without pensions, the Yeltsin team was investing billions of dollars in its reelection campaign.

Since it was clearly illegal for Yeltsin to use budgetary funds to finance his election campaign, these funds were laundered through the big industrial empires of oligarchs.

Some oligarchs, like Boris Berezovsky, enjoyed personal and professional relationships with such Western billionaires as News Corp. CEO Rupert Murdoch and junk bond king Michael Milken, reflecting the reach of the syndicate. Berezovsky was reportedly was one of the few guests at Murdoch's 1999 wedding.

Fugitive financier Marc Rich, a prominent member of the syndicate, advised the oligarchs on strategy. Klebnikov reports that Rich taught them how to loot and launder money.

Through Istok, a Russian-state company, Rich smuggled four million tons of petroleum out of Russia for a reported half a billion dollars in 1990. As head of the second largest commodities firm in the world, Marc Rich & Co., Rich was Russia's largest provider of grain and number one raw materials exporter.

By 1993, his yearly turnover on ex-Soviet territory was $3 billion, up half a billion over the year before, Klebnikov reports. Only a tenth of this went into Russia's treasury. Ironically, while looting Russia, Rich presented himself as a benefactor dedicated to serving the Russian public interest.

The trick Rich employed and which the newly minted oligarchs emulated was that of acquiring Russian assets for pennies on the dollar and then selling them overseas at huge mark ups; or exploiting embargoes and sanctions against countries and then circumventing the sanctions to sell goods at top dollar.

Throughout his criminal career, Rich exported hundreds of millions of dollars worth of Russia's aluminum, oil, and other assets at pennies on the dollar – even though it wasn't his to sell.

One British executive reported that Rich's profits on Russian oil and aluminum were "a factor of two or three higher than the average profit on world markets." as is befitting a thief. The Russians, the owners of those assets, were "losing about thirty percent on this trade."

Russia Vice President Alexander Rutskoi reported that in 1992, the country was stripped of over $17 billion in raw materials. Rutskoi then remarked that had Russia's assets not been looted, the country wouldn't have needed foreign aid – including the $13 billion committed by the G-7 industrial nations in 1993.

One overnight Russian billionaire, Roman Abramovich, was a pauper who transformed overnight into an oligarch worth over $13 billion. Born an orphan, Abramovich would never have achieved this level of success without the support of the hidden hand, suggesting that he was a Rothschild bloodline or somehow connected through blood or alliance to the syndicate's power structure.

According to investor Bill Browder, Abramovich – and other oligarchs – were holding their billions for Putin. The *Kommersant* went one step further to report that Putin was holding the assets for Jacob Rothschild.

Abramovich was mentored by Boris Berezovsky, who reportedly partnered with Summers to secure the election of Vladimir Putin as President of Russia.

Abramovich later acquired Berezovsky's media and oil empires – after the latter had the audacity to criticize Putin. In 2013, Berezovsky was founded dead, hanging from a noose in his bathroom.

The power structure in Russia formed "a symbiotic relationship," Klebnikov writes. "The oligarchs' economic power buttresses the political power of the Russian president and the president's power buttresses the economic power of the oligarchs, like a medieval king getting tribute from his aristocracy in exchange for his protection."

Abramoff, Soros, and Gates

During the Cold War, Jack Abramoff partnered with the National Endowment for Democracy, which was bankrolled by billionaire financier George Soros, to overthrow African governments and install puppet regimes in the interests of "spreading democracy" and "fighting Communism." Their paths would cross again during the Russian elections.

After the Republicans reclaimed both Houses of Congress in 1994, Abramoff was hired by the Seattle office of Preston Gates, Microsoft's lobbying firm of record. Microsoft CEO Bill Gates' father was Partner. As lobbyist, Abramoff counted among his lobbying contacts the Clintons, Congressman Tom DeLay, House Speaker Newt Gingrich, members of the Bush political dynasty, Sen. Harry Reid, among others.

While working for Preston Gates, Abramoff and Patrick Pizzella registered to lobby on behalf of Chelsea Commercial Enterprises Ltd., a Bermuda-based firm which represented NaftaSib, a Russian company whose principal, Marina Nevskaya, was involved in diverse business interests, including oil exploration throughout the world. The group retained Preston Gates to "support the policies of the Russian government for progressive market reforms and trade with the United States."

According to reports, NaftaSib had "tight connections to the Russian security establishment."

NaftaSib advised the Russian government while Abramoff engaged Russian Prime Minister Viktor Chernomyrdin, the founder of Gazprom, managed the auction of Yukos.

NaftaSib oversaw the transfer of Yukos' shares to Jacob Rothschild, *Kommersant* reports. (*Kommersant* has since been acquired by billionaire Russian oligarch Alisher Usmanov, a close friend of Larry Summers and Russian mining mogul whom the *Guardian* has described as "Putin's favorite oligarch.")

The American Prospect reports that Summers' policies led to the "rise of corrupt oligarchs as a path to Putin's dictatorship in post-Soviet Russia." At the Treasury Department, Summers "fought with State and Defense Department officials for control of Russian policy."

Summers' "secret weapon was the IMF whose assistance Russia urgently needed as its economy was collapsing," *The American Prospect* reports. As Undersecretary, Summers was the main U.S. liaison with the IMF (and) not shy about using that leverage."

Russian Influence

Among the organizations which linked Abramoff to the oligarchs was the U.S. Family Network (USFN) and the Alexander Strategy Group, both of which had close ties to Congressman Tom DeLay who formed a power alliance with Abramoff. The USFB was funded by Abramoff's corporate clients at Preston Gates.

The Washington Post reports that Russian energy executives caused $1 million to pass through a London-based law firm, James & Sarch, Co. – and into the USFB to fund DeLay and Abramoff's travel to Russia.

As lobbyist, Abramoff replicating the strategies he had observed in the Kremlin, helping to transform Capitol Hill into a cesspool of greed and corruption. The $1 million the group received reportedly influenced DeLay to support legislation, granting the IMF public funds to bail out the Russian economy. Outraged critics suggested that Russia raise taxes instead to cover its own debt – to which DeLay responded, conservatives should never support raising taxes. Yet, the IMF was bankrolled by the United States, transferring the debt burden onto the American people.

"In the end, the Russian legislature refused to raise taxes, the IMF agreed to lend the money anyway, and DeLay voted on Sept. 17, 1998, for a foreign aid bill containing new funds to replenish the IMF account," the *Washington Post* reports.

The money the Russian government received from taxpayers was laundered back to the USFN which then used it to influence DeLay. All parties reportedly denied that money was a factor in their decision making, that all legislative actions were performed with the highest levels of integrity. "Whatever the real motive for the contribution of $1 million -- a sum not prohibited by law but extraordinary for a small, nonprofit group -- the steady stream of corporate payments detailed on the donor list makes it clear that Abramoff's long-standing alliance with DeLay was sealed by a much more extensive web of financial ties than previously known," the *Washington Post* reports.

The $1 million was reportedly intended to influence the federal government to secure between $10 billion and $15 billion in international loans as part of a bailout for the Russian government while the oligarchs were looting Russia, with assistance from the reformers whom Abramoff, Soros, and others had helped install.

Establishing a Bank Holding Company for Gates

In 1970, United California Bank (UCB) President and CEO Paul Erdman set up shop in the offshore jurisdiction of Bermuda and acquired control of Electronics International Capital (EIC) through a hostile takeover.

According to Securities and Exchange Commission News Digest, the EIC was "a closed-end investment company of Bermuda," which had applied to the SEC for an order under the Investment Company Act "with respect to certain transactions involving an exchange of securities and other property."

In 1963, Erdman, who was a Swiss banker, boasted to the New York Times that he was "making a killing in sterling" through UCB, which was investing in stocks in European and U.S. markets and trading in precious metals and commodities.

While the banks were making out like bandits, "the (British) pound had been devalued, the dollar was under fierce attack, the price of gold was at the launching pad, silver was already in orbit, and jittery investors were dumping their funds into Switzerland, afraid of a monetary catastrophe," The New York Times reports. "For years, Swiss banks had prospered on financial troubles elsewhere in the world, and while (United California) Bank was new and brash, it was full-fledged member of the exclusive Swiss banking club, with a license to make killings."

It was no longer after that the bank lost $30 million over "unauthorized" transactions in commodities, and Erdman was arrested on fraud. "Since Swiss banks not only act as brokers but also trade on their own account, they can become highly exposed in any misjudgment of market trends," The Times reports. "The bank, with a modern facade looking out over St. Jacobs-Strasse near a busy intersection, is in a town perhaps best known as the inner sanctum of the Western world's central bankers. These discreet, publicity-shunning men meet monthly at the Bank for International Settlements and in comfortable hotels by the railroad station to try to solve the world's monetary problems."

Once the smoke had cleared from the scandal, United California was rebranded as First Interstate Bank – a bank holding company over which Mary Maxwell Gates – the mother of, Bill Gates – would preside as Director. Bill Gates would go on to become a monopolist in the tradition of the robber barons who captured over 90 percent of the market share for the world's personal computers by the 1990s while his political consultants were partnering with the oligarchs and he was partnering with the Communist Chinese government.

Microsoft and Human Trafficking

A sexual compromise operation came to the surface in the United States in with the Nixon Administration, coinciding with the launch of the petro-dollar, the normalization of U.S.-China relations, and the appointment of Secretary of State Henry Kissinger, a Rothschild protégé through whom the City of London dictated policy to the federal government.
The Watergate scandal was spurred by a recovery operation involving a black book of political leaders who had been sexually compromised and were being blackmailed, according to New York Det. "Jimmy Boots" Rothstein.
The British had their Jimmy Saville, a close advisor to the Crown and Prime Minister Margaret Thatcher. Within the United States, the syndicate's compromise operation began with Meyer Lansky, progressed through Roy Cohn, and then exploded in the media with Jeffrey Epstein.
Abramoff, an influential and well connected Rothschild asset, was reputed to have run a sex trafficking operation out of his office at Preston Gates, the lobbying firm for Microsoft. Journalists at the National Press Club confirmed that this was the case. Indeed, while working with the Department of Justice as part of a wider investigation into his activities, Abramoff connected Congressman Tom DeLay to an opportunity to lobby Capitol Hill to support the prosecution of Joris Demmink, Secretary-General of the Ministry and Justice – and suspected pedophile. Perhaps this effort was undertaken as part of a plea deal.
Once federal charges were dropped against DeLay, the Congressman established his firm, "First Principles," and registered to lobby on behalf of Argus Global, a firm specializing in discrete investigative services and executive protection security detail for media

personalities, celebrities, political figures, athletes, musicians, and corporate executives. Among the lobbyists who registered to lobbying on behalf of Argus Global during at least part of the time in question were DeLay; Patrick O'Donnell, former Special Assistant to President Richard Nixon and member of the Reagan Transition Team; and Chase Kroll a former legislative aid to Zionist Congresswoman Michele Bachmann from Minnesota.

Bachmann appeared alongside Abramoff, in Park Avenue: Money, Power, and the American Dream, *a documentary directed by Alex Gibney, a film partner of Jemima Goldsmith, a Rothschild.*

During the Trump Administration, Kroll was named in the federal government's investigation of alleged fraud involving Abramoff's AMLBitcoin project in which the superlobbyist was accused by his partner, Marcus Andrade, of enlisting the federal government to steal the businesses right out from under him on behalf of Jared Kushner and the Trump Administration. Among the interests working with Abramoff and Andrade, according to legal documents, were Rothschild Public Affairs; Kroll Global; and George O'Neil, the great grandson of John D. Rockefeller, Jr.

Abramoff wanted to "spread the money around," Andrade said.

Kroll had also established two successor firms – including K2 Intelligence, which acquired Thatcher Associates – a company that oversaw the cleanup of the World Trade Center following the terrorist attacks of September 11, 2001. A K2 intelligence opened an office in London and expanded to New York City, Madrid, and Tel Aviv.

One of Kroll's most controversial clients was Hollywood mogul Harvey Weinstein who retained the firm for assistance in wiping evidence of his sexual abuse of women from electronic devices and uncovering compromising information on his accusers to discredit them.

Harvard Law Professor Alan Dershowitz, a friend of the Rothschilds who had represented Trump, (Michael) Milken, and Epstein, joined Weinstein's defense team.

Perhaps Andrade's biggest disclosure was that the federal government's case against him and Abramoff started with Special Counsel Bob Mueller's investigation into whether the Trump presidential campaign had colluded with Russia to interfere in the 2016 presidential election as part of an effort on behalf of Russian oligarchs to circumvent or repeal the Magnitsky Act which curtailed their money laundering. In a statement, Andrade said, by this point, Abramoff "was under federal investigation for his foreign ties (which had) national security implications."

*Rense has reported on the alleged child sex trafficking ring at Preston Gates. (*https://rense.com/general74/mother.ht ml*)*

According to this article a mother by the name of Patricia Johnson-Holm claims that in 1985, her 12-year-old son was kidnapped by a pedophile ring connected to the Bush family.

Johnson-Holm believes that the White House had been used as cover for the sexual exploitation of children. The mother claims to have seen a picture of her son as a teenager bound, gagged, and lying on a "double bed between two other boys also bound and gagged," Rense *reports.*

Reports documented "15-year-old call boys wandering through the White House in the middle of the night," connected to the "Franklin cover up," in which a Republican operative named Larry King had allegedly procured boys and girls from Boys Town in Nebraska, and "entrapping them in a child sex-slave and espionage ring."

When Johnson-Holm sought legal advice concerning her son's disappearance, Abramoff, then an attorney at the Seattle office of Preston Gates, Microsoft's lobbying firm, reportedly informed her that she had a "very good case."

According to the Rense *report, a colleague pulled Abramoff aside and whispered something into his ear, prompting Abramoff to drop her "like a hot potato."*

At first Abramoff couldn't make out what the colleague was saying and so the colleague repeated himself, this time louder.

*The words Johnson-Holm heard were: "You took her kid." (*https://rense.com/general74/mother.htm*)*

On June 29, 1989, The Washington Times *ran a cover story on a human trafficking ring under the headline of "Homosexual Prostitution Inquiry Ensnares VIPs from Reagan, Bush: 'Call Boys' Took Midnight Tour of White House."*

*(*https://educate-yourself.org/tg/franklincoverupexcerptwashtimesphotos.html*)*

Among the alleged clients, identified by prostitutes and escort operators, were government officials, locally based U.S. military officers, businessmen, lawyers, bankers, congressional aides, among others.

The inquiry into the matter was coordinated by the Harvard-educated U.S. Attorney Jay B. Stephens, former deputy White House counsel to President Reagan who served as assistant special prosecutor on the Watergate prosecution team, which never publicly acknowledged the pedophile/sexual compromise elements behind Watergate, as reported by Rothstein.

Stephens was general counsel for the Overseas Private Investment Corporation, the U.S. Government's Development finance institution until it merged with the Development Credit Authority of the USAID. The OPIC mobilized private capital to "solve development challenges to advance the foreign policy of the United States and its national security objectives," raising questions of why private capital was even influencing foreign policy and involved in national security issues in the first place.

"Several former White House colleagues of Mr. Stephens are listed among clients of the homosexual prostitution ring," The Washington Times *reports. "Mr. Stephen's office, after first saying it would cooperate with* The Times' *inquiry, withdrew the offer late yesterday and also declined to say whether Mr. Stephens would recuse himself from the case because of a possible conflict of interest."*

Among the concerns raised by senior top-ranking military intelligence offices was that "hostile foreign intelligence services were using young male prostitutes to compromise top administration homosexuals, thus making them subject to blackmail," The Times *reports.*

Harvard's Stolen Patent

The harvesting of data – to track and trace each individual from cradle to grave is part of an agenda – that of Silent Weapons for Quiet Wars, *which was launched by Prince Philip and the Rothschilds to coincide with the coronation of Queen Elizabeth II.*

The data has been harvested from emails, online bank accounts, social media, and various other channels. Widespread data harvesting may not have been possible without the patent of Leader Technology's Michael McKibben who reportedly made social media, online banking, etc. scaleable.

According to McKibben, his patent attorney shared the patent with IBM – and wound up in the hands of Larry Summers at Harvard. Summers then allegedly directed Facebook founder Mark Zuckerberg – whose COO, Sheryl Sandberg, had served as Summers' chief of staff while he was Treasury Secretary, to establish a social media site.

The tech companies who have profited from the patent were the seedlings of IBM, and Summers has been the greatest promoters of Facebook. A Russian-born Israeli tech investor, Yuri Milner was Facebook's largest investor.

Miler, in turn, has invested in Chinese tech companies – including a number of online platforms, like Spotify, AirBnb, Alibaba (Chinese version of Amazon), JD.Com, and the mobile phone maker, Xiaomi.

After McKibben's intellectual property was shared with IBM Eclipse, the code was passed on to DARPA which then passed it along to Eric Schmidt, the CEO of Google, who then launched GMAIL, using the code.

Once the the technocrats acquired McKibben's source code, "they carved up the globe and the markets in each region, giving each a piece of the market using Leader Technologies' stolen trade secrets," aim4truth.org reports. Schmidt acquired America and Europe; Chandler was assigned South America, Summers and Sandberg join Schmidt America in managing the American market; James Breyer was given China; and Yuri Milner, Alisher Usmanov and Summers got Russia.

"A host of fake tech lords became the front men for all the various social networks we see cropping up everywhere in the world – the richest companies in the world – Google, Facebook, Amazon," aim4Truth.org reports. "Usually, we see them stealing oil, gold, uranium, and other resources, but this time they stole the very software code that is utilized by the largest tech companies in America, Europe, Russia, China, South America, and anywhere else they could market it —making trillions of dollars in the process. The criminals got filthy rich."

Just as the USSR was broken up into satellite states that appeared to be separate nations while each was controlled by the same Soviet apparatus, social media companies cropped up everywhere, each appearing to be separate from each other while all were controlled by a network of technocrats surrounding IBM.

"A front man is assigned to lead the company, like Zuckerberg," aim4truth.org reports. Companies were then "built upon stolen

technology and then weaponized against the public. The dummy company gets tens of millions of dollars in initial investments. Its underwriters then inflate valuations that turn into billions when the fake private corporation later hits the stock market. These fake front-men, pseudo-military corporations, stolen patents, and corrupt defense contractors then magically become the largest corporations in the world—Google (NSA), Facebook (NSA and CIA programs), Amazon (NSA and CIA) and on and on down the line of the huge tech corporations that are consuming everything around them in league with the ill-intent of the military and intelligence agencies.

"Leader Technologies' inventions fueled dozens of the largest corporations in the world. It was out-right industrial espionage at the highest governmental levels that led to the theft of Leader's trade secrets, copyrights, and patents."

Given Summers' role in shoring up wealth for the oligarchs, it is perhaps no mystery as to why the Russians are the leading investors in tech companies.

VIII.
The Syndicate's Mask Slips

"Power always thinks ... that it is doing God's service when it is violating all His laws."

President John Adams
American Founding Father

    Jack Abramoff was groomed from childhood to assume his place among the global elite as a reward for faithfully serving the interests of the syndicate, particularly its chieftain, Jacob Rothschild, by way of his father's connections. There were two sides to him. One part wanted to do the right thing, the other, doing the exact opposite as if his will to wealth and power overtook him and he understood there was only one road there. For a while, he was on the fast track to becoming the nation's most influential, well connected, and prodigious rainmaker. Whatever ideals he might have espoused, times had changed, the syndicate was in control – and the road to riches and power, even if illusory, was paved in gold in service to it. In the end, Abramoff characterized the people he had served as "unspeakably evil."

    Abramoff was a conflicted man. He believed he could outwit, outlast, and outplay the competition, but he played the double game – that of saying one thing and doing another. The more the elite looked to him to solve their problems, the wealthier and more influential he became. He envisioned himself with a portfolio filled with casinos, hotels, and real estate spanning the globe. As a golden boy for the shadow hand that secretly controlled the levers of power, he expected no harm would ever come to him, that he would remain above the law and would be protected at all costs while success, wealth, and power magically fell into this lap.

    Following his path is vital to our discovery if only revealing how history moved around him, that he was the catalyst, or at least a car in the train driving the agenda against the United States.

The Best Laid Plans

    American author John Steinbeck once opined, "The best laid plans of mice and men oft go awry." Even the so-called elite, with the world's power at their fingertips, have seen their agendas derailed, timelines broken, plans devoured. And so it was with the ill-fated SunCruz deal.

In 1999, an attorney at Preston Gates introduced Abramoff to its client, Gus Boulis, a Greek shipping tycoon. The federal government was pushing Boulis out of the shipping business over his numerous scrapes with the law. Would Abramoff, like to purchase the fleet, the attorney inquired.

Driving the federal government's effort against Boulis was the Seminole Tribe of Florida, which had ambitions of dominating the Florida casino market. The Clinton Administration had even convened the National Gambling Impact Study Commission (NGISC), bringing together leaders of the religious right with MGM and other casino interests to map out the nation's casino strategy for Rothschild, Inc. dba as the federal government.

The NGISC specifically took aim at "cruises to nowhere," alluding to SunCruz, a casino fleet which posed competition to the Seminoles. The fleet took patrons into international waters to gamble legally at a time when casino-style gambling was forbidden on the mainland, thus accounting for why the business consisted of "cruises to nowhere." Representatives of anti-casino groups whose organizations were affiliated with MGM and Rockefeller groups lobbied Congress to put an end to SunCruz.

Virginia Rep. Frank Wolf, an ally of Congressman DeLay convened hearings in Congress to sink SunCruz, a business in Florida, raising all sorts of red flags among observers who couldn't help but notice that the federal government was trying to intervene in a state matter and that a legislator from Virginia was a little too passionate about a matter concerning Florida. So much for being discreet.

Wolf attempted to legislate the NGISC's recommendation, failed, and then quietly tabled the matter. The Cruise to Nowhere Act was dead on arrival. Back to the drawing board.

Abramoff had come to Preston Gates in 1994 after the Republicans aligned with the "religious right" reclaimed control of Congress. His value to the firm was that he had influence with the newly elected faction stemming from his days meddling in South Africa and running the College Republicans. As Abramoff understood, the religious right was another manufactured construct to manufacture consent for the syndicate. While appearing to defend Christian morality, the religious right actually exploited Christians for fundraising purposes and then cynically mobilized them on behalf of political causes that advanced the power and interests of the shadow elite.

With the NGISC stymied on the SunCruz matter, Preston Gates appealed to Abramoff for assistance.

The good-natured Boulis, who made deals with friends on a handshake, never anticipated Abramoff's double cross. Abramoff presented himself a savior, with all the false sincerity he could muster. Given Abramoff's influence with the Clintons and religious right, Boulis might have had a decent chance of reaching a satisfactory resolution. Instead of besting the federal government, Boulis wound up swimming with the fishes.

Abramoff was indirectly involved in the deal – he delegated the matter of negotiating the acquisition to Adam Kidan, a political operative he had known for decades.

Boulis had agreed to sell SunCruz for $148.5 million. As a bankrupt, disbarred attorney – a qualification that rendered him "compromised," Kidan could not qualify for a loan, much less one for a multi-million dollar casino business – and so the Abramoff served as a guarantor.

Abramoff could not qualify for a loan on his own either. "To get the loan, Abramoff specified that he (held) a $1.4 million investment jointly with his father, in the parking lot of an Atlantic City gambling casino, the legacy of Volpe-Bonanno," *Executive Intelligence Review* reports.

Paul Volpe was a member of the Cosa Nostra, a powerful Italian-American branch of organized crime. In his youth, Abramoff was involved in Atlantic City real estate deals with his uncle who managed properties for a developer associated with Volpe, whose "men were pouring Mafia millions into Atlantic City through the Abramoffs," the *EIR* reports.

An Italian-American crime boss who presided over the Sicilian Bonanno crime family and specialized in illegal gambling, loan sharking, and narcotics, Joseph "Joe Bananas" Bonanno was assigned the Brooklyn territory by Mafia Commission founder Charles "Lucky" Luciano. Yet, Bananas was so slippery and treacherous, even by organized crime standards, that the Commission expelled him.

Abramoff carried himself like a mobster. Professing a preference for "killers," he dressed in pinstripe suits, replete with a black fedora and flamboyant tie.

His brother, Robert Abramoff, worked on *Gotti*, an underperforming film starring John Travolta as mob boss John Gotti; the film was released in 2018, nearly two decades after Boulis was shot dead at the hands of Gotti and Gambino mobsters employed by Abramoff's team at SunCruz. *Gotti* deifies "the Teflon Don" over his ability to evade the law while hinting at the Abramoffs' celebrated ties to the mob and Hollywood elite.

The details surrounding the SunCruz fraud can be found in the bankruptcy proceedings, providing important clues and connections to unraveling the crime syndicate overtaking the United States: *Citadel Equity Fund, Ltd., vs. Wells Fargo Foothill,* "Boulis Creditors' Notice of Filing of Complaint filed by Citadel Equity Fund, Ltd., against Wells Fargo Foothill, Inc.*

Taking a Page out of the Oligarch Playbook

It should surprise any that the tactics Abramoff employed in the SunCruz deal mirrored those that the Russian oligarchs employed, given that he worked on behalf of the interests of the oligarchs as a Microsoft lobbyist. The SunCruz loan was structured in such a way as to enable Abramoff's team to purchase the fleet for no money down – essentially to provide IOUs in lieu of actual payment, or collateral.

This was a tried and true strategy the Russian oligarchs used to transform themselves into overnight millionaires and billionaires, as Paul Kleibnikov reveals in *The Godfather of the Kremlin*:

"The sale of Logovaz (did not involve) cash, but some kind of promissory note."

"In March 1994, a Berezovsky-led investment fund called Avva had placed money with Mostorg Bank, buying two 500-million-ruble short-term promissory notes. Mostorg Bank was controlled by Sylvester; the bank did not pay back the obligation on time, having transferred the money abroad."

"The cash-strapped Russian government (paid for) collective farms with promissory notes."

Abramoff's team convinced Boulis to sign off on the IOUs, with a promise that the Greek shipping tycoon would be allowed to retain an (illegal) stake in SunCruz. Once the paperwork was signed, Wells Fargo proceeded to process the loan. Curiously, the bank failed to take routine steps required to confirm whether the equity contribution had been received.

In vintage oligarch fashion, a fake wire transfer was finessed to lend the appearance that an equity contribution had been made. According to the legal documents, the banks listed on the schedule of the loan did not match. Wells Fargo allegedly didn't even bother to check and confirm the federal reference numbers on the purported wire transfer nor did it reach out to either of the banks involved to determine whether the funds had gone through, per standard operating procedure.

Abramoff's attorney defender the superlobbyist on grounds that Wells Fargo couldn't have been defrauded by Abramoff as the bank had signed off on the fraudulent loan.

Compare Abramoff's strategy with the strategies of the Russian gangsters, for example in the case of "The Great Chechen Bank Fraud," as reported in *Godfather of the Kremlin:*

"This was a famous scandal. In 1992-93, using a network of corrupted officials inside the Russian Central Bank, several organized-crime groups and gangster-connected banks carried out the biggest bank fraud in Russian history. Incredibly, it was a simple check-kiting scheme. There was so much chaos in the Central Bank's payments department, and the bank's employees were so susceptible to bribery that the criminal organizations were able to make a fortune. The typical scheme involved two shell companies, usually registered banks. Using codes purloined from the Central Bank, the first bank would send a fake wire transfer to the second. The second bank would then present the wire transfer to one of the 1,400 Central Bank payment centers and receive the money in cash. By the time government officials realized what was happening, both banks had disappeared along with the Central Bank's money."

The SunCruz loan was structured by Wells Fargo, and signed off on by Abramoff, who claimed to have received blank signature signature sheets in lieu of actual closing documents (perhaps for the purposes of plausible deniability).

Of note, according to Alaska common law Judge Anna Von Reitz: "The U.S. ATTORNEY GENERAL played with the Wells Fargo Bank Trademark while using WELLS FARGO BANK as a securities broker. As always, it isn't just a matter of what appears in front of your nose, it's a matter of what should be there ---- and isn't. For example, while all these 'banks' appear to be banks, they are all actually acting in a different capacity --- that of credit brokers. Remember how I told you that although they continued to use the name and logos of 'Wells Fargo Bank'--- as if it was still functioning as a bank, the cretins in charge of the U.S. Attorney General's Office who used 'Wells Fargo Bank' to monetize land assets that don't belong to them, were in fact acting as Securities Brokers and not as a bank at all? This is because only a few Eastern and Muslim banks deal in actual money--- money that has intrinsic value in and of itself. The rest all deal in "monetized credit'." https://annavonreitz.com/bigsteal.pdf

Whatever the case, the loan appears to have been designed to eliminate SunCruz as a viable business. For example, per legal documents, Wells Fargo withheld nearly $5 million from the $32.5 million in term financing, contributing to the subsequent defaults, and to SunCruz's loss of its valuable trademarks. "Rebranding every aspect of the business and rebuilding consumer goodwill under a different brand would have required enormous expenditures and resulted in significant lost revenue," the bankruptcy documents reveal. "These additional costs and lost revenue, including the cost of removing the trade name and trademarks from every aspect of the operation coupled with the loss of revenue while doing so would make it impossible to service the lender loans."

Moreover, Abramoff's team appeared to have had no intention of paying Boulis. Like the oligarchs, they appeared to have attempted to steal the business through legal legerdemain. They accomplished this by devaluing the fleet in a post-sale inspection by the amount owed, thereby technically ensuring they didn't owe any money. (This allegation was made by SunCruz President Ben Waldman.) In this way, Abramoff's team had acquired a multi-million dollar casino fleet without having to pay for it, leaving Boulis with nothing but IOUs.

Boulis was justifiably outraged, though he received a concession that he wanted – a stake in his business. What he wanted was his money – the $20 million promised.

Since Boulis had been party to the fraud, he could not sue without revealing his own complicity. His business partners now owned his business, with the federal government and powerful interests now backing them.

Lacking what appeared to be any legal recourse, Boulis stormed into the office of the Adam Kidan and demanded to be paid. When Kidan refused, Boulis threatened to stab him with a pen, according to witnesses. The moment Boulis threatened violence, Kidan had the justification to hire Gotti and Gambino gangsters from Brooklyn, New York "for protection," again taking a page from the Russian gangster playbook.

As Kleibnikov writes:

"The main reason for the explosion of organized crime in Russia, in other words, was neither poverty nor unemployment. It went back to the earliest days of Communism. Lenin and his heirs understood the gangster mentality, and their secret police had used gangster methods to intimidate or eliminate political opponents. With privatization, Russia's political bosses and industrial managers found themselves in control of the nation's prime industrial enterprises. To operate these companies in their own interests (rather than the interests of the Party or the state), they needed protection."

Not long after, Boulis threatened to come forward with the fraud, Boulis was murdered in cold blood by Kidan's security detail, again reflecting tactics of the Russian mobsters. Kleibnikov writes:

"Murder had become a form of dealing with business competition. (Businessmen), instead of deciding their differences in the market or in court, are hiring professional killers and deciding their differences with guns."

Abramoff's network overlapped with the oligarchs – as did Donald Trump's. One prominent oligarch, Aras Agalarov, an Azerbaijani who was worth a reported $1.7 billion and flies around in a private Gulfstream jet valued at $44 million, had brought Donald Trump's 2013 Miss Universe pageant to Moscow.

During this trip to Moscow, Trump may have been filmed by Russian intelligence with prostitutes at the Ritz Carlton Hotel – an accusation Trump rejects. However, the Ritz Carlton is known for its connections to the Crown and intelligence, including MI6. The Ritz Carlton in London was frequented by British Royalty and celebrities while the Ritz Carlton in Paris was the venue in which arms trafficker Adnan Khashoggi negotiated his arms deals for the Saudis.

Intelligence is known to monitor these hotels and capture prominent people in compromising situations, with human trafficking being a recurring theme. Trump's sexual dalliances are renowned. Whether the allegations made against Trump in MI6 agent Christopher Steel's dossier were true or not, the fact is, that Trump was heavily involved with the global networks of the transnational crime syndicate – and one of its leading beneficiaries.

While working on the SunCruz deal, Kidan resided at Fisher Island – an area in Florida where Russian oligarchs reportedly have acquired billion of dollars worth of real estate. Fisher Island is a "hot spot" for Russian investors, Kleibnikov writes. As a disbarred, bankrupt attorney, how could Kidan even afford to live there?

Agalarov's name came up in the federal investigation of Russian interference in the 2016 presidential election when Abramoff was seeking business with the incoming Trump Administration. At the time, oligarchs close to Abramoff were working behind-the-scenes to lobby the Trump campaign on the Magnitsky Act, which was interfering with their ability to move money around the world.

According to counsel representing the mobsters, Kidan did not have a prior relationship with the gangsters; however, the Seminole Tribe connection was "suspected, but not explored," he said.

Even if Kidan had paid mobsters from proceeds of SunCruz, why would Gotti and Gambino mobsters want to protect opportunistic political operatives from Capitol Hill trying to get into the casino business? It's not like the mafia is hard up for money. Why waste time on small fish like them, much less murder a man over a squabble concerning a business contract? On principle, the mafia should have sided with Boulis, who was robbed in this deal. However violent its reputation, the Italian-American mafia is not known to indiscriminately kill people, unlike the Russian mobsters who have succumbed to such tactics as burying rivals alive and paving roads over their victims, among other sick, twisted behavior.

Typically the Italian mafia only murder when family honor is at stake, out of revenge, or when the target has reneged on a deal. Boulis was well liked by many and trusting to a fault. He was also an incredibly successful, self-made businessman. He hadn't reneged on promises. The other side had.

The wider strategic purpose for engaging Boulis was to advance the casino interests of the Seminole Tribe of Florida. It just so happens that the Seminole's casino was bankrolled by Meyer Lansky, the founder of the National Crime Syndicate. Lansky was also connected to Trump's Resorts International in Atlantic City, and his lieutenant, James Weisman, ran the Seminole Management Association which ran the tribe's Hollywood-based casino.

Lansky has been credited with convincing Seminole Chief James Billie to pursue gambling as a viable business strategy for the tribe in 1979. By Billie's own accounts, Lansky said that the Seminoles could make as much as $3 million in six months. "That was a lot of money back then, so I thought, maybe we should try it," Billie told reporters.

Already Jim Allen, a former Trump executive from Atlantic City who was spearheading casino efforts at the Seminoles, was speaking with the Hard Rock about a possible partnership with the Seminole Tribe of Florida. The amount of money that stood to be made through the deal was astronomical. The big players did not want Boulis to join them as they moved forward. He was a liability who knew too much and who was not content to just tag along and accept crumbs. The people he was up against were polished, suave, sophisticated and completely and utterly ruthless; these people prided themselves in conning others whereas Boulis was a down-to-earth, hard working entrepreneur who genuinely cared for his community.

The Executive Intelligence Review reports that prosecutors had attempted to "interrogate Abramoff five years after the Boulis murder," but were "blocked under ambiguous and baffling circumstances, despite the obligation under a Federal plea agreement to cooperate with all investigations."

According to *EIR*, "The problem may stem from a potential international political fallout were Abramoff to open up about the sources and destinations of the mammoth cash flows at stake in control of SunCruz (as) tens of millions of dollars" passed through the business "away from regulators and law enforcement."

After Abramoff fell into legal trouble, casino mogul Donald Trump curiously mocked him in the media, much to Abramoff's confusion. "Why is he saying such horrible things about me," the superlobbyist asked. At the same time, he was very tight lipped about his relationship with Donald Trump, but with a little sleuthing, the connections were discovered.

The Trump Connection

Before Abramoff connected to SunCruz, Trump retained Greenberg Traurig as legal advisor on his efforts to secure a lucrative casino compact for the Seminoles Tribe.

During the period in which Abramoff had engaged Boulis over the SunCruz acquisition, Preston Gates was representing Ikon Public Affairs, a firm that employed Trump's casino lobbyist, Roger Stone, who was then representing the Trump Organization. Among the Trump Organizations interests at the time was a casino for the Seminoles Tribe of Florida.

It was not immediately known what business Preston Gates had with the Trump Organization or Roger Stone during this period in question. However, while Preston Gates was representing Ikon Public Affairs, Abramoff's teams was engaged with the Seminoles. Abramoff's team had acknowledged that Abramoff's team had approached the Seminole Tribe during their negotiations with Boulis.

Abramoff was also enlisted to provide counsel to Philippine dictator Imelda Marcos, who was famous for owning 3,000 pairs of shoes – after she was indicted with arms trafficker Adnan Khashoggi, who had provided Seminole Chief Billie a jet previously owned by Marcos while Trump acquired one of Khashoggi's yachts. When Stone was defending Trump's casino interests in Atlantic City, Stone's firm, BMSK, was representing Marcos. These overlapping connections suggest that the superlobbyist may have acquired the business with Marcos through his Trump connections.

By the time Abramoff got involved, Imelda Marcos was under investigation for laundering $231 million she stole from the treasury and through kickbacks; she was being prosecuted for absconding with earnings from secretly owned private corporations and laundering money. Since 1972, Ferdinand and Imelda Marcos embezzled, stole, purloined, and diverted "to their personal use and the use of others certain Philippine government funds," the indictment read.

Counsel representing Wells Fargo in the SunCruz deal had Seminole connections too, reflecting, perhaps, a confluence of interests that might have implicated Trump. While negotiating the SunCruz deal, Wells Fargo received counsel from Schulte Roth Zabel, a law firm that also represents Merrill Lynch, the Seminole Tribe's financial advisor; and Invesco, a firm founded by Trump (and Rothschild) advisor Wilbur Ross.

Meanwhile, Kidan was appointed General Counsel for St. Maarten's Beach Club, a Seminole establishment where the Seminoles were "quietly investing money in a casino on the tiny Caribbean island of St. Maarten," according to the *St. Petersburg Times*. Trump had also reportedly "stayed at (an) estate" on St. Maarten, Le Chateau des Palmiers. Trump once described the property as "one of the greatest mansions in the world, (one that) blends the elegance of a private chateau with the service of a five-star resort." Situated just east of Puerto Rico, St. Maarten is administered by the Netherlands. The State Department has identified the area as a center for cocaine and heroine trafficking through which drug money is laundered.

After the SunCruz debacle, Abramoff's team at Preston Gates was invited to represent the Saginaw Chippewa Indian Tribe of Michigan alongside Larry Rosenthal, a lobbying ally of Scott Reed, Roger Stone's business partner who was later involved in coordinating the federal investigation into Abramoff's lobbying after Abramoff fell out with his own co-conspirators as he moved to claim their business for himself.

Rosenthal had effectively lobbied the Clinton Administration to intervene in the Saginaw Chippewa election of 1999 to install a favorable slate of candidates in the Tribal Council. Having interfered in elections in South Africa, Yugoslavia, Russia, and elsewhere to secure candidates who could then be enlisted to serve his interests and those of his clients, Abramoff concluded he could claim wealthy tribal casino interests through tribal election meddling.

With this realization, Abramoff promptly intervened in the next Saginaw Chippewa election, secured the victory of a friendly slate of candidates for himself, ousted the previous lobbyist, and claimed the client – a pattern he replicated throughout Indian Country.

This betrayal and act of bad faith led his fellow partners to align against him. The people who were ultimately responsible for bringing the SunCruz fraud and Boulis murder to the nation's attention were Abramoff's own partners. Upon being engaged, the federal government prosecuted Abramoff, allowing the lobbyists to reclaim their clients.

After falling out with Preston Gates, Abramoff promptly joined Greenberg Traurig as Government Affairs Director in Washington, DC. Even though Abramoff was never named as a suspect in the murder, how many people associated with the taint of murder, much less a mammoth fraud, like that surrounding SunCruz, would even be considered an attractive hire for a politically connected firm? My most accounts, he would have been rendered unemployable, regardless of the level of money he was bringing in. By 2023, Greenberg Traurig was eyeing a $2.2 trillion private credit market, *Bloomberg Law* reports.

According to its own press releases, in 2024, Greenberg Traurig reported its 10th year of record revenue, hitting $2.3 billion. The firm didn't need Abramoff to make money. What it needed was for the SunCruz problem to go away.

According to Jon Van Horne, a Harvard-educated Partner at the firm, Greenberg Traurig offered to negotiate a settlement for Abramoff on the SunCruz matter only to turn the case over to the Department of Justice, in what Van Horne characterized as a "violation of attorney-client privilege."

Greenberg Traurig was able to successfully guide the investigation away from itself and its well-heeled clients and onto Abramoff, as the main instigator. Greenberg Traurig's influence with the Bush Administration's Department of Justice could be attributed, in part, to its successful representation of Bush-Cheney in the contest for Florida's electoral votes, helping to secure the White House for the Republicans.

Among the attorneys who partnered with Greenberg Traurig in the election contest were Ted Olson, who became Solicitor General in the Trump Administration; Tim Flanigan, a candidate for Deputy Attorney General in the Bush Administration; and George Terwilliger, III, whom Attorney General Alberto Gonzalez retained to represent him in the mismanagement of the increasingly "partisan" Department of Justice.

The federal investigation into Abramoff's career revealed numerous kickback schemes. While the firm claimed to have been "victimized" by Abramoff and oblivious to his schemes, Van Horne said that Greenberg Traurig had negotiated all of his contracts and signed off on all of his paperwork; the firm even received kickbacks from the money Abramoff brought in, he said. Abramoff confirmed that this was the case in prison interviews. William Worfel, a Council Member for Louisiana Coushatta, a former Abramoff client, said that whatever corruption Abramoff had participated in, Greenberg Traurig was equally as complicit.

Microsoft Seeks Cover

Abramoff's rivals relentlessly pursued his prosecution, weaponizing the government against him while smearing his reputation in the media and throughout the political establishment. In response to growing scrutiny of the Florida scandal, Microsoft immediately moved into damage control. As evidence of this, Microsoft advisor Mark Penn, a senior media strategist for the Clintons, established the reform group, Citizens for Responsibility and Ethics in Washington (CREW) in 2001, for the express purpose of removing Abramoff and his chief legislative ally, Congressman Tom DeLay, from power. The group was supported, in part, by billionaire financier George Soros, who had backed previous Abramoff undertakings.

In 2001, Boulis was gunned down, Kidan had filed for bankruptcy protection, and political operatives were put on notice. The syndicate needed to move fast to cover up its role in Abramoff's affairs and find a scapegoat. As the man at the center of the scandal, Abramoff was the obvious person and also among the most expendable of the powerful players involved. Discoverthenetworks.org, a website run by the David Horowitz Freedom Center, reports that the reforms group's "Form 990 for 2001" lists as a founding CREW director, Mark Penn, a key strategic advisor for Bill Gates and Microsoft since the mid-1990s. Penn later became Corporate Vice President for Strategic and Special Projects at Microsoft Corporation; he reported directly to Microsoft CEO Steve Ballmer.

Notice that by this point, the *Washington Post* hadn't even broken the wider Abramoff scandal, but the foundations were being laid for the eventual public relations and legal assault against Abramoff.

In, 2003, when the *Washington Post* broke the story surrounding Abramoff's lobbying, CREW moved ahead to market Abramoff's guilt, while deflecting attention away from other parties, such as Microsoft and Preston Gates. The scandal was marketed by way of PR firms, one of which was the Soros-backed Fenton Communications. As Larry Rosenthal of Ietan Consulting, one of Abramoff's rivals told the Saginaw Chippewa Indian tribe that once the story broke in the *Washington Post,* "we took it to important PR people."

No one has come forward to take credit for orchestrating the wider Abramoff PR extravaganza which resulted in the lobbyist generating more news articles than Osama bin Laden, the al Qaeda terrorist credited with being the mastermind behind the terrorist attacks of September 11,2001.

The firm in question was likely Burson-Marsteller, which was later presided over by Penn, who became the firm's CEO in 2005, the year the Abramoff hearings were wrapping up with the Senate Indian Affairs Committee. By this point, the superlobbyist had been delivered into the hands of the Department of Justice. Crisis averted.

Reflecting a nexus of interests surrounding these parties, Burson-Marsteller's parent company -- Wire and Plastic Products (WPP) – owns such powerful PR firms as Hill & Knowlton, which expanded its operations to China in 1984 and represented BCCI during its money laundering scandal. WPP represents the Hong Kong and Shanghai Banking Corporation (HSBC), a bank that was originally established in 1865 in Hong Kong to finance growing trade between Europe, India, and China. HSBC was listed in the credits of *Casino Jack*, the film directed by George Hickenlooper and starring Kevin Spacey which dramatizes the SunCruz fraud, reinforcing the guilt of Abramoff and his team while deflecting attention from his powerful collaborators.

Roger Stone's firm, BMSK, which had represented Marcos and Donald Trump's casino interests in Atlantic City, transformed into BKSH & Associates, which was acquired by Burson-Marsteller. BKSH marketed the false intelligence reports that led the United States into war against Iraq after the Twin Towers were targeted for terrorist attacks. As PRWatch.org reports, "in 2003, BKSH & Associates (was) hired by The

Lincoln Group, one of the three firms selected (by) the U.S. Special Operations Command to wage psychological warfare on behalf of the Pentagon in Iraq and other hot spots. (BKSH) was credited with promoting the lies of Ahmed Chalabi and the Iraqi National Congress."

There were other overlapping interests too – involving, for example, the Carlyle Group.

While Greenberg Traurig was representing Bush-Cheney in the 2000 Florida recount, Stone was working with James Baker to execute strategy to prevent Democrats from successfully contesting the recount. Baker was advisor, senior counselor, and strategist for the Carlyle Group, a multi-billion dollar private equity that profits through government grift and access capitalism. Baker, who had served as Secretary of State for President George H.W. Bush – another investor in the firm – helped Carlyle expand overseas into Asia and the Middle East.

Baker's grandfather founded the firm, Baker Botts, whose clients included Berkshire Hathaway – the company of billionaire Warren Buffett, a mentor, partner, and investor with Bill Gates. Both Osama bin Laden and billionaire George Soros were investors in Carlyle.

Baker Botts, in turn, has defended the Saudi Arabian government against litigation filed by American whose families were killed and injured in the attacks of September 11, 2001. The firm also defended Michael Scanlon, Abramoff's partner, in the federal government's case against him.

Add to this that the journalist Naomi Klein reported for the *Nation* in 2004 that as an unpaid Special Presidential Envoy, Baker used his influence to secure "an extraordinary $1 billion investment from the Kuwaiti government."

The deal, she wrote, "involves a complex transaction to transfer ownership of as much as $57 billion in unpaid Iraqi debts. The debts, now owed to the government of Kuwait, would be assigned to a foundation created and controlled by a consortium in which the key players are the Carlyle Group, the Albright Group (headed by another former Secretary of State, Madeleine Albright) and several other well-connected firms. Under the deal, the government of Kuwait would also give the consortium $2 billion up front to invest in a private equity fund devised by the consortium, with half of it going to Carlyle."

Burson-Marsteller provided crisis management for Erik Prince's Blackwater after the mercenary company was investigated for killing 17

Iraqi civilians. Reflecting a nexus of overlapping interests, Prince had worked for Alexander Strategy Group, a firm that represented Microsoft and which had assisted Abramoff and DeLay in their efforts on behalf of the Russian oligarchs. Prince's name would later reappear during the Trump Administration in connection to the Russian investigation. While providing security for the Communist Chinese along the Belt and Road Initiative in China, Prince helped secure government funding for the government's response for the coronavirus pandemic and then carved out markets throughout the world to cash in on vaccines with Paul Behrends, who had worked for both Blackwater and the Alexander Strategy Group.

Whatever the case, Wells Fargo allegedly went to incredible lengths and assumed incredible risk to accommodate all parties in the SunCruz loan. Another factor the media misses is Bill Gates' connection to Wells Fargo by way of First Interstate Bank, a bank holding company presided over by Mary Maxwell Gates, Bill Gates' mother – which the former acquired in 1996.

Wells Fargo, Bill Gates, and the Saudis

In 1996 – three years before Abramoff was connected to the SunCruz loan as Microsoft lobbyist, Wells Fargo acquired First Interstate Bank (FIB), a bank holding company over which Bill Gates' mother, Mary Maxwell Gates, presided as Director.

FIB's rich history traces to Amadeo Pietro Giannini, the son of Italian immigrants who established the Bank of Italy in San Francisco in 1904.

The Bank of Italy eventually became the Bank of America, the world's largest bank and partner of the World Economic Forum.

Of note, Giannini was the inspiration for American Madness *– a film by Frank Capra, who also created the* Why We Fight *propaganda documentary series for the War Department. After the Soviets had massacred millions of their own people, Capra helped market the USSR as a benevolent force and friend of the United States. The following are quotes from Capra's* The Battle of Russia:

"History knows no greater display of courage than that shown by the people of Soviet Russia." – Henry Stimson, Secretary of War

"We and our allies owe and acknowledge an everlasting debt of gratitude to the armies and people of the Soviet Union." – Frank Knox, Secretary of the Navy

The gallantry and the aggressive fighting spirit of Russian soldiers command the American army's admiration." – George C. Marshall, Chief of Staff, U.S. Army

"I join ... in admiration for the Soviet Union's heroic and historic defense." – Ernest King, Commander in Chief, US Fleet

"The scale and the grandeur of the (Russian) effort mark it as the greatest military achievement in all of history." --Gen. Douglas MacArthur. Commander in Chief, Southwest Pacific Area

The film describes the numerous attempts undertaken over the centuries to "conquer Russia," ranging from the Teutonic Knights and Charles XII of Sweden to French Emperor Napoleon Bonaparte and the German Empire.

The narrator in the film then salivates over Russia's vast resources. "Seven hundreds years of trying to conquer Russia," with its nine million square miles," the film's narrator says. "The sun never sets" in the Soviet Union. Among the resources the narrator identified were gold, silver, copper, tin, magnesium, nickle, timber, fuel, goal, iron, lotus, tea, tobacco, cotton sugar, vast pastures with which to feed livestock.

The blood-soaked Russian Revolution that unleashed tyranny upon the world, was waged with the complicity of Rothschild, Inc. dba as the U.S. federal government; and Wall Street..

The film even quotes Nazi leader Adolph Hitler: "When we think of new territory, we think of Russia. Destiny itself points that way," revealing a longstanding agenda driven by the interests surrounding the City of London to stake its claim on Russia's natural resources.

In 1929, Giannini formed a holding company, Transamerica Corporation, which spun off Bank of America in 1953 under the Clayton Anti-Trust Act – legislation written by Samuel Untermeyer, who also penned the Federal Reserve Act; its banking operations became Firstamerica Corporation, which changed its name of Western Bancorporation; its retail operation was United California Bank of Basel, Switzerland, whose President and CEO was Paul Erdman.

Erdman had previously served as a financial analyst for the European Coal and Steel Community (ECSC), a nascent European common market established by the Rothschilds after World War II to chip away at national sovereignty to advance globalism on behalf of the interests of the City of London. In an interview, Baron Robert Rothschild said the ECSC was established as a next step towards global dictatorship. First, Europe, then the world, he said.

Through a hostile takeover in 1970, Erdman acquired the Electronics International Capital (EIC), which was established in Bermuda for investments in European tech companies.

Three years later, executives from JP Morgan, whose operations had bankrolled the Russian Revolution, secretly met in Bermuda to resurrect the House of Morgan. The House of Morgan and the Rockefellers, who had destroyed Russia's oil industry during the Russian Revolution so that they could control it afterward, provided the financial backing for Merrill Lynch, Banks of America's investment arm, which acquired G.H. Walker & Co., an investment bank founded by George Herbert Walker, a member of Bush clan.

Merrill Lynch was the Seminole Tribe's financial advisor – and the bank in which, according to Nations in Action's Maria Zack, money was diverted from Obama's Iranian deal through Rome to influence the 2020 presidential election.

^^^

In 1986, around the time narcodollars were flooding the financial system and federally recognized Indian tribes were anticipating a deluge of casino dollars, Goldman Sachs and Morgan Stanley simultaneously decided to go public to receive outside capital – capital that would enable them to dramatically outpace the competition in the mergers and acquisitions departments, creating the entities that became "too big to fail." The capital arrived circuitously by way of Japan's Sumitomo Bank.

During merger-mania, First Interstate Bank unsuccessfully attempted a $3.2 billion hostile takeover of Bank of America., a spin-off of its parent company.

In 2009, Bank of America acquired Merrill Lynch. Through this deal, Bank of America acquired a 34 percent stake in BlackRock, the world's largest asset manager, with $11 trillion in assets. BlackRock, in turn, acquired a stake in Sumitomo Mitsui Financial Group, Inc. which International Investing describes as "bigger than BlackRock" and "Asia's biggest asset manager" in terms of Assets Under Management.

Sumitomo invests with the Saudis.

Wells Fargo has been a "proud supporter" of Native Americans since the 1950s, around the time that Saudi Arabia and the World Bank partnered to develop the world as part of a wider effort to consolidate the world's wealth, power, and commercial enterprise within the hands of the select few.

By its own accounts, Wells Fargo has established banking relationships with 40 percent of federally recognized tribes, committed $3 billion in credit, and holds $3.9 billion deposits for tribal governments and tribal-owned enterprises.

Wells Fargo and the Boston Consulting Group have teamed up to collaborate on the economic imbalances within tribal communities by "highlighting the wealth and economic opportunities for investment and value creation that achieve resiliency." Yet for all the investment in Indian Country, to the tune of billions upon billions of dollars, the Natives remain the poorest people in the land.

Since the Obama Administration, federally recognized Indian tribes have become partners with the federal government to advance a Green New Deal in line with Saudi Arabia's Vision 2030.

Boston Consulting Group has been enlisted to help Saudi Crown Prince Mohammed bin Salman consolidate power in Saudi Arabia to advance Agenda 2030, that of moving away from an oil-based economy to alternative fuels, with an emphasis on creating Smart Cities. At the same time, Saudi Arabia has aligned with Russia and China to join BRICS to dethrone the dollar. BCG designed the economic blueprint for Vision 2030 – for complete economic diversity away from oil.

The plan involved: 1.) making Saudi Arabia "the heart of the Arab and Islamic worlds;" 2.) transforming the Kingdom into a global investment powerhouse; 3.) establishing Saudi Arabia as a hub linking Africa and Eurasia.

BCS partnered with Harvard to study AI. Of note, After Epstein earned an MBA from Stanford, he went to work for Boston Consulting Group.

Since 2021, Boston Consulting Group has been led by a German executive Christoph Schweizer, a member of the Business Roundtable and the World Economic Forum's International Business Council which is dedicated to fighting climate change, perfectly in line with Saudi Arabia's Vision 2030.

A Closer Look at Citadel

The secondary lender in the SunCruz debacle was Citadel Equity Fund, a multinational hedge fund and financial services company. Citadel reportedly said it hadn't received the closing documents until months after closing.

The definition of Citadel is a "fortress" or "last line of defense." The name evokes images of a castle surrounded by an alligator-infested moat in which battle-scared warriors returning from a pillage retreat to the castle and draw the bridge to protect themselves and their cherished loot.

Citadel's previously name, before it was changed in 1994, was the Wellington Financial Group, which was named after the Duke of Wellington, a celebrated figure in Rothschild history, who prevailed over Napoleon in the Battle of Waterloo – an event Nathan Rothschild leveraged to tank the British stock market by lying about this victory so that the dynasty could claim Britain's assets for pennies on the dollar; when the anticipated upswing occurred, Rothschild became the wealthiest man in Europe, the owner of Great Britain and the British Empire, and the recipient of a 200-year contract to control and breed itself into the British Monarchy. With offices that stretch across Europe, Asia, the Americas, Wellington has generated more than $74 billion in profits since its founding.

Wellington has also emerged as a major investor in climate change solutions. "Climate change is an existential threat to society and touches every sector of the global economy," Greg Wasserman, the head of Wellington's Private Climate Investing team, said in a public statement.

Wellington's research partner in this endeavor is Woodwell Climate Research Center, whose previous president, Dr. Philip Duffy, is currently advising the Biden Administration through the White House Office of Science and Technology Policy.

In addition to participating United Nations climate negotiations and helping to "shape U.S. global change policy and research," Duffy was Senior Policy Analyst and Senior Advisor on Global Climate Change for the Obama Administration.

Wellington serves over 2,500 clients in more than 60 countries and manages $1.2 trillion for pensions, endowments, foundations, global wealth managers, and other clients.

Much can be said for shrewd investing and creating multi-generational wealth, but what the world is witnessing is outright pillage and kleptocracy – that of shoring the world's wealth into the hands of the few.

Wellington is one of the world's largest independent investment management firms, with assets valued at more than $1.2 trillion, under management and whose client list includes central banks.

One of the firm's former chairmen, John Bogle, established the Vanguard Group, which reportedly holds more than $7.7 trillion in global assets under management as the largest provider of mutual funds and the second-largest provider of exchange-traded funds after BlackRock.

In 2015, former Federal Reserve Director Ben Bernanke became a financial advisor to Citadel on global economic and financial issues.

As one of the largest "market makers" in the United States, Citadel paid Secretary of Treasury Janet Yellen $800,000 in speaking fees from 2018 to 2020 after she served as Federal Reserve Chair.

Citadel acquired more than $2 billion in assets under managements within its first eight years of existence – an amount that has blossomed to over $58 billion.

In 2014, Citadel became the first foreign hedge fund to complete yuan fundraising as part of a program to allow Chinese investors to invest in overseas hedge funds.

In 2021, Citadel became the second top money managers for net gains. Citadel's Kensington Global Strategies – one of the largest private funds in the world, requires a minimum investment of over $10 million to become a client.

Citadel's founder, Ken Griffin, has amassed an estimated net worth of $35 billion. Griffin, in turn, has contributed tens of millions of dollars to political candidates and causes, mostly Republican or conservative in ideology – with the notable exception of Obama, who has collaborated with the Republicans to advance globalism.

Griffith gave the Obama Foundation $1 million when Obama was running against Sen. John McCain, whom Abramoff blamed for his criminal prosecution. "But for McCain," Abramoff lamented, his criminal grift with DeLay and the gang would have continued.

The other surprise donor to Obama in the last stretch of the 2008 presidential campaign was the Bill and Melinda Gates Foundation, which also donated $1 million.

∿∿

The corporate headquarters of Citadel is based in Miami, where at least three billionaire oligarchs own property. Florida is home to "Little Moscow."

Oligarchs are snapping up real estate with stolen public assets while Americans are losing their homes. Consider how the oligarchs acquired that wealth and whom they stole it from – along with the generous spirit in which Americans provided it, and the absolute contempt and disregard oligarchs have demonstrated towards the good American people, their values, and their society as they pursue a materialistic life in the United States, as if they were kings walking among peasants.

Little Moscow is located on a small strip of land near Miami called Sunny Isles Beach. "Among these developments are several Trump Towers," Business Insider *reports. Trump's brand has "held huge appeal among Russian investors looking to move their money in the post-Soviet economy. Real estate agents told the (*Washington*) Post that Trump's name carries weight among the European, South American, and Asian elite, but especially among the Russian oligarchs."*

Reuters reported in 2017 that at least 63 members of Russian so-called elites invested $100 million buying property in Trump buildings in the region. These were "politically connected businessmen," according to Reuters. "Russian men make money at home; they visit their Miami property just for a few months in winter. Some of these rich daddies are in their fifties or older, while their women are in their twenties; the beach is packed with really young pregnant Russian girls, girls with babies."

Russians reportedly hold more than $1 trillion in offshore accounts, which are "disproportionately held in South Florida property," Business Insider *reports. Meanwhile, U.S. taxes and the cost of living for Americans are dramatically increasing to pay the debt accrued for reasons that not do not serve the debtors.*

The federal government – and now increasingly, state and local governments, are shoveling the wealth of the American people out the door to politically connected individuals, reflecting a toxic, insidious alliance between private industry and governments that live off the fat of the land. The plunderers give little back beyond flaunting their ill-gotten gains in the face of those they have robbed while making strategic donations to politicians who can kick even more back to them.

∧∧∧

In 2022, Citadel signed a deal with Vornado Realty Trust and Rudin Management Co. to master lease a new $1.2 billion office tower on Park Avenue in Manhattan to establish Citadel's headquarters in New York City.

Vornado previously owned 660 (formerly 666) Fifth Avenue, which was acquired by Kushner properties, a firm connected to Jared Kushner, Trump's son-in-law. The property was established by Tishman Realty and Construction, Co. which built the World Trade Center – and sold the 666 address to Sumitomo Reality and Development, which then sold it to Tishman Speyer, which which passed it along to Kushner in 2007.

The headquarters for the Saudi central bank, SAMA, was designed by American architect Minoru Yamasaki, who also designed the World Trade Center in New York City, the Federal Reserve Bank of Richmond, and the Temple Beth El synagogue for the oldest Jewish congregation, led by Rabbi Isaac Mayer Wise who, in 1889, established the Central Conference of America, a central body of authority for American Judaism.

Coincidentally, Tishman Speyer's first project in Europe was launched in Frankfurt, Germany, the origins and center of Rothschild financial power, where the group established the Messeturm Trade Fair Tower – identified as a site to serve, ironically, as the European Union's anti-money laundering authority.

Rudin Management represents a real estate empire comprised of over 40 buildings valued at $2 billion. One of its investors, Lewis Rudin, established the Real Estate Roundtable – a nonprofit public policy think tank which bills itself as "an exclusive group of real estate leaders *focused on coordinating a national policy agenda focused on the continued prosperity of our industry and our economy."*

Despite being a Jew, Rudin was awarded the Benemerenti Award by Pope Benedict XVI for his service to the Catholic Church, in the tradition of a "Papal Army."

IX.
Saudi Arabia Comes Clean

"Property monopolized or in the possession of a few is a curse to mankind."

President John Adams
American Founding Father

In the late 1990s, Saudi Arabia, the principal development partner of the World Bank, sought to change course to diversify its economy. Its oil fields had been overproduced and were not sufficient to provide the revenue or resources need to develop the world as envisioned by the syndicate, when gas was readily available and cheap.

It was never the responsibility of the nations of the world to fund the lavish lifestyles of the parasitic elite or indulge their lust for power. With a mandate granted to the World Bank to alleviate poverty, the syndicate has spread it around while amassing greater wealth for itself. The quality of consumer goods, homes, vehicles, lifestyles, even farm products has rapidly declined, salaries have dropped, and living expenses, taxes, and inflation have increased – the result of the syndicate's strategy of squeezing every last dollar out the economy for themselves as they establish a global monopoly, that of owning and controlling everything – and everyone. Theirs was a fool's errand from the start.

Sure there was money to be made, but at what cost? Could the rape, pillaging, exploitation, human rights abuses, and government corruption justify accommodating their insatiable greed?

Behind the high-minded rhetoric of lifting up the poor, the agenda was geared as stripping nations and people of their resources and properties so that a small, charmed group of pirates could enjoy unlimited wealth, power, opportunities, and influence. There were even talks of "breakaway civilizations" supported by advanced technologies while everyone else was left with with societal rot and regression in an obsolete world.

Sustainable development, led by a wise hand, could have ensured that progress unfolded in a measured way through thoughtful deliberation and respect for national sovereignty and the rights of others; wise, ethical, competent, and *legitimate* leaders could engage each other in trade, exchange, and diplomacy to serve their nations and their people, rather than plunder them. Together humanity could explore the stars and work together for the betterment of society and each other.

Instead the so-called elites have proceeded to plunder behind endless virtue signaling. Anyone can see that the elites who profess a deep concern for the environment have polluted the world over, poisoned the foods we eat, and tainted the air we breathe. They are pushing for mass migration at unsustainable levels, fueling unemployment, societal disruption, and a need to move people off of the land and into cities to establish a global monopoly on power. Immigrants are pouring across borders faster than the destination countries can absorb them. The result has been further environmental degradation.

Before the Nixon Administration – and arguably, before the World Wars – and even before the Civil War, the United States was on a trajectory to becoming a truly prosperous, self-sufficient nation, a beacon of light upon the hill, where freedom, culture, and free enterprise thrived. The United States offered a well functioning society for free, God-fearing people with a common culture, language, and history to pursue their God-given talents.

This was a society from which anyone, regardless of his or her station in life, could live a life of one's choosing, where children were protected, parents respected, and teachers, doctors, executives, and others served the public good. There was an extant social contract between the governed and government. The public served its civil duty and the government managed society, protected rights, performed needed services, and served the greater good. The United States offered quality universal education, medical care, and even a high standard of living, with limited taxes. Indeed, the income tax had not even been instituted until the World Wars – which was waged on behalf of the City of London, not the national interest, to fund the war. The American people were promised that the tax would be temporary, only it remained, another promise the so-called leaders broke.

From the ashes of the World Wars, Saudi Arabia emerged as a leading global oil producer, the United States was transformed into a fat calf to be slaughtered; and the World Bank became a vehicle through which the elites redistributed the wealth of the United States and other nations to themselves, mortgaging the futures of American and other citizens without their informed consent, in the process.

The American people had rejected Rothschild's central banks, repeatedly and consistently. The Federal Reserve, upon which the so-called elite have based their fraudulent banking system in the United States, was created by their corporation – without a proper Congressional quorum in place. The legislation supporting the Fed never passed since the government was not even in session – and hasn't been since the Civil War.

Therefore the Federal Reserve Act arguably exists under color-of-law, therefore absolving the American people of the debt the syndicate has accrued. The shadow hand who influenced Wilson to sign off on the Federal Reserve Act was Edward Mandell House who wrote this to the President:

"Soon, every American will be required to register their biological property in a National system designed to keep track of the people and that will operate under the ancient system of pledging. By such methodology, we can compel people to submit to our agenda, which will affect our security as a charge-back for our fiat paper currency.

"Every American will be forced to register or suffer not being able to work and earn a living. They will be our chattel, and we will hold the security over them forever, by operation of the law merchant under the scheme of secured transactions.

"Americans, by unknowingly and unwittingly delivering the bills of lading to us, will be rendered bankrupt and insolvent, forever to remain economic slaves through taxation, secured by their pledge. They will be stripped of their rights and given a commercial value designed to make us a profit, and they will be none the wiser, for not one man in a million could ever figure out our plans; and if by accident one or two would figure it out, we have in our arsenal plausible deniability.

"After all, this is the only logical way to fund government, by floating liens and debt to the registrants in the form of benefits and privileges. This will inevitably reap to us huge profits beyond our wildest expectations and leave every American a contributor to this fraud, which we will call Social Insurance (SSI)."

"Without realizing it, every American will insure us for any loss we may incur, and in this manner every American will unknowingly be our servant, however begrudgingly. The people will become helpless and without any hope for their redemption; and we will employ the high office of the President of our dummy corporation to foment this plot against America."

Talk about psychopathic, anti-human mindset. Americans, indeed people the world over should reject this agenda in no uncertain terms. We have the legal wherewithal to do it.

All the propaganda, media spin, history rewrites, slander of genuine historians and debasement of historic records in the world do not change the fundamental facts. Worse, the American people were lied to about how their money was being spent. They were being fleeced, without their informed consent. Their wealth was being redistributed to the Rothschild crime syndicate – by way of a currency reduced to "debt currency" that could be printed out of thin air and which had no intrinsic value.

The people were left holding the debt for the syndicate's wars, rapacious acquisitions, land and resource grabs, luxurious homes, yachts, planes, and crimes while they advanced their treasonous, subversive agenda against the United States and other countries. The agenda involved nothing short of claiming all the real assets in the world through fraud, pillage, and outright deception..

The United States (dummy corporation) is a member of the World Bank, which contributes funds to its operations. The World Bank, in turn, extends loans and grants for development projects and programs throughout the world and provides bilateral aid.

While poverty is increasing throughout the United States, America's infrastructure crumbles, and the country's education, legal, and health care system, that used to be the envy of the world, have become unspeakably corrupt. Meanwhile, the syndicate pollutes and desecrates America's once pristine environment as the United States, through the World Bank, pledges the wealth of the American people to specific initiatives and programs administered by the World Bank and other multilateral development organizations.

Consider that the United States gives aid to foreign countries, including, for example, Nigeria, South Africa, Japan, Brazil, India and China. Ask yourselves why it's the responsibility of the United States to mortgage out the future of its own citizens on behalf of foreign nations to establish markets and monopolies for private, predatory corporations who owe no allegiance to any country or anything beyond themselves.

These corporations have supported a system that few want – beyond the unaccountable criminal elite who nurse delusions of grandeur. Not only is the United States pouring money into these nations, but it is spending billions annually for hundreds of federally recognized Indian tribes – that is, closed, captive, tax-payer supported markets established as corporations for the syndicate. There is no accountability for how the money is spent, much of which is misdirected and stolen, creating a class of rich oligarchs presiding over impoverished wastelands and monopolies. While U.S. citizens are told to tighten their belts, their future is being mortgaged for such purposes as described below:

1. **Nigeria**: The United States provides aid to Nigeria to support various initiatives, including health programs, education, economic development, security assistance, humanitarian aid, and governance reforms;
2. **South Africa**: U.S. assistance to South Africa focuses on areas such as health, education, economic development, democracy and governance, and support for marginalized populations;
3. **Japan**: While Japan is a major economic power and donor country in its own right, the U.S. and Japan have engaged in various forms of cooperation and assistance, including in areas such as disaster relief, security cooperation, and development assistance in third countries;
4. **Brazil**: U.S. assistance to Brazil has focused on areas such as environmental protection, healthcare, education, economic development, and governance;
5. **India**: The United States provides aid to India to support a wide range of programs, including health initiatives, education, economic development, agricultural productivity, environmental sustainability, and collaboration on science and technology;
6. **China**: While China is not a traditional recipient of U.S. foreign aid, and is a strategic adversary built up with with the wealth and technology of the United States, the federal government has provided assistance to China in areas such as public health, environmental protection, disaster response, and initiatives to address climate change and infectious diseases.

How often is aid granted to foreign countries –and even Indian tribes – misdirected? How often do public funds fail to reach their intended destination while political insiders disbursing the aid grow increasingly rich? How is it possible that the United States gives money to countries for infrastructure while America's infrastructure crumbles?

Through such investments, the syndicate is establishing its dominance over national and global markets – to disseminate its propaganda, distribute its films, acquire real estate, internationalize hospitals, schools, governments, and technology – and secure monopolies over power, commerce, and resources.

The global control system is being consolidated within the hands of an increasingly small number of people who dominate all markets and distribute products based upon patents subsidized by taxpayers – if not stolen, ensuring criminal elites reap all the profits through public-private partnerships, tax avoidance schemes, and a weaponized government that redistributes the public's money and assets to them.

The World Bank's members include a vast majority of the world's nations, ranging from large industrialized countries to small developing nations, ranging from the United States, China, India, and Brazil to Germany, Japan, Nigeria, South Africa, and many others.

The United States gives money to these countries – which then subsidize the World Bank, raising questions of institutional double dipping. How can a country so desperately in need of American, turn around and give that money to the World Bank? The answer is that money is passed around and not used for its intended purpose – that is, to benefit the countries and their people, but to line the pockets of a criminal elite.

The World Bank borrows funds from international capital markets by issuing bonds. These bonds are backed by the creditworthiness of the member countries and the bank's own resources. The United States is being treated as an ATM, even though the money taken out isn't theirs to have. Global planners have just signed on to the accounts and helped themselves. In turn, the creditworthiness of the United States has fallen – with fewer and fewer nations willing to accept the dollar and actually taking advantage of the Unites States to enrich themselves while leaving this nation behind. At the same time the World Bank relies upon its own funds for investment purposes – but where did it get those funds? From the taxpayers by way of their color-of-law governments.

An abstract for an article entitled "Plundering the Poor: The Role of the World Bank in Third World," which critiques Cheryl Payer's recent book, *The World Bank: A Critical Analysis,* is instructive. The abstract analyzes the World Bank's role in the Third World and explains why poverty, hunger, and malnutrition, unemployment, and "adverse social phenomena associated with them," are increasing.

According to the abstract: "The World Bank, the most important so-called development assistance agency, annually dispenses billions of dollars to Third World governments, ostensibly to develop their economies through a variety of loan projects. But even a superficial analysis reveals that the Bank is the perfect mechanism to help (i.e., subsidize) the large transnational corporations from the industrial countries to expand their industrial, commercial, and financial activities in the Third World, at the expense of the latter and particularly at the expense of the rural and urban (worker)."

The once fiscally responsible U.S. government now holds debt of over $34 trillion. There are around 337 million Americans – so that averages out to over $100,000 per each U.S. citizen. Yet, with all the assistance the United States has provided to Saudi Arabia in the form of arms sales, training, and logistical support, Saudi Arabia has amassed trillions of dollars in its Sovereign Wealth Fund. Instead of giving back, the Saudis are gobbling up U.S. assets and businesses and investing in BRICS, an alternative global economic system that seeks to dethrone the dollar.

Despite being a high-income country with substantial oil wealth, Saudi Arabia receives development assistance from the United States in education, healthcare, and economic diversification at the expense of its own citizens. The United States has also provided humanitarian assistance to Saudi Arabia. How much has Saudi Arabia or any other country provided the American people in return?

The World Bank provides loans, grants, and technical assistance to Saudi Arabia to support projects in areas such as infrastructure, education, healthcare, agriculture, and private sector development. With money, comes strings. The World Bank provides policy advice and technical assistance to Saudi Arabia to support the development goals of the shadow elite.

Saudi Arabia Realigns Oil Priorities

"Crown Prince Abdullah stunned the energy world when, in the autumn of 1998, he announced that he was interested in what American oil companies could do for Saudi Arabia, during a high profile visit to the United States," Matthew Simmons writes in *Twilight in The Desert*. "In one fell swoop, he seemed to have reversed the Kingdom's 25 yr-old hydrocarbons strategy of maintaining a national monopoly on upstream development. The visit came towards the end of what had been a disastrous year for the Kingdom economically, and which contained uncomfortable or even alarming implications, both for domestic stability and foreign relations."

At the end of the Clinton Administration, the Saudis launched the Saudi Gas Initiative. "With its flagship investment potential, its credibility and, more widely, its expected contribution to standards of governance in the Kingdom, the gas initiative has become an important benchmark of the fortunes of economic reform in Saudi Arabia," Simmons writes. "The initiative was born in the United States, the center-piece visit of a six week world tour by Abdullah. The tour itself was a high profile, almost triumphant, display of Abdullah's new found political authority, aimed at projecting his role as a statesman to a domestic audience and demonstrating abroad that he was now King in all but name. The U.S. leg of the tour was the most important, with Abdullah and his technocratic commoner allies preoccupied with a long agenda of economic reform and Abdullah himself most concerned with the need to safeguard the political transition,"

Simmons argues that Saudi Arabia had vastly overstated the size of its oil reserves and that Saudi oil fields could no longer support the development of the world in a sustainable way. Simmons wanted the world about "peak oil," – that global oil production had peaked.

A global plan was then hatched to decrease U.S. oil production and economic prosperity while elevating the energy production and wealth of other countries, particularly China and Saudi Arabia.

U.S. energy production peaked in December of 1970 during the Nixon Administration. "Out of the blue and totally unexpectedly, U.S. oil production ended the century-long run during which the United States dominated global oil supply," Simmons writes.

Secretary of State Henry Kissinger had tightened the nuzzle on American oil production while unleashing Saudi oil production in service of global development. He also decoupled the dollar from gold, launching the petrodollar, in which all oil purchases were to be denominated in dollars, with the World Bank setting the price.

As Saudi oil production soared, U.S. production dropped, Simmons writes. "The decline of U.S. oil production enabled Saudi Arabia to take advantage of its resource potential as the world's appetite for oil grew. Saudi Arabia had both the opportunity and the need to increase its oil output as fast as possible."

By the fall of the 1985, Saudi Arabia oil production had notably fallen. By the late 1990's, almost all OPEC producers, with the exception of Saudi Arabia, were reaching peak sustainability rates. At the same time, the Saudis remained "firmly committed to the role they were playing as the sole stabilizer of world oil markets."

By 2004, Saudi Arabia had become the only country in the world with any meaningful unused production capacity, Simmons writes.

The only meaningful non-OPEC oil additions from 1977 through 2003 came from the Russia/former Soviet Union. "And these surprising and anticipated gains were mainly the result of reworking existing fields in which faulty waterflooding had bypassing massive amounts of oil," Simmons writes. "By mid-2004, the Russia oil miracle was also beginning to fray. Pipeline capacity to export oil was not full. Political turmoil erupted over the fall of Yukos. Concerns were also being raised in some circles that most publicly traded Russian oil companies might now be overproducing these field to maximum current profits."

In late 1998, Saudi Arabia launched a "highly visible, widely publicized effort to enlist western oil company capital and technical expertise to help the kingdom address its increasingly urgent need for additional supplies of natural gas," Simmons writes.

The Gas Initiative was "the first publicized attempt to bring major international oil and gas companies into Saudi Arabia since the original SOCAL concession issued in 1933," he writes. "(The) seed for the gas initiative was planted in late 1998 when Crown Prince Abdullah visited Washington, DC. (The) Saudi ambassador hosted a reception for the Crown Prince. Senior representatives of every major oil company were invited."

Given that Rothschild is at the pinnacle of this global shit show, the syndicate would have been aware of the problem before it was made public, and prepared to provide a solution to keep the wider agenda on track, particularly with regards to the role of Saudi Arabia as the key strategic partner of the World Bank.

In 1996 – two years before the Gas Initiative was launched, Richard Perle, a staunch neoconservative and former Assistant Secretary of Defense for Global Strategic Affairs under President Ronald Reagan, led a study group which produced a document, *A Clean Break: A New Strategy for Securing the Realm*. The report was produced for Benjamin Netanyahu, the future Prime Minister of Israel, a state wholly created and owned by the Rothschilds where the dynasty had planned to establish the seat for the world government.

A case could be made that *A Clean Break* was a response to a as-yet unannounced decision to end of the petro-dollar, which Kissinger had established,. With the launch of the petro-dollar, the Secretary of State promised that the United States would provide for Israel's energy security and protection in perpetuity.

Clean Break promoted "a clean break from the past (to) establish a new vision for the U.S.-Israeli partnership, based on self-reliance, maturity and mutuality—not one focused narrowly on territorial disputes." Israel's new approach was one in which the Jewish state would no longer rely upon American troops, but could defend itself, even by way of launching pre-emptive strikes (for oil).

In 2024, the Council of Foreign Relations (CFR) reported that "Israel has been the largest cumulative recipient of U.S. foreign aid since its founding, receiving about $300 billion (adjusted for inflation) in total economic and military assistance."

Most of the aid – around $3.3 billion a year – was given to Israel as a grant under the Foreign Military Financing program – requiring Israel to purchase U.S. military equipment and services. Military contractors produced weapons, subsidized by taxpayers. The weapons are then sold them to Israel and other countries, which receive U.S. aid, thereby forcing the taxpayers to support both the creation and purchase of these products, revealing that the Pentagon was little more than an arms sales shop for the world.

Other nations that receive such block grants are also required to purchase U.S. military equipment, raising questions of why the United

States is arming the world. Of course, the syndicate is heavily invested in toppling foreign governments to establish puppet regimes for the purposes of establishing monopolies, seizing resources, thinning out populations, siphoning public money, and reorganizing the world under its own control.

With increased global destabilization, the elite can justify more security to curtail freedoms and surveil citizens, with money doled out to the syndicate's contractors. Israel is the only country provided an exemption, that allows the Jewish state to use financial support received from the United States to purchase weapons from its own contractors instead.

Israel's new self-reliance – involved no longer needing U.S. troops for defense purposes. In lieu of strategic retreat, it sought preemptive strikes to advance its strategic interests and will to power. The terror attacks of September 11, 2001, set this agenda in motion.

Please note that this author is no way advancing "conspiracy theories," that would even presume to suggest that the terror attacks on U.S. soil were deliberate or waged as part of a response to the Saudi oil issue. Instead, the facts concerning the financial relationships and networks at play are being presented so that the reader can come to his or her own conclusions.

In 1997, the Kyoto Protocol extended the 1992 United Nations Framework Convention on Climate Change, committing nations around the world to reducing greenhouse gas emissions, based on the "scientific consensus" that global warming is occurring and that human-made CO_2 emissions are driving it."

That year, the Project for the New American Century (PNAC) was established to "promote American global leadership." To this end, PNAC called for increasing defense spending, promoting political and economic freedom abroad, and pre-emptive strikes against "regimes hostile to our interests and values" in the interests of preserving "an international order friendly to our security, our prosperity, and our principles."

Among the signatories of PNAC's founding statement of principles were Texas Governor George W. Bush, before he became President; and Paul Wolfowitz, who became the President of the World Bank in June of 2005.

A few months later, starting in November, the United Nations held a Climate Change Conference, the first meeting the first Meeting of the Parties to the Kyoto Protocol since their initial meeting in Kyoto in 1997.

Wolfowitz had signed on to an agenda that involved pre-emptive strikes against countries, in the interests of seizing oil for Israel, before assuming the titular head of the World Bank, which was in partnership with the Saudis to advance the syndicate's agenda.

In 2000, PNAC issued a report entitled *Rebuilding America's Defenses* in which it promoted "advanced forms of biological warfare to target specific genotypes to transform biological warfare from the realm of terror to a politically useful tool."

Immediately after the terrorists attacks of September 11, 2001, PNAC lobbied the Bush Administration to "remove Saddam Hussein from power in Iraq" through a pre-emptive strike.

Politicos alternatively blamed the Saudis and the Israelis for the terrorist attacks on the Twin Towers. The individual ultimately credited with being the mastermind behind the attacks of September 11, 2001 was al Qaeda terrorist Osama bin Laden, a CIA asset who had invested in the Carlyle Group alongside billionaire financier George Soros, Presidents George W. Bush and George H.W. Bush, and Secretary of Defense Donald Rumsfeld.

PNAC called for building up America's military to wage multiple theaters of war simultaneously, reflecting perhaps, the desperate agenda to seize oil around the world or overthrow governments from which this could be possible. High among the concerns of the neoconservatives was the loss of American global leadership – which was being sustained, in part, by the petrodollar, which was on its way out.

During the Gas Initiative, "various various oil company attendees soon began whispering among themselves that something extraordinary seemed to be underway," Simmons writes. "(Saudi) Arabia was about to invite the daughters of the Seven Sisters – Exxon, Mobil, Chevron, Texaco, Gulf, BP, and Shell – back into the kingdom. (The) perceived invitation came at a time when these major companies were struggling to gain access to prospective areas where they might hope to find enough oil to halt their now steeply accelerating production declines. Out of the blue and to the astonishment of all the oil moguls attending this Saudi reception, the gates of the Kingdom seemed about to open, and this elite group would again enter into a land where easy oil could more be found.

(The) Prince had spoken about gas and the downstream sector. The U.S. oil executives seemed to have heard something far more to their liking."

The attack of the Twin Towers spurred the War on Iraq – and the wider War on Terrorism, which came at a cost of over $6 trillion dollars and over 900,000 lives over the course of 20 years, *Vox* reports.

After the United States invested billions of dollars destroying and then rebuilding Iraq, enriching Alaska Native Corporations and other parties connected to the syndicate, Iraq's oil was claimed by Israel. "Yes, the Iraq War was a war for oil, and it was a war with winners: Big Oil," CNN reports. "In 2000, Big Oil, including Exxon, Chevron, BP and Shell, spent more money to get fellow oilmen Bush and Cheney into office than they had spent on any previous election. Just over a week into Bush's first term, their efforts paid off when the National Energy Policy Development Group, chaired by Cheney, was formed, bringing the administration and the oil companies together to plot our collective energy future."

According to *Israel-Palestine News*, oil insider Gary Vogler, the agenda behind the Iraq war was "to supply Iraq oil to Israel."

Among the key figures involved in driving this agenda were the neoconservatives within the Bush Administration, Dr. Ahmed Chalabi, and the Israeli government, he writes. "Israel was paying a huge premium for its oil imports, and this premium had just started in the late 1990s," Vogler writes. "The agenda called for the reopening of the old Kirkuk to Haifa pipeline and its significant expansion. When this pipeline plan became unattainable in the 2nd half of 2003, then Chalabi took other actions to get inexpensive Iraqi oil to Israel."

In March of 2003, Israeli Infrastructure Minister Joseph Pritskzy acknowledged that the Pentagon was planning to reopen the pipeline between Kirkuk in Iraq and Haifa, Israel, the only export pipeline in Iraq from 1934 to 1948. A pipeline through Syria, which neoconservatives had also targeted for "regime change," was constructed to replace the Haifa pipeline.

Israel was paying a 25 percent premium for its oil imports and "the reopened pipeline to Haifa would eliminate the premium," Pritskzy writes.

In 2003, Netanyahu – then, Israeli Finance Minister –appealed to investors in London to fund the expansion of the pipeline from Kirkuk to Haifa, raising questions of why a country which has received billions of dollars in aid from the federal government would need to panhandle to establish a pipeline – or whether this was an appeal for greater government-sponsored opportunities through which the syndicate could further grift.

Chalabi had promised to reopen the Kirkuk to Haifa pipeline, according to Mark Zell, a law partner of Undersecretary of Defense for Policy Doug Feith.

While BKSH was blanketing the U.S. media with disinformation from Chalabi – that Iraq was harboring weapons of mass destruction, as pretext for a pre-emptive strike, Scooter Libby, Vice President Dick Cheney's Chief of Staff, opened communications channel to Chalabi.

Coincidentally Libby was counsel to Marc Rich while the oil trader generated billions of dollars between the 1970s and 1990s, transporting Iranian crude oil by way of "a secret pipeline through Israel."

The Clintons, through their Clinton Foundation, have received tens of millions of dollars in donations from Saudi businessmen, princes and their associates. Later, when Hillary Clinton was Secretary of State, the federal government approved arms sales, worth more than $29 billion for Saudi Arabia.

By January 2004, four small gas concessions were awarded to companies that were not on Aramco's original list. Among them were a number of Rothschild-affiliated oil companies, including Russia's Lukoil and China's Sinopec. Concessions were also awarded to the Spanish oil company Respoil and the Italian energy conglomerate, Eni.

By 2004, Simmons writes, Saudi Arabia had become the only country in the world with any meaningful unused production capacity that was accessible (The syndicate had blocked U.S. production). Every other key oil producer around the globe had started acknowledging that they were producing at peak sustainability rates," he writes.

If the Abramoff saga intersected with the syndicate and its wider agenda, then finding ties linking the SunCruz fraud in Florida with the terrorist attacks of September 11, 2001 might be expected. To find out more about the ties that bind the two, read on....

Strange Coincidences

There are some interesting ties between Abramoff's notorious team and the wider events surrounding September 11, 2001.

Astonishingly, the federal government escorted Saudi Royals out of the United States immediately after the attacks on the Twin Towers. The flights and some of the individuals involved reveal the hand of the syndicate – and the ubiquitous Abramoff connections.

The mastermind behind the terrorist attacks was identified as Saudi al Qaeda leader and CIA asset, Osama bin Laden, an investor in the Carlyle Group. Afterward, Saudi elites were quickly flown out of the United States. One of these flights was called the Universal Weather Flight (UWF), an interesting name considering the syndicate's pretext of "climate change" to advance the greed energy agenda and end of the petro-dollar. The flight escorted an "unnamed Saudi Sheikh out of the United States from Rhode Island to Paris on September 14, according to *Executive Intelligence Review.*

After the terrorist attacks, Adnan Khashoggi promoted John Gray's *Men are from Mars, Women are from Venus*, transforming the book into an international best seller, *EIR* reports.

The son of a CIA agent who committed suicide under "exceptionally bizarre circumstances," Gray then funded the 9/11 "Truth Movement."

Numerous conspiracy emerged around 9/11 – including stories of "dancing Israelis" who allegedly celebrated fall of the Twin Towers, reports that Jewish workers were given instructions from Mossad not to go to work that day, sparing their lives while sacrificing others. Some claimed that Clinton had "keys," or "patents" to remote-control the planes. Some claimed the Pentagon and Twin Towers hadn't been hit by planes at all, but by missiles. Others circulated stories that CGI, or Deep Fake images, were used, creating the illusion of planes, and that the Twin Towers were destroyed through controlled demolition. Others promulgates stories of a nuclear strike. And then there were stories that documents concerning trillions of dollars that had been siphoned from the federal government were destroyed at the precise area where the Pentagon was struck by a plane, or as some have alleged, "a missile." Some conspiracy theorists blamed the Israelis, others the Saudis. Still others claimed the entire event was "an inside job" orchestrated by the federal government.

One 727 plane, with the Christian symbol of a dove on its tail, flew 18 members of the Saudi Royal family from Las Vegas to Stamstead

Airport (London) England on September 20, 2001. "The tail number (read) 727PX," *EIR* reports.

The PAX plane was registered in Clearwater, Florida to "Classic Designs of Tampa Bay," a company owned by Lowell Paxon, the founder of the Christian broadcast network, PAX-TV and the Home Shopping Network. Paxon "found God in a Las Vegas hotel room," the Rothschild-backed *Financial Times* reports in a feature highlighting the pastor's acquisitions that include "a $12 million, 35-room oceanfront mansion;" "his and hers Rolls Royces" for Paxon and his wife; three airplanes, a 132-foot yacht; and "a considerable collection of autographs of former U.S. presidents, kings, queens and entertainers.

Paxon bought the Burt Reynold's dinner theater in Jupiter, Florida – an area that was developed by Averill Harriman who reportedly launched the National Security State there with George H.W. Bush, according to Webster Tarpley and Anton Chaitkin's *George Bush: The Unauthorized Biography.*

According to Tarpley and Chaitki, Jupiter is the area from which the syndicate plans dirty tricks and propaganda campaigns against the American people. Among those who have owned properties on the exclusive Jupiter Island are Victoria's Secret founder Les Wexner, a close associate of Jeffrey Epstein; and members of the Trump family. Trump's Mar-a-Lago clubhouse is a stone throw's away.

Pax-TV was bought out by Citadel Investment Group – the secondary lender in Abramoff's fraudulent SunCruz loan, *EIR* reports..

Around the area of the demolished Twin Towers, the passports of the Saudi terrorists who had allegedly hijacked the planes were found at the scene of the crime as if someone had simply thrown them there. One of the passports reportedly identified Mohammed Atta, the alleged hijacker who allegedly flew American Airlines Flight 11 into the World Trade Center.

Before September 11, 2001, Atta was reportedly seen partying at SunCruz. Fifteen of the 19 hijackers were reportedly Saudi nationals.

Atta's father, el-Amir Atta, was a close associate of Mohammed al-Fayed, who funded al-Qaeda, the terrorist organization blamed for the attacks. Al Fayed provided the venue in Paris for Khashoggi's arms deals and was the father of Dodi, who was dating Princess Diana before his death. Al-Fayed's first wife was Adnan Khashoggi's sister, who conceived Dodi.

Wally Hilliard, whose flight school reportedly trained the pilots who flew into the World Trade Center, supported Khashoggi's casino interests in the Bahamas.

While the ADL was raising the alarm over the increase in anti-Zionism and antisemitism, a Muslim rights group, CAIR, announced "Islamophobia is now mainstream." The end result was that free speech was silenced so no one could speak about the syndicate's activities without incurring the wrath of an identity group and somehow risk being called a racist.

In 1998. the year the Saudi Gas Initiative launched, Americans for Tax Reform (ATR) President Grover Norquist, a lobbying partner of Jack Abramoff, established a private firm, Janus Merritt. Norquist established the Islamic Institute, with the ATR as its headquarters. The Islamic Institute was a key center through which Muslims directly lobbied the federal government.

Through the Institute, Norquist led efforts to bring Muslims into the Republican Party and provide them opportunities to influence with the Bush Administration and worked to neutralize criticism of Muslims after the terrorist attacks of September 11, 2001. Abramoff performed a complementary function for Zionists – by advancing causes within the Bush Administration and providing funding for such Zionist groups as JINSA and AIPAC.

At the same time, Norquist's firm, Janus-Merritt, represented News Corp., a Zionist news organization that spread some of the most vitriolic hate speech against Muslims – which resulted in calls to place them into positions of power to eradicate Islamophobia. At the same time, the federal government ramped up security efforts by stripping Americans of civil liberties through the Patriot Act and other measures. Yet, to avoid profiling Muslims, ordinary Americans were subjected to dehumanizing searches and an increase in surveillance, generating lucrative contracts for contractors to buff up security at airports, schools, and elsewhere.

Norquist's sought to secure fast track trade negotiations authority while promoting the Koran as being compatible with capitalism. "People should remember that Mohammed and his wife were businessmen," Norquist told reporters.

A key Muslim rights group, the Council of American-Islamic Relations (CAIR) sent its members to Norquist meetings. CAIR supported Osama bin Laden and blamed Mossad and Egyptian intelligence for terrorist attacks. Some of Norquist's Muslim affiliations had terrorist ties, which isn't surprising considering that they were extensions of the syndicate.

Whoever was truly behind the attacks of September 11, 2001, this watershed moment ushered in a new era of automation, track-and-trace surveillance in line with a post-oil world filled with 15-minute cities. It also provided the pretext to pre-emptively invade nations to grab oil at a time when the elites were up facing oil scarcity.

Within the United States, the syndicate was pitting Muslims against Judaeo-Christian while goading Muslims to believe that they were destined to establish an Ummah or caliphate over the United States and world – by outbreeding Americans.

Muslims were entered the West by the droves and having large families, with many children while their Western supporters, who subsidized the welfare to support their families had less disposable income with which to support and grow their own families.

The syndicate's Jewish arm, the ADL, created a a CAIR profile, stating, "key CAIR leaders often traffic in openly antisemitic and anti-Zionist rhetoric." At the same time, the Zionists in the media were spewing viciously anti-Muslim rhetoric, casting Islam as the religion of terror.

Meanwhile, Soros – who has partnered with Zionists on other issues – donated $1.8 billion through his Open Society Foundation (OSF) to fund a Muslim legal group. DC Leaks posted internal documents revealing that between 2008 and 2010, OSF spent $40 million to undermined the United States by weakening U.S. counter-terrorism policy – while the syndicate was actively promoting terrorism to destabilize the United States. (Source: https://www.algemeiner.com/2016/10/10/how-george-soros-money-and-a-muslim-rights-group-undermined-homeland-security/)

By spreading terrorism, the syndicate had the opportunity to expand warrantless surveillance against American citizens, as revealed by Edward Snowden. Hateful, incendiary rhetoric was promoted by opposing sides, as American were split into identity groups, pitted against each other, and then muzzled to avoid offending, thereby preventing an honest, informed, and open dialog about true origins and appropriate responses to the terrorism as the syndicate's war against the American people advanced..

In 1998, Soros admitted to confiscating Jewish property during Nazi occupation, stating and that he had no guilt over what he had done. After all, if he hadn't done it, someone else would have. The truth is, many wouldn't have – theft of assets and human rights abuses are the *modus operandi* of the Rothschild crime syndicate. Under Nazi Germany, led by Adolf Hitler, who was a Rothschild bloodline, Jews were targeted for this very purpose.

The Saudis Lead the Way

Reflecting efforts to diversify the Saudi economy in a post-oil age, the Saudi Arabian Fertilizer Company (SAFCO) expanded its operations as part of the Gas Initiative. SAFCO, a major player in the petrochemical industry, uses natural gas as a feedstock for fertilizer production.

The company has since changed its name to SABIC Agri-Nutrients. In a short promotional video entitled "Why We Farm," which was posted on its website, SABIC describes its global designs:

"The story of agriculture is one of progress, but the way we manage our land and grow our food cannot continue unchanged, not with our population growing by a million extra people per week. Not with environmental crises unfolding around us. SABIC Agri-Nutrients brings SABIC science in collaboration to the big agricultural questions of our times. We are here to help farmers in more places access new science and smart tech, to help a growing world do more with less land so people can get the nutrition they need and to work closely with farmers, scientists, economists, governments, and (nongovernmental organizations), so that together we can strengthen the relationships that matters most of all – the ones between us and the land we depend on."
(https://www.sabic-agrinutrients.com/en#modal-31113)

With designs on becoming "the preferred global leader in agri-nutrients by 2025." SABIC professes to offer sustainable agri-nutrient solutions to produce higher yields of quality crops "to feed an ever growing global population." (SABIC's agent in the U.S. is Burson-Marsteller.)

Another Saudi company, Rabigh Refining & Petrochemical Company (Petro Rabigh) was established in 2005 as a joint venture between Saudi Aramco and Sumitomo Chemical, a part of the Sumitomo Group. Petro Rabigh has launched projects in the billions of dollars "at the hub of an upsurge in economic and technological development in line with Saudi Arabia's Vision 2030," according to its promotional literature.

Established in 1995 as "one of the first privately owned petrochemical companies in Saudi Arabia," the Saudi Industrial Investment Group has invested in such companies as Saudi Chevron, Phillips (SCP), the National Petrochemical Company (Petrochem), Jubail Chevron Phillips Company (Saudi Arabia), Saudi Polymers Company (Saudi Arabia), Gulf Polymers Distribution Company (UAE), and Aromatics Distribution Company (UAE).

SCP was established by Royal Decree in 2000 as a joint-stock company, Marafiq, that is owned by four major shareholders, including the Royal Commission for Jubail and Yanbu (RC), Saudi Basic Industries Corporation (SABIC), Saudi Arabian Oil Company (Saudi Aramco), and the Public Investment Fund (PIF), Saudi Arabia's sovereign wealth fund.

The PIF is one of the largest investment funds in the world, with a valuation of near $1 trillion. The fund was launched in 1971, around the time of the launch of the petro-dollar and just years before establishing its formal technical partnership with the World Bank. While poverty has spread throughout the world, Saudi Arabia has grown increasingly rich, pursued preferential hiring to foreigners over its own citizens, and moved the poor out of areas where it is investing money in luxury accommodations.

Marafiq, in turn, has "revolutionized the power and water industries by consciously designing strategies for climate change" and incorporating environmental, social, and government (ESG) systems to mark its "sustainability progress," and advance "the global green revolution."

Another entity, the Royal Commission for Jubail and Yanbu, is part of a development strategy to "diversify (the Saudi) economy and minimize dependence on raw oil income."

With the syndicate clear on its vision, the Saudis moved ahead to advance their agenda to lead the world into a new post-oil, automated age, towards global development that promised to be technologically advanced, but somehow inhuman.

X.
Betrayal of Trust and Innocence

"Liberty can no more exist without virtue and independence
than the body can live and move without a soul."

President John Adams
American Founding Father

Pedophilia is a recurring theme among the syndicate for reasons this author cannot understand. It's unconscionable that anyone would want to harm, much less molest an innocent child. While Judaeo-Christian society was geared toward protecting a child's innocence and shielding children from harm, some esoteric circles believe that through sodomy and child abuse they can absorb the life force of the underage victim for spiritual purposes and to feel powerful.

When Secretary of State Henry Kissinger was negotiating the petro-dollar with the Saudis, the CIA learned that the Saudi Royals were preferential to little boys and reportedly supplied them to help "sweeten deals." That the CIA would even descend to such depravity, even in the interests of acquiring a strategic advantage, reflects that the United States has been hijacked. Can anyone imagine the founders of the United States, much less the Americans of yesteryear entering such an agreement or sacrificing children for profit?

The criminal elites who were overthrowing and subverting governments throughout the world in the interests of establishing global monopolies, embraced the principles of the "rational Enlightenment" – that is, they rejected conventional Judaeo-Christian standards as limiting and instead embraced rational self-interest – that of pursuing one's pleasure, power, and profit without being restrained by other considerations, like moral and legal limits, a belief in God, empathy, or even consequences. This was a Satanic "do as thou wilt" materialistic ethos that eventually found expression in Marxism, Communism, Fascism, and Ayn Rand's cold objectivism.

Since even the thought of violating a child betrayed conventional wisdom and standards of humanity, the elite used child abuse as a means to compromise people and toughen them up for the treasonous service expected them. Who but a hardened psychopath could set out to sexually abuse and willfully inflict trauma upon an innocent child? Those would prove able were worthy of membership within the syndicate -and subsequently controlled. Betraying the clique, falling out of favor, or becoming a liability could result in exposure with the damning truth, with devastating legal and social consequences.

The relationship between Bill Gates, Microsoft, and Jeffrey Epstein is far more extensive that has been reported in the mainstream media, as investigative journalist Whitney Webb reports. "The individuals who founded tech giants such as Google, LinkedIn, Facebook, Microsoft, Tesla, and Amazon all have connections with Jeffrey Epstein, some closer than others," she writes.

Nigel Rosser reports in the *Evening Standard* that Epstein "made many millions (of dollars) out of his business links with the likes of Bill Gates, Donald Trump and Ohio billionaire (Victoria's Secret founder) Leslie Wexner, whose trust he runs."

Rosser reports that Epstein once claimed to have "worked for the CIA," an assertion the pedophile later retracted.

The *Washington Times* reported child/human trafficking connected to powerful members who operated within Bush and Reagan political circles. "Both Wexner's and Trump's relationships with Epstein prior to 2001 are well known and date back to 1985 and 1987 respectively," Webb writes.

In the *Columbus Free Press*, Bob Fitrakis, the author of *The Fitrakis Files: Spooks Nukes and Nazis*; and *The Fitrakis Files: Cops, Coverups, and Corruption*, connects Epstein and Wexner to criminal activity in Ohio. "Not many people know that the infamous Jeffrey Epstein spent a lot of time in Columbus in the 1990s and owned the second most valuable house in Franklin County, in the plush Stepford suburb known as New Albany," Fitrakis writes.

Among Fitrakis' sources was State of Ohio Inspector General David Sturtz, who was investigating Wexner and Epstein over "public corruption, bribery, and information related to the murder" of Columbus attorney Arthur Shapiro" in 1985.

The Daily Beast reports that "The shy, secretive lawyer - a partner in the Columbus, Ohio firm of Schwartz, Shapiro, Kelm & Warren - was under investigation by the Internal Revenue Service for failing to file income tax returns for seven years and for possible investments in shady tax shelters."

In March of 1985, Shapiro "was due to testify before a grand jury over his tax dodging - and whether anyone had helped him hide money," the *Daily Beast* reports. "What he might reveal, no one knew, but he and his firm had several high-profile clients and a long history in Columbus. But Arthur Shapiro never made it to the stand. A day before his scheduled testimony, someone fired two bullets point-blank into his head as he fled from a secretive breakfast meeting - held in his red BMW - at a Columbus cemetery."

The firm, which became, Schwartz, Kelm, Warren & Rubenstein in 1987, represented Wexner's "personal investment company" and Limited Brands, *Smart Business* (sbonline.com), reports. By the 1990's, attorneys were leaving the firm en masse. (Victoria's secret was connected to Limited Brands, which, Fitrakis writes, is "linked with associates reputed to be organized crime figures."

Shapiro managed the Limited account for the firm. In an article for FreePress.org, Fitrakis reports that the police "accidentally released a report linking Leslie Wexner and the Mob."

The report documented "unusual interactive relationship among" the Limited, the law firm, and Omni Oil Company. A search for Omni Oil online produces a website identifying Omni as "a wholly owned Malaysian Company." (https://ootm.com.my/about-us/company-profile/) Bayt.com lists its industrial production in Dubai, United Arab Emirates. (https://www.bayt.com/en/company/omni-oil-technologies-449949/?ysclid=lx4v1iggwo666689683) Among Omni Oil Technologies' "notable clients" are Murphy Oil Corporation, Petrofac, KPOC, Hess, ExxonMobil, CPOC, Mubadala Petroleum, Ophir, Weatherford, Coastal Energy, ConocoPhillips, Nippon Oil & Energy, Vestigo, Roc, Lundin Petroleum, Shell, Schlumberger, SapuraKencana, Repsol, Petronas Carigali.

Omni's stated mission is "to create a product development and manufacturing organization that serves the oil and gas industry and grows profitably and independently into the global markets in an environmentally friendly manner while maximizing value to its shareholders and surrounding community, and become the preferred organization of choice to its employee."

Other businesses connected to this group, Fitrakis reports, are Edward DeBartolo Company of Youngstown, Ohio; which describes itself as "a leader in American retail development for almost half a century" which has "owned and/or operated over 78 million square feet of retail space by the early 1990s, (with) commercial assets (exceeding) 95 million square feet." This company's holdings includes "over 100 retail malls and community shopping centers, nine office projects in operation or under development, and three hotels. Aside from its real estate and commercial holdings, the company has also dabbled in horse racing facilities and owned professional sports team."

An individual named in association with this group is developer John Kessler, who founded the New Albany Company with Wexner. Kessner has served on the Board of Directors of JPMorgan Chase & Co., The Limited, Inc., Commercial Vehicle Group, Abercrombie & Fitch, Columbus Regional Airport Authority, the Columbus Downtown Development Corporation, and Cleveland Federal Reserve, to name a few of his affiliations. The New Albany website describes Kessner as "one of central Ohio's most accomplished real estate developers and influential civic leaders."

In 1998, documents identified Epstein as President of the New Albany Company, Fitrakis reports.

Making the Harvard connection, the New Albany site affirms that Wexner, whose estimated worth is $6 billion, was inaugurated by Harvard University into the Society of John Harvard Fellows and has served as a visiting lecturer at Harvard's Kennedy School of Government. The Wexner Foundation has been a long-time financial supporter of Harvard University.

Other connections identified were Wexner's business relationship with Francis J. Walsh, the owner and chief executive officer of the New Jersey-based Walsh Trucking Company – which reportedly "has done an excess of 90 percent of the Limited's" trucking business around the time of Shapiro's murder." The Limited, Inc. was described as "Walsh's single largest customer."

Per the report, National Westminster Bank of New York, the address of Frank Walsh Financial Resources, was "One Limited Parkway," the address of The Limited. According to a police report obtained by Fitrakis, Walsh was "an associate do the Genovese-LaRocca crime family in Pittsburgh."

Among those associates was Anthony "Fat Tony" Salerno of the Genovese crime family who owned S &A Construction – which has done business with Donald Trump.

According to the report, "From the predicate facts presented, it appears that Les Wexner had established contact with associates reputed to be organized crime figures, one of whom was a major investment partner and another was using The Limited headquarters as a mailing address," Fitrakis reports. "It is not known whether there are other such figures among Wexner's associates, but it can be hypothesized that the Genovese/LaRocca crime families might consider Wexner a friend."

The Shapiro report concedes that "the primary illegal activity of the LaRocca family is gambling.... Its operation extends into the West Virginia panhandle and eastern Ohio. The family has also become well entrenched in legitimate businesses. These include, but probably are not limited to, construction, trucking, food service and vending businesses."

The Genovese crime family was considered "second in strength, power, and wealth to the Gambino LCN family."

Ohio State Inspector General David Sturtz referred to Epstein as Wexner's "boyfriend," Fitrakis writes.

Epstein and Wexner reportedly met in 1985 by way of Bob Meister, an insurance mogul who once told Epstein to "get the f*** out" after the pedophile brought five models to his apartment as a sexual enticement, *Vanity Fair* reports. Wexner reportedly was aware of Epstein's activities but retained him as a "financial advisor" anyway – possibly as Epstein was a key agent of the Rothschild crime syndicate through which incredible fortunes are made. Wexner granted Epstein power of power over his economic affairs in 1991.

Epstein, who served a function similar to that of Adnan Khashoggi, flew with President Clinton on a jet obtained from The Limited, Fitrakis reports, adding that the pedophile "moved Wexner's billions around the globe." Similarly, , Khashoggi took influential people into international waters on yachts where they were sexually compromised or otherwise invited to participate in scandalous activities with prostitutes.

Sturtz provided files identifying Epstein as a person of interest in the death of media mogul Robert Maxwell, the father of Ghislaine Maxwell and known Mossad asset."As the logistics man for Wexner, Epstein arranged the arrival of Southern Air Transport (SAT) to Rickenbacker Air Force Base in Columbus, Ohio,: Fitrakis reports. "The airline, formerly Air America, was infamous as an illegal gun- and drug-running operation. SAT filed for bankruptcy in Columbus on October 1,

1998, the same day the Central Intelligence Agency Inspector General issued a report linking the cargo hauler to allegations of drug-running in connection with U.S.-backed Contra rebels in Nicaragua in the 1980s."

Fitrakis also revealed that "Epstein helped his mentor, Wexner, sell the war in Iraq through the Wexner Foundation"

A leaked document from the Wexner Foundation, *Wexner Analysis: Israeli Communication Priorities, 2003* was "was prepared to sell the war in Iraq.," he writes (https://rense.com/general38/communi.htm)

The Wexner Foundation offers leadership training programs, like "Birthright Israel" to offer free trips to Jewish-Americans to travel to Israel through the Luntz Research Company, a PR firm; and the Israel Project. Led by Marcus Sheff, a spokesman for the IDF, the Israel Project is a U.S.-headquartered 501(c)(3) non-profit group that describes its mission as being 'devoted to educating the press and the public about Israel while promoting security, freedom and peace' (and providing) journalists, leaders and opinion-makers accurate information about Israel.'."

Among the clients of Luntz Global are MGM Mirage, Pfizer, Anheuser Busche, News Corp., Wynn Resorts, GE, McDonalds, Fed Ex, Hilton, 20th Century Fox, Pfizer, NBC, Merrill Lynch, FritoLay, BBC, Kroger, FedEx Corporation, Lowe's, Continental Airlines, Pepsi, and Westfield.

In the case of Trump, In 1987, around the time was connected to Epstein, the future reality-TV star, acquired a 93 percent stake in Resorts International, a Meyer Lansky-connected casino with deep ties to the Rothschilds, Rockefellers, and Mossad.

Reflecting ties that further link the technocracy with the Crown and pedophilia, Webb reports that the BBC "has received millions in funding for years from the Bill & Melinda Gates Foundation."

The BBC was created to disseminate propaganda in service of the British Monarchy, starting with Queen Elizabeth II, an illegitimate Queen who, according to Royal historians, was the daughter of a maid allegedly impregnated by Prime Minister Winston Churchill, the biological father of President Bill Clinton.

The Crown, in turn, has ties to the Seminole Tribe of Florida, whose financial advisor is Merrill Lynch and whose casino efforts were bankrolled, in part, by Lansky and Trump. The Seminoles purchased the

Hard Rock brand name for $1 billion, with Merrill Lynch and Abramoff's employer, Greenberg Traurig, negotiating the deal. Previously Hard Rock was controlled by the Rank Group, which released a promotional film for the coronation of Queen Elizabeth II.

Narrated by Laurence Olivier, *A Queen is Crowned* immortalized the events surrounding the coronation. The documentary starred the Queen, Prince Philip, and Prince Charles, reflecting Rank's tight relationship with the Monarchy. "I have to be seen to be believed," Queen Elizabeth II once said.

Under new management, the Hard Rock has donated money, through its philanthropic arm, Hard Rock Heals, to such organizations as the World Wildlife Fund (WWF) which was founded by Prince Philip, the Queen's consort and trillioniare; and Prince Bernhard of the Netherlands, the founder of the Bilderberger Group who was implicated, along with Adnan Khashoggi, in the Lockheed Martin bribery scandal. The WFF is also funded by Amazon founder Jeff Bezos (Bezos Earth Fund), the Rockefeller Fund – and has entered partnerships with Johnson & Johnson and China's Belt and Road project. The WWF is active in 33 of the 64 countries connected through the Belt and Road Initiative (BRI).

In a public statement, the WWF announced: "Several offices met to discuss further work on greening the BRI. As well as the core projects building transport infrastructure, chiefly railways, ports and fiber optic connections, BRI will open up locations for economic development and stimulate investments in extraction, electricity generation, shipping and commerce. Infrastructure development can generate enormous economic benefits.....Projects should be planned and implemented using the framework of the UN Sustainable Development Goals, and China's own philosophy of ecological civilization. It is also important where possible to direct investment towards ecological infrastructure and renewable energy."

Saudi prince MBS, Trump/Rothschild bankruptcy advisor Wilbur Ross, former World Bank economist Larry Summers, Harvard Law Prof. Alan Dershowitz, and Microsoft CEO also ran in Epstein's circles. From 1995 to 1996, an Epstein victim claimed to have overheard Epstein mention Gates in a manner suggesting that "they were close friends" and "which gave her the impression that the Microsoft co-founder might soon be visiting one of Epstein's residences."

Webb reports that Gates had a "documented connection to a business run by (a sister of Epstein's advisor and sex-trafficking collaborator) Ghislaine Maxwell (in which) Ghislaine had a financial stake." The sister, Isabel Maxwell, "has ties to the PROMIS software espionage intelligence."

Webb writes that Ghislaine Maxwell and Epstein cultivated the Clinton Foundation and the Clinton Global Initiative in the early 2000s. President, Bill Clinton was "the main focus" of Epstein's sexual blackmail operations, she writes.

Isabel, Ghislaine's twin sister, and their respective spouses created "the McKinley Group in January 1992," Webb reports. After their father, media mogul Robert Maxwell was slain, the twins joined Information on Demand as a front group through which they sold "the backdoored PROMIS software to the U.S. government," Webb reports.

Fitrakis reports that Epstein was identified as a "person of interest" in the murder of Robert Maxwell. While the oligarchs were stealing money and amassing fortunes as Rothschild front men, Ghislaine "throughout the 1990s, (was) discreetly building up a business empire," Webb reports. This was the period in which Ghislaine was "operating an intelligence-linked sexual-blackmail operation with Jeffrey Epstein."

"There was considerable overlap of (Epstein and Ghislaine's) finances," Webb writes, adding that "McKinley created what became known as the Magellan Internet Directory." The directory attracted several large corporations, resulting in major alliances with AT&T, Time-Warner, IBM, Netcom, and the Microsoft Network (MSN) that were all negotiated by Isabel Maxwell – and which overlapped with the emerging technocratic network around the Rothschilds, she reports.

Through deals finessed within these circles, Ghislaine "not only obtained a multi-million-dollar payout (but) also forged close connections with Silicon Valley high rollers," she writes. "Isabel's ties to Microsoft also persisted following the sale of the McKinley Group. She became president of the Israeli tech company CommTouch, whose funding was linked to individuals and groups involved in the Jonathan Pollard nuclear spying affair."

Webb writes that Gates and Microsoft co-founder Paul Allen "put CommTouch on the map" and invested in Maxwell enterprises. Trump, in turn, purchased his elegant, gold-plated Boeing 757 airplane in 2010 from Allen. Six years earlier, Allen established an "elite online community," whose membership included Epstein and Petrina Khashoggi, the daughter of Adnan Khashoggi -- a former client of Epstein's," Webb reports.

The group's "largest shareholder," she writes, was Hollywood film mogul Harvey Weinstein, an Epstein business partner who moved within Abramoff's circles.

Nathan Myhrvold, Microsoft's Chief Technology Officer and one of Gates' closest advisors "traveled on Epstein's plane from Kentucky to New Jersey, and then again, (the following year) from New Jersey to Florida," Webb reports.

Harvard University Law Professor Alan Dershowitz, attorney for Epstein and Trump, joined Myhrvold on flights. In the 1990s, Myhrvold traveled to Russia with Epstein and Esther Dyson, a digital consultant and agenda contributor to the World Economic Forum.

Dyson, Webb writes, had "close ties to Google as well as the DNA testing company, 23andme."

At Microsoft Russia in Moscow in 1998, Epstein and Myhrvold "explored the state of post-Soviet science," Webb writes, adding that when Myhrvold left Microsoft to establish Intellectual Ventures, he reportedly greeted Epstein at the firm with "young girls, " who appeared to be "Russian models."

Linda Stone, Microsoft's Vice President, introduced Epstein to MIT Media Lab's Joi Ito. In 2000, Gates attended the White House "Conference on the New Economy," whose attendees included close Epstein associate Lynn Forester (de Rothschild), Larry Summers, Janet Yellen, and Thomas "Mack" McLarty, "whose special assistant Mark Middleton met with Epstein at least three times at the Clinton White House."

McLarty, whose firm was established by Kissinger, is linked to MIT Media Labs. According to *The MIT Technological Review,* Nicholas Negroponte, the founder of MIT's Media Lab, tapped Epstein to raise $200 million for a "Frankenstein-like plan" to analyze human DNA and "sequence people's genomes" to sell DNA data to drug manufacturers, with the goal of creating a search engine capable of pinpointing genetic links to diseases.

Nicholas Negroponte is the brother of John Negroponte, a former U.S. Deputy Secretary of State, U.S. Representative to the United Nations, and Director of National Intelligence – the executive head of America's intelligence community.

A Kissinger disciple, John Negroponte managed secret negotiations under President Richard Nixon. After leaving public life, John Negroponte became Vice Chair of McLarty Associates, a firm that has serves over 300 clients in 112 countries. "We've also assisted at the local/regional level as well as with multilateral and international organizations from the United Nations to the European Union and APEC to the World Health Organizations," according to McLarty's website.

Serving on McLarty's Board of Directors is Stuart Eizenstat, a former U.S. Ambassador to the European Union, who received a high civilian award from Larry Summers.

Founded by Thomas "Mack" McLarty III, the former Chief of Staff and Special Envoy for the Americas to President Bill Clinton; and Nelson Cunningham, Clinton's former Special Advisor for Western Hemisphere Affairs, McLarty manages public perception and engineers public consent by way of theater productions and the media.

In 2019, the *MIT Technology Review* reported that Nicholas Negroponte prided himself in knowing more than 80 percent of the billionaires on a first name basis, and that it was through these relationships that he came to know Jeffrey Epstein. The inevitable child sex trafficking allegations followed.

In an article entitled "Was Aaron Swartz Killed by an MIT Satanic Child Porn Ring," science journalist and former *Japan Times* Weekly Editor Yoichi Shimatsu reports that "child porn was orchestrated and produced by acclaimed professors (at the MIT Lab) and distributed to their wealthy sponsors." (https://rense.com/general95/swartz.html)

According to Shimatsu, "the MIT cyber-pimps cater to a clientele that includes the highest echelon of the State Department, major corporations, intelligence agencies, the military brass, and the White House." The network he reportedly uncovered follows "a torturous path that leads from the hallowed ivy halls in Boston to the outskirts of Phnom Penh, where a world famous professor arranged underage sexual services for visiting dignitaries and sent encrypted child porn via satellite to illicit databases on the MIT campus."

Reflecting the role of the network within the wider military industrial complex, MIT Lab performs military-related services for the U.S. Air Force, Space, and Naval Warfare Systems, Google, DARPA, and the Technion Institute for the Israeli Defense Forces, Shimatsu writes, adding that MIT Media Lab is "just another spin off of MK Ultra and DARPA."

MIT trained Israeli Prime Minister Benjamin Netanyahu, who studied at Harvard University before joining the Boston Consulting Group (BCG), which has been retained to help Saudi Prince MBS consolidate power. According to OpenSecrets.org's online database, Boston Consulting Group retained the Carmen Group – a firm that represents Silverstein Properties, chaired by Larry Silverstein, who collected a reported $4.1 billion from insurers after the World Trade Center was demolished on September 11, 2001.

Epstein attempted to convince the Gates Foundation to partner with JP Morgan on a multi-billion dollar global health charitable fund that "would have resulted in hefty fees paid out to Epstein, who was very involved with JP Morgan at the time," Webb writes. "Though that fund never materialized, Epstein and Gates did discuss Epstein becoming involved in Gates's philanthropic efforts."

In 2013, Ghislaine Maxwell's TerraMar Project, which supports UN Sustainability Development Goals – in line with Saudi Arabia's Vision 2030, made a $1.25 million commitment to the Clinton Global Initiative. The son of Christian Maxwell, Xavier Malina interned at the Clinton Global Initiative – and worked for the Office of White House Personnel within the Obama Administration, and, later, Google.

Isabel Maxwell's son, Alexander Djerassi, was Chief of Staff at the Bureau of Near Eastern Affairs in the Clinton-run State Department, Webb writes.

Epstein was also involved with Amazon founder Jeff Bezos who met with Gates in Seattle before launching Amazon.

Elon Musk, and "other prominent Silicon Valley empires" were connected to Epstein, Webb writes. "One key reason for this is that the Epstein network's blackmail operation involved not only sexual blackmail but *electronic* forms of blackmail, something used to great effect by Robert Maxwell on behalf of Israeli intelligence as part of the PROMIS operation."

Among Epstein's contacts was the Saudi Prince, MBS, whose image adorned Epstein's wall. MBS visited MIT in 2018 around the time "Epstein said he was investing his money in the United States" – and right before the pandemic struck that forced a global lockdown to establish a "new normal" in line with a post-oil economy and Saudi Arabia's 2030 Vision.

Some speculate that Epstein's wealth may have derived from the Saudis or even Russia. Not only did he have a fake Saudi passport, but *Business Insider* reveals that Epstein possessed a counterfeit Austrian passport bearing Epstein's photo under a different name.

Epstein's passport stamps reveal "travel to and from Saudi Arabia – along with France, Spain, and the United Kingdom. The passport listed Epstein's residence as Saudi Arabia too."

Epstein was even photographed with Saudi prince Mohammed bin Salman and Emirate prince Mohammed bin Zayed, "some in beachwear and with snorkel gear," *Business Inside*r reports, adding that Epstein expressed a desire to "buy a house in Riyadh, since that was becoming the new center of international finance."

∧∧∧

Federal whistle-blower Stew Webb reports that "a long-time senior intelligence agent" divulged that the Washington, DC Hilton, Ritz Carlton, and Sheraton Hotels were the venues in which House and Senate members, national media hosts ... had sex with children in a legislative and media blackmail ring."

According to Webb, Microsoft lobbyist Jack Abramoff "provided male and female heterosexual, homosexual, lesbian, bisexual and child prostitutes sexual services to numerous U.S. Congressmen, U.S. Senators, national media hosts, and (various) federal officials who were compromised and made susceptible to blackmail at three Washington hotels."

Many Capitol Hill reporters who covered Abramoff made similar allegations against the superlobbyist. Webb quotes a federal agent, saying, "Poppy Bush and Abramoff were up to their eyeballs in this kid shit."

One of the hotels, the Washington Hilton, "was specifically used for sex with children because it has what the agent termed a 'super secure section' for VIPs that is out of public view and which reportedly employs no camera surveillance, an area able to hold around 6-10 vehicles so that no one could observe abducted, abused or drugged children flown in from other states who were coming to or leaving the hotel'," Stew Webb reports. "I was told that Hilton employees began to become suspicious of Abramoff's operation, so children were moved to the Washington Ritz-

Carlton according to other intelligence officials. The operation was organized by convicted Republican lobbyist Jack Abramoff."

After the *Washington Times* reported on the sex trafficking ring implicating high level Bush and Reagan officials, a follow up article reported on "abducted children, 23 now dead – abused by 20-30 pedophile members of Congress at child sex parties held at Embassy Row mansions."

That the leaders of a free nation founded of, by, and for the people of God would violate children in this manner – not only to abuse, but to murder innocent children, reveals how evil and illegitimate the government really is. This act alone reflects that the Rothschild corporation dba the federal government has severely and irreparably broken its social contract with the governed.

Smack in the middle of the sex trafficking operation was reportedly President George H.W. Bush. Stew Webb writes, "The U.S. shadow government (is) tied to organized crime. (The network has) blackmailed, imprisoned, murdered, defamed, and tried to destroy the reputations (of) those who have exposed their crimes or got in their way."

The Bush family, around which much of this alleged pedophilia activity was taking place – had longstanding ties with the Saudis. As Craig Unger writes in *House of Bush, House of Saud*, the Saudi Royal family cut deals with the Bush dynasty for over three decades. In exchange for protection, the two sides family have cut lucrative oil and investment deals. "Never before has an American president (George W. Bush) been so closely to a foreign power that harbors and supports our country's mortal enemies," Unger writes.

Launching Microsoft

In a properly functioning representative democracy, with checks and balances firmly in place, the federal government would be able to draw upon its anti-trust powers to keep the monopolists and the money trusts in check. Instead, under Rothschild Inc. dba as the federal government, anti-trust law has been weaponized by the syndicate to restrain, break up, or eliminate corporations who dominated markets so that the syndicate could dominate instead. That this strategy was in play is evidenced by Samuel Untermeyer's role in crafting the Clayton Anti-Trust Act. Untermeyer had also crafted the Federal Reserve Act, solidifying the money trust's hold on Capitol Hill while appearing to do otherwise.

Since the 1960's, IBM had faced anti-trust litigation from the Department of Justice for controlling some 70 percent of the computer market, thereby establishing what constituted a monopoly. After 20 years of litigation and millions of dollars in legal fees, IBM finally convinced a judge that the company's share of revenue within the industry had dropped sufficiently to provide room for new entrants to compete effectively in the market. In 1982, a judge dropped the case, concluding that the federal government's "anti-trust" claims against IBM were "without merit."

As the syndicate tightened its grip on the federal government, regulators were stripped of their anti-trust enforcement powers in an increasingly rigged system. Once the syndicate established a monopoly, anti-trust legislation was neutered. By this point, the competition had been eliminated and the syndicate was moving toward consolidating power.

Writing for The Antitrust Law Journal *in 2001, Larry Summers argues that technology, innovation, globalization, and market competition resolved the issue of market consolidation and that anti-trust enforcement was no longer necessary.*

Since monopolies ensure that consumers would pay lower prices for goods and services, there was no need for anti-trust actions, he argues. In actuality, once monopolies are established, prices increase and quality of goods and services decrease. Prices have actually increased to the point where Amazon, which has established a monopoly in online sales, can set prices based upon one's buying habits and financial history.

For decades, Judge David Edelstein had presided over the IBM anti-trust case. A former Assistant United States Attorney for the Southern District of New York, Edelstein held IBM's feet the fire and refused to relent. As Edelstein observed, IBM repeatedly engaged in anti-competitive behavior that included restricting competition, controlling supply chains, maintaining high barriers to entry for competitors, and repeated offenses. IBM bundled its software products in its mainframe hardware, effectively making it difficult for customers to purchase software from other vendors – thereby limiting customer choice and creating insurmountable barriers of market entry for rival software companies.

IBM had also engaged in discriminatory pricing practices by offering preferential pricing to certain customers or regions while charging higher prices to others, thereby disadvantaging competitors and impeding fair competition in the market.

Moreover, IBM forged exclusive contracts with customers, thereby contractually shutting out potential competition. Ironically, these were the very sorts of practices to which Microsoft would later be accused.

The elites plan decades in advance. Given their control over the levers of power, the media, and vast pools of wealth, they are able to plan with great efficiency. In this case, the federal government would not relent against IBM until new entrants claimed some of IBM's market share. This would all be well and good, except for the fact that the syndicate created its own competition, essentially multiplying its own power and market dominance.

Over the course of the IBM anti-trust litigation, the number of legal documents and court filings eventually reached into the millions of pages. Then, after 20 years, the case was assigned to a new judge - Horace Greene, who rejected the government's anti-trust cause of action on grounds that new entrants into the market reflected that IBM no longer held a monopoly. Little attention was given to the fact that IBM ostensibly had its hand in the launch of the new entrants.

Coincidentally, Greene was born Heinz Grünhaus, a German from Frankfurt, the origins and center of Rothschild banking activity. According to Rothschild's own promotional literature, Frankfurt played *"a central role"* in the history of the Rothschild family. It was here that Mayer Amschel Rothschild, an aspiring monopolist, first established himself as a *"trustworthy"* investor and custodian in the 1760s. *"Frankfurt was home to the first of the five original Rothschild banking houses."*

More famously, Greene supervised the consent decree that broke up AT&T into seven regional operating companies in 1984, thereby opening opportunities for Internet services to enter markets previously dominated by Ma Bell.

Once the anti-trust action was resolved against IBM, Microsoft picked up where IBM left off. Somehow Bill Gates, the seventh cousin of George H.W. Bush, one time removed, fell into the opportunity of a lifetime. As luck would have it, his father, William Gates, Sr., served on the Board of Directors of the United Way of America, an international *network of nonprofit fundraising affiliates; his mother, Mary Maxwell Gates, was a member of the national United Way's executive committee where she had the ear of IBM CEO John Opel.*

In July of 1980, as the anti-trust case against IBM was winding down, Opel invited Microsoft to provide an operating system for the IBM PC. Gates obliged. Microsoft then went on to dominate the market, employing the very anti-competitive strategies over which IBM had been prosecuted.

A year after the IBM anti-trust case was settled, Microsoft acquired access to the British market. By 2005, the Rothschild-backed Queen Elizabeth II knighted Gates for his "contribution to enterprise in Britain," which no doubt included his contribution to the Silent Weapons and Quiet Wars (SWQW) *agenda driven throughout the world by the Rothschilds and Prince Philip – that of tracking and tracing all of humanity.*

Microsoft in China

President George H.W. Bush, who had worked with Kissinger during the Nixon Administration to normalize U.S.-China relations, salivated over the money that stood be made in China's vast, untapped markets. With government funding, the syndicate could provide the Chinese with all the products corporations could produce, cheap labor, lax environmental standards, and an market of over one billion consumers, ensuring that whoever conquered the Chinese markets would acquire a level of wealth that would eclipse all others.

Even better, the syndicate controlled the Communist Chinese government, ensuring that the new markets, with the syndicate in control, could be dominated by the politically connected criminal elite. From China, the syndicate would rule the world, establishing itself as a global market leader while the United States was eclipsed.

With Bush opening the doors, Microsoft entered and dominated China's technological development. In turn, China granted Microsoft the privilege of maintaining a Web-run search engine. in China. "Microsoft has had a presence in China for more than 25 years, entering the market in 1992," a Microsoft press release announced. "Our founder, Bill Gates, had the foresight to establish an office in Beijing, accurately predicting the country's transition to the booming economy we see today." That same year, Microsoft launched subsidiaries in Russia, South Africa, and the Middle East.

Microsoft licensed its MS-DOS software to Chinese PC makers. To succeed in China, Microsoft established a "collaborative approach" with the Communist Chinese government, that included a "Chinese Immersion tour" in which its senior executives were inculcated into the Chinese way of thinking. "Microsoft wanted to help China develop its own software industry, an urgent government priority," Fortune *reports.*

In 2007, Gates predicted that China would become Microsoft's biggest market within 10 years. <u>"Microsoft has its own five-year plan in China, formulated to match up with the government's,"</u> Fortune *reports. Microsoft set up "a global center to respond to customer emails" in Shanghai.*

By 2006, Communist Chinese authorities were collaborating with American Internet companies to censor websites and collect and pass along identifying information about individual users, including dissidents. Yahoo, Google, and Cisco have since joined Microsoft to construct the Great Firewall of China to track, trace, censor, and imprison critics of the Chinese government. One of the few surviving search engines in China is Microsoft's Bing.

XI.
The Green Years

"The Hebrews have done more to civilize men than any other nation. The doctrine of a supreme, intelligence sovereign of the universe, I believe to be the great essential principle of all morality, and consequently, of all civilization."

President John Adams
American Founding Father

In 2005, as McCain's Abramoff hearings within the Senate Indian Affairs Committee were winding down, Mark Penn, the Clinton's leading PR strategist, was appointed CEO of the powerful PR firm, Burson-Marsteller.

Trump held a fundraiser for Florida Gov. Charlie Crist at his private club, Mar-a-lago – after Roger Stone introduced Trump to Crist. The governor then moved forward to approve a lucrative state casino compact for the Seminole Tribe of Florida.

The Florida House of Representatives blocked the Seminole's compact by filing a petition with the Supreme Court, and Crist was charged with exceeding his authority by moving to approve it, without having first received approval from the state assembly.

The Seminole deal was table, for now – as Trump moved ahead to celebrate his marriage to his third wife, model Melania Knauss, with Hillary Clinton attending. Soon Clinton would be launching her presidential campaign to realize her dream as "the first woman President."

By 2006, the Senate Indian Affairs Committee were over and the storm surrounding Abramoff's activities had passed. Abramoff quietly entered prison while Democrats campaigned on the mostly Republican scandal to win seats in Congress. With Abramoff out of the way, business carried on as usual.

"For more than 21 years, (Trump) and his company have been on record trying to get casino deals in one form or another in Florida," *Politico* reports. "The gaming industry is so cutthroat in Florida that lobbyists from different companies have almost come to blows protecting their turf and trying to get an edge." With the Abramoff scandal safely behind them, the Seminoles moved ahead with plans to acquire the Hard

Rock franchise for $1 billion, with Greenberg Traurig and Merrill Lynch negotiating the details.

Jim Allen, a former Trump Properties and Park Place casino executive from Atlantic City, was the new Chairman of Hard Rock International and CEO of Seminole Gaming in 2000. "When I presented (the idea to acquire Hard Rock) to the tribe, they frankly thought I was a little crazy," Allen told reporters. "We didn't have that kind of money at all, and it was somewhat of a risk. The Seminoles got a taste of the Hard Rock brand power in 2004 when the tribe licensed the rights to call its hotel-casinos near Hollywood and Tampa Hard Rock." Hamish Dodds was then appointed Chairman of Hard Rock International.

As Clinton charged triumphantly toward the White House and the matter cleared in the legislature, Crist proceeded in April of 2008 to sign the Seminole's casino compact. Paul Huck Jr., – the son of the Clinton-appointed judge who presided over Abramoff's SunCruz case, represented the state in negotiations with the tribe that resulted in a lucrative casino compact. Abruptly Penn resigned from the Clinton campaign over what NPR characterized as "conflicts between his PR business and his candidate's interests."

As politicos attempted to make sense of the sudden departure, *The Huffington Post* reported that Penn was "dragging Clinton down," over his controversies:

"Clinton's Mark Penn problem does not lie in the strategist's advice and counsel -- it lies in Penn himself. As the CEO of powerhouse PR giant Burson-Marsteller Penn heads a bipartisan corporate conglomerate specializing in influence peddling, lobbying, phony front groups, and manufactured hype. Penn, the network of companies that he oversees, and the corporations to which he answers, represent precisely what voters have come to dislike most violently about Washington: the relentless cultivation and manipulation of political connections to generate wealth for a handful of operatives, all at taxpayer expense and in blatant defiance of the public will.

"There is no one in politics today who has ascended the special interest ladder as steeply as Penn. He's no Jack Abramoff, but in the public mind, **Penn**, *and the corporate structure that supports him, are an integral part of the same lucrative and corrupt system that produced Abramoff.* (The) problem Penn poses for the Clinton campaign is reflected in the numerous stories in the media about Penn's conflicts as CEO of Burson-Marsteller Worldwide, on the one hand, and as chief strategist for Hillary Clinton, on the other."

And just like that. Barack Obama, an obscure African-American Senator from Illinois, was on course to become President.

A case could be made that Obama was immensely more charismatic and likable than Clinton, but had the establishment preferred her instead, Clinton arguably would have emerged as the Democratic nominee.

The establishment marketed Obama, nearly deifying him as a Savior of mankind. He received unabashed, undeserved, and uncritical praise from the media and even top-down support from the churches by way of the ecumenical World Council of Churches. Obama was a product who promised to cleanse America of the taint of Bush and restore integrity to the government.

In June, Jim Messina, a longtime aide to Montana Senator Max Baucus (D-MT), signed on as Obama's Chief of Staff, helping to lead the campaign to victory. Baucus was the Chair of the powerful Senate Finance Committee for whom Abramoff had raised nearly $19,000 as lobbyist. Carlyle Consulting lobbyist Tom Rodgers who claimed credit for manufacturing the Abramoff scandal, had worked as a Congressional aid for Baucus, the chief lobbying contact on Capitol Hill for PhRMA (Pharmaceutical Research and Manufacturers of America), a client of the DeLay-linked Alexander Strategy Group.

That Messina was even working for Obama vexed many as he was not "of the Obama movement." Messina didn't resonate with Obama's message of "hope and change."

Facebook, which was created with support from Larry Summers, helped mobilize the youth behind Obama. "Eric Schmidt and Mark Zuckerberg used Google and Facebook to manipulate users," Aim4Truth.org

Facebook's *Template for Winning Elections* was curiously written in Russian. "Obama set up a political war-room that utilized the Template to Win officially under the aegis of the U.S. Digital Service," or what was first called 'the Eric Schmidt Project'," Aim4Truth.org reports. "

In the last leg of the presidential race, Ken Griffin, the founder of Citadel and heavy GOP contributor, began pouring money into the Obama campaign – as did the Bill and Melinda Gates Foundation.

With the establishment in his corner, Obama prevailed over his rival, Sen. John McCain who had delivered Abramoff to the Department of Justice. As much as McCain threatened to weaponize the information he held on Abramoff against political rivals, his campaign ran scared once the prosecution was exposed as a lie (by yours truly). I had revealed that Abramoff had been scapegoated through an investigation based upon half truths and disinformation that contradicted the paperwork in order to shield Abramoff's co-conspirators from liability and scrutiny. The entire scandal had been manufactured and driven by political operatives, who, were, in fact, Abramoff's partners in crime.

As Director of Personnel within the Obama-Biden Transition Team – and later as Deputy Chief of Staff, Messina advised on the placement of key personnel within the Obama Administration and rammed through the Affordable Care Act, which transferred control over the healthcare industry to the government.

He reported directly to Obama Chief of Staff Rahm Emanuel, whose political efforts were bankrolled Griffin, whose company had served as secondary lender in Abramoff's SunCruz deal. A $10 million grant from philanthropist Ken Griffin helped "support a transformative new initiative to reduce violent crime in Chicago, through a collaboration with Mayor Rahm Emanuel, the Chicago Police Department and the University of Chicago Crime Lab," according to the University of Chicago. *The New York Times* even commented on "Chicago's odd couple, Mayor Rahm Emanuel and a Billionaire Republican," Ken Griffin who had established headquarters for Citadel in Chicago in 1990 before relocating to Miami. After Emanuel left the White House, Citadel poured millions into Emanuel's mayoral campaign, helping him win the election.

Hedge Clippers reports that after lobbying "for loosening regulations on high-frequency traders," Emanuel "landed a $55 million TIF subsidy for a high-end convention center hotel managed by a company in which Griffin has a major investment."

Perhaps reflecting an ideological kinship, Emanuel's father was part of Irgun, a Zionist paramilitary organization, which carried out terrorist acts within Mandatory Palestine between 1931 and 1948 – the year in which Israel was established. The United Nations, U.S. federal government, media and Anglo-American Committee of Inquiry – even the Zionist Congress and Jewish Agency characterized Irgun as a terrorist organization. Renowned physicist Albert Einstein, who was offered the Presidency of Israel, compared Irgun and its successor organization, Herut party, to Nazi and Fascist parties, describing it as "a terrorist, right-wing chauvinist organization." Irgun was absorbed into the Israeli Defense Forces.

∧∧∧

It was not long after that the Seminoles made a move on Abramoff's former clients. One month before the 2008 presidential election election, the Saginaw Chippewa Indian Tribe made a "one time exception to normal policy" to authorize six Council Members to meet the Seminole's Assistant Chief Larry Harrison," according to Tribal Council minutes dated October of 2008.

A Tribal Minute dated April 15, 2009 reflects that the Saginaw Chippewa Tribal Council "moved to approve the Wells Fargo Banking Agreements to create bank accounts for the Investment Trusts; and approve the Money Market Account Agreements with (Merrill) Lynch Funds for each of the Investment Trusts, contingent upon fully executed contracts."

The Saginaw Chippewa Tribal Council then announced "a bold vision" to transform the tribe's sleepy reservation in bucolic Mt. Pleasant, Michigan into an eco-friendly tourist destination replete with indoor water and motor sports facilities, indoor ski slopes, a fishing pond, waterfalls, a lodge, theme park, bowling alley, a Cineplex movie theater, and expanded gaming operations under the Hard Rock brand name, the tribe's newsletter revealed. The new businesses were to run on green energy.

The Tribal Council projected that it could create conference facilities would rival those in Detroit, Lansing, and Grand Rapids for convention business. The Tribal Council then formed a Migizi Economic Development Company to "oversee the acquired business and any possible business acquirements or developments."

Once Migizi was created, the tribe's billion dollar portfolio was injected into this new company, according to Dr. Ahmed Kooros, who had guided the Saginaw Chippewa to $1 billion portfolio status.

The Seminoles, he said, proposed launched a Hard Rock casino in Michigan. The idea was for the Saginaw Chippewas to provide the capital while both tribes split the profits. All the Hard Rock was willing to bring to the table was a brand name. After evaluating the plans, Kooros concluded that Hard Rock's proposal was financially unsound, but his concerns went unheeded.

On January of 2009, Migizi informed the Saginaw Chippewa Tribal Council that it had engaged Hamish Dodds about a "Letter of Intent," outlining "the terms of the agreement." And then after a short engagement, the entire Saginaw Chippewa $1 billion portfolio vanished into thin air, Kooros said.

By 2016, the Seminole tribe was reportedly worth $12 billion, *Forbes* reports. "At the behest of the Seminoles, (Seminole Gaming CEO Jim) Allen presides over an expanding, privately owned global business that spans 71 countries and owns 168 Hard Rock cafes, 23 hotels and 11 casinos. Including franchisee sales, system-wide revenue is slightly more than $5 billion. Another 25 Hard Rock hotels are in the pipeline—from Dallas to Dubai to Shenzhen—and the company just acquired the rights to the flagship Hard Rock Las Vegas....And though the Seminoles are guarded about the information they share with outsiders, it's clear that their rapid expansion in the hospitality and gambling industry under Allen's stewardship has created a money machine that generates operating profits estimated at $1.5 billion per year. That's enabled the tribe to send revenue-sharing cheques to the state of Florida amounting to more than $1 billion over the past five years."

Tribes, which are federally subsidized, and can determine their own membership. "Today every man, woman and child in the tribe receives biweekly dividend payments totaling about $128,000 a year," *Forbes* reports. "Indeed, by the time a Seminole child today turns 18, she is already a multimillionaire." No thought has been given to repay the federal government, pay down the debt, or share that revenue with tribal members (and increasingly many others) throughout the nation who languish in poverty. The Seminole Hard Rock Hotel & Casino Tampa reportedly accounts for 40 percent of the Seminoles' $2.2 billion in annual gambling revenues.

When Obama became a viable presidential candidate, the Epstein pedophile fundraising operation took an interest in him. Roy Black, one of Epstein's attorneys held a fundraiser for the Senator in 2007 – and had attempted to host a second fundraiser for Obama in Miami Beach before this effort with nixed over the taint and growing awareness of Epstein's sordid activities.

Based upon circumstantial evidence, it would appear that Obama was firmly embedded within the Epstein network – and its agenda. For example, according to court filings, Obama's White House counsel, Kathryn Ruemmler, was a key contact between Epstein and JP Morgan.

Court filings reveal that weeks after Epstein was arrested, Epstein's personal assistant reached out to senior executives at JPMorgan Chase in 2019 to request that they open an account for Kathryn Ruemmler who was described as an ideal client. By this point, JP Morgan claimed to have severed all ties with Epstein over internal concerns. The filing reveals that JP Morgan acknowledged Epstein's role in "establishing JP Morgan's) customer relationship with Kathryn Ruemmler."

Epstein cultivated relationships with a number of individuals who would later appear in the Administration of Joe Biden, including, for example, CIA Director William Burns, who met with the pedophile on three separate occasions.

Green Boondoggles

One of the first actions Obama took upon becoming President was to address the issue Simmons raised on peak oil. To this end, Obama unveiled a new "cash-for-clunkers" program in which the Administration set aside $1 billion – and then, later, an additional $2 billion, to take gas guzzlers off the road in the interests of fuel efficiency.

Beyond remaking the healthcare industry, Obama advanced a green agenda, setting aside billions of dollars for failed green projects. While the City of London was keen to advance the green energy agenda, politically-connected individuals and companies rushed out with little planning or foresight, to grab as much money as possible. One of the most notable initiatives was the American Recovery and Reinvestment Act (ARRA) of 2009, which allocated around $90 billion for clean energy investments, including renewable energy production, energy efficiency upgrades, and advanced vehicle technologies.

In total, the Obama Administration's investment in green energy projects surpassed several hundred billion dollars. To cite an example, A123, which makes rechargeable lithium ion batteries for electric cars, received $249 million. Billions more were invested in electric vehicles and batteries – even though the United States was not close to having an electric grid to support them.

The Washington Post reported that "The American taxpayer has gotten precious little for the Administration's investment in battery-powered vehicles, in terms of permanent jobs, or lower carbon dioxide emissions. There is no market, or not much of one, for vehicles that are less convenient and cost thousands of dollars more than similar-sized gas-powered alternatives – but do not save enough fuel to compensate. The basic theory of the Obama push for electric vehicles – if you build them, customers will come – was a myth. And an expensive one."

A Chinese company purchased the distressed A123.

Ener1, an American lithium-ion battery manufacturer, which used $55 million from a $118 million federal grant before declaring bankruptcy in 2011 was purchased by Russian executive Boris Zingarevich's company, Interros, in 2012.

As a presidential candidate, Obama promised to have one million electric or hybrid vehicles on the road by 2015 – a promise he attempted, but failed to deliver.

Another high profile embarrassment was Solyndra, which made cylindrical solar panels. "Perhaps you thought the Solyndra scandal amounted to a $535 million government loan that will never be repaid," the *Wall Street Journal* reports. "No such luck. In the latest twist, Solyndra's investors could be rewarded for their failure, thanks to a tax benefit the Administration handed out in a bid to evade political accountability."

Obama's Energy Secretary, Steven Chu infamously said, "We have to figure out how to boost the price of gasoline to the levels in Europe," with seemingly no concern for how American citizens would be impacted. Rather it appeared as though the Administration had received instructions – to cut back on oil and then just half-assed it while shoveling money out the door.

Solyndra laid off 1,100 workers after losing billions of dollars attempting to deliver a workable product.

Another company, Abound Solar, which donated generously to Obama's presidential campaign, received a $400 million loan guarantee only to file for bankruptcy.

Ecotality, a San Francisco-based green-tech company received around $115 in loan guarantees only to teeter toward bankruptcy.

Evergreen Solar received $527 million before filing for bankruptcy, closing its factory, and laying off 1,800 employees.

Yet, despite these failures, the nation failed to have an honest discussion about the problems surrounding Saudi peak oil. Former House Speaker Newt Gingrich, a foreign policy expert, whose wife was appointed Ambassador to the Vatican during the Trump Administration, exploited Obama's failures for political mileage. In an article he accused Obama of "hating oil."

Obama promised to "end the age of oil" while failing to explain the reasons why. Perhaps if he had been honest with the American people, effective, workable, cost-efficient solutions could have been forged in lieu of endless, wasteful grifting.

Obama's Department of Energy provided billions of dollars in loans to green start ups. The Department of Treasury received $9 billion to "give away" for green projects. The Department of Labor was allotted $500 million for a "green jobs" training program.

The Inspector General of the Labor Department discovered, for example, that many of the grants went to Obama cronies, including $1.5 million for La Raza ("the race"), a military Hispanic group whose radical activists preach anti-American hatred and a desire to reclaim and conquer North America for Hispanics. This group failed to place any people into permanent jobs whereas BlueGreen Alliance, a large labor union and environmental group) received $3 million in exchange for securing employment for 230 people.

Yet, Obama was celebrated among elite circles, including the Rothschild-controlled Vatican as a great savior. In 2015, Pope Francis I visited the White House to champion "our shared values and objectives."

Obama joined the Vatican to promote "Sustainable Development Goals" in line with UN Agenda 2030 for Sustainable Development, setting out "a vision and shared commitment by 193 countries to pursue a common path to reduce poverty and increase opportunity over the next 15 years."

Chillingly, Saudi Arabia, which is leading Agenda 2030 sought to "empower people through welfare" – an objective Obama seems to have advanced quite handily.

The Sudden Death of Simmons

Matthew Simmons should have been hailed as a hero for warning the nation about "peak oil," in his best selling book, *Twilight in the Desert*. His research should have prompted a national discussion to explore how the United States arrived at this position, with an honest, representative government engaging the citizenry towards workable solutions that served the public interests. The government might have drawn upon the finest intellectual talent to determine the best course of action for the American people.

The globalists were clearly panicking as the public was growing tired of them. The collapse of the economy in 2007-2008, spurred by subprime mortgages – followed by the bailout of Wall Street, gave rise to the populist Tea Party movement on the right and the Occupy Wall Street movement on the left – both of which were controlled and managed by their respective party apparatuses.

High atop the global agenda was to transform society's relationship with oil. Americans had long appreciated the car – and cheap gasoline as a symbol of freedom, independence, and individualism. Young adults were anxious to obtain their driving permits to improve their mobility – to drive themselves to school or to events they wished to attend without constant parental supervision. Adults enjoyed being able to hop into their cars and travel cheaply wherever they wished to go, if even on a whim. A car was vital for most people as a reliable form of transportation.

Americans didn't concern themselves with politics or global affairs as a group as there was simply no need to. Society was safe and stable – and most were content to enjoy and build their lives interspersed with a little bit of escapism in the form of reality-TV, a sports game, a good book, or a day at the park. Some observed, to their dismay, that the typical American could name all NFL sports teams, and yet not be able to identify their state, much less their country on a map. Of course, this is a hyperbole, but as a whole, Americans are busy, productive people who are focused on making a living, enjoying their lives, and applying themselves to their individual pursuits.

How could complacent Americans, who were growing increasingly skeptical of their government, be mobilized into taking action on peak oil? The political classes believes that arguments were won, not by laying out the facts to the people, but through sound bites, emotional appeals, and clever marketing. One ploy may have involved the Deep Horizon Gulf oil spill.

In *Disaster on the Horizon: High Stakes, High Risks, and the Story Behind the Deep Well Blowout*, oil industry expert Bob Cavnar reports that prior to the devastation to the Gulf, safety systems had been turned off, among other anomalies. Matthew Simmons, a long-time energy expert – and the founder and Chairman of Simmons & Company International who created an investment banking firm to support oil companies following the 1973 energy crisis, raised the alarm too.

Speaking to Simmons credibility, he held memberships within the Council on Foreign Relations and the National Petroleum Council. He also served as energy advisor to President George W. Bush. Simmons' arguments that the Saudi oil fields had been overproduced are outlined in his book, which drew upon hundreds of internal documents obtained from Saudi Aramco, professional journals, and other credible, authoritative sources.

Reports that Saudi oil had increased by more than one million barrels a day may be attributed to any number of factors. Perhaps the Saudis had found a way to extract the oil after all – or repair the wells. Perhaps the oil was obtained circuitously to retain the illusion that all was well. For example, while efforts were made to prevent the United States from tapping its own oil reserves, to render the nation reliant on foreign reserves, the U.S. shipping oil to China and other countries. Following oil distributions, it becomes clear that oil was moved around the world, just as money is laundered, making it a challenge to determine the origins or destination of the resource or asset. Whatever the case, the world acted *as if* peak oil had occurred and took the precise countermeasures Simmons recommended.

At the same time, the idea for BRICS – Brazil, Russia, India, China, and South Africa – as a separate common market that would emerge and dethrone the dollar was conceived towards the end of the

Clinton Administration and beginning of the Administration of George W. Bush, with the establishment hyping an urgent need to respond to "climate change." At the same time, the petrodollar was being phased out. Somehow, somewhere there was duplicity involved and the government refused to come clean with the American people.

When Kissinger attempted to block development of Prudhoe Bay, Alaska, oil spills were heavily marketed to turn public sentiment against oil. A similar dynamic appeared to be unfolding around the BP oil spill. Simmons was somehow able to anticipate, if not predict, that the spill would occur.

The Deepwater Horizon (BP) oil spill refers to the environmental catastrophe that unfolded on April 20, 2010 in the Gulf of Mexico in the British Petroleum (BP) -operated Macondo Prospect. The spill was deemed as the largest marine oil spill in the history of the petroleum industry. Once the catastrophe stuck, the media was filled with images of beautiful sea birds and other sea life soaked in oil – and pundits rallying against America's reliance upon oil. Simmons made the media rounds to discuss the spill. He appeared on Bloomberg-TV to warn, for example, "If it were my family, I'd evacuate now, while you still have time."

Before his death, on August 8, 2010, he had disparaged BP in the media, spurring conjecture that he might have been assassinated. His death was ruled an "accidental drowning, with heart disease a contributing factor."

In an obituary, Tom Whipple, a retired CIA analyst and Editor of the E*nergy Bulletin* (formerly entitled *Peak Oil News* and *Peak Oil Review*), who is considered "one of the most highly respected analysts of peak oil issues in the United States," describes Simmons as "unique among those talking and writing about peak oil in that he came from the very heart of American capitalism, a self-made investment banker for the oil industry, unlike most who are outspoken on the issue of peak oil."

Simmons, Whipple writes, "commanded the attention of the financial and mainstream media."

His sudden death was attributed, by some, to "assassination at the hands of the CIA or BP," Whipple writes.

Simmons was even referenced in cables leaked from the U.S. State Department in which the Saudis were apparently denying that they had reached peak oil. "While (Sadad) al-Husseini, (the founder of Husseini Energy Company) believes that Saudi officials overstate capabilities in the interest of spurring foreign investment, he is also critical of international expectations. He stated that the IEA's expectation that Saudi Arabia and the Middle East will lead the market in reaching global output levels of over 100 million barrels/day is unrealistic, and it is incumbent upon political leaders to begin understanding and preparing for this 'inconvenient truth'."

Al-Husseini, a leading Saudi oil and gas industry expert, was Senior and Executive Vice President for Exploration and Producing at Saudi Aramco. He is credited with launching the field modernization and state of art reservoir management and development of the Saudi oil fields.

Yet al-Husseini, in 1996, was called upon by King Abdullah ibn Abdul Aziz to advise him on expanding the Saudi economy through exploration of its proven reserves, resulting in the Natural Gas Initiative in which international oil companies were invited to participate in the development of the Kingdom's non-associated gas reservoirs and the expansion of its power generation, desalination, and petrochemical sectors.

According to the cables, al-Husseini stated that he disagreed with analysts, like Simmons, who raised alarms over "peak oil," and that he remains optimistic and pragmatic with regards to available energy resources. His views were considered at odds with Aramco.

"The real history of Saudi Arabia oil exploration has been rather different than conventional wisdom has assumed," Simmons writes. "The lack of additional great finds since the late 1960s was not due to lack of effort. The effort was there. The oil was not."

Al-Husseini is also Senior Energy Consultant to the King Faisal Foundation, which was established in 1976 to preserve King Faisal's legacy and which is considered one of the largest charities in the world.

So, Simmons and al-Husseini held diametrically opposing views, and yet, somehow the world was following Simmons' recommendations for peak oil – most notably during the pandemic when World Economic Forum founder Klaus Schwab promoted "a new normal" and "Great Reset;" and World Bank economist Larry Summers advocated "permanent lockdowns."

Consider these recommendations and insights from Simmons, reflecting an agenda consistent with Saudi Arabia's Agenda 2030:

"We need to reduce the quality of goods we ship over long distances and transport the goods we must ship in the most energy efficient ways possible. Workers need to begin working closer to their residence and reduce the hours now wasted by commuting ever greater distances to their corporate environments. We need to grow our food supplies closer to where we live and raise the fish and meat we consume closer to home.

"In a sense, the world of the 21st century needs to evolve back to the village. By making these changes, we can improve productivity and lifestyles, and the global economy can actually become stronger on a more sustainable basis than the current course which will no longer work once oil suppl peaks.

"The easiest and swiftest change the developed world and particularly the U.S. can make is to alter the rules under which most people still have to work...The technology to enable flexible work hours, flexible office space, and flexible work locations is available today. The only change needed is a new mindset by employers to pay people according to their productivity instead of the antiquated check in system where compensation reflects the amount of time one spends in the workplace. Too many people are now spending up to a third of their workday crawling along freeways to get to the office or plant.

"The fuel efficiency of even high miles per gallon vehicles diminishes abruptly when traffic congestion begins. Those companies that take the lead in liberating their skilled workers will create not only create a far happier workforce, but also a far more productive one. The first corporation to effect the change could emerge as the biggest economic winners in a world that as passed peak oil...

"In a globalized world, we have created over the past several decades, vast amounts of the products bought in Europe, Canada. and the (United States) come from Asia. The embedded fuel used to transport goods from China to where they are purchased by European and North American consumers now rivals motor gasoline use. Some forms of transporting goods over long distances are fuel efficient while other means are perhaps at least efficient ways of fuel use.

"Another adjustment ...involves changing the sources of a great deal of the food we consume. Until two decades ago, most vegetables, meat and produce available year round. Produce was canned, bottled or frozen where it was at its freshest so it could be eaten throughout the year.

Over time the food business went global. Bottling and canning vanished. It became commonplace for attractive food from around the world to be found to the farthest corners of any prosperous country.

"As long as fuels were cheap, no one thought of the energy embedded in good globalization. While much of this food looks attractive, shipping requirements means that it never has a truly fresh and wholesome taste. To keep shipped food fresh it is subjected to a series of additives and refrigeration. Every step of the process increases the energy intensity of the food we eat."

The adjustments Saudi Arabia, and indeed the world made following the covid pandemic, followed Simmons' prescriptions, with the Saudi Kingdom positioning itself to lead the AI revolution and promote sustainable development, including global control of food production.

If Simmons assessment were incorrect, why did the world take his prescriptions so seriously? Why did they cover up the peak oil assessment and blame other factors, attributing the urgent need to follow his recommendations instead to climate change, global warming or pandemics?

The lockdown served to propel Saudi Arabia to a global AI leader, with one of the largest sovereign funds as it transitioned away from an oil-based economy into AI, invested heavily in start up companies, and even spoke of the end of the petro-dollar, while at the same time, purchasing weapons from the United States. On the one hand, Saudi Arabia was working closely with the Untied States as a partner. On the other, it had joined BRICS to decouple the dollar, with a view to ending the petro-dollar, while still partnering with the World Bank, its global development partner. The policies Saudi Arabia and other nations were pursuing made no sense. They were contradictory and at odds with the explanations given. The truth behind the cover up, if there indeed was one, may have been revealed in disclosures surrounding Italian Prime Minister Matteo Renzi who had met with Obama to discuss strategies on how they could keep globalism on track in the wake of rising nationalism that was poised to derail the New World Order.

Former Italy prime minister Matteo Renzi characterized Saudi Arabia as the place for the "new renaissance." He also participated in the Future Investment Initiative, the nonprofit arm of the Saudi Public Investment Fund, Saudi Arabia's sovereigns fund, which is controlled by

Saudi Prince MBS and leading global efforts to promote Smart Cities, AI, and high tech solutions in a post-oil world.

While the victims of the terrorist attacks of September 11, 2001, were turning their eyes to Saudi Arabia, Obama vetoed a bill that would have allowed families of the victims to sue Saudi Arabia over the attacks. As *Politico* reports, "Many of the same U.S. lawmakers, who are happy to make it easier to sue the Saudis, green-lit a $1.15 billion arms sale to the country." On the one had, politicians were grandstanding to retain the support of the public, while on the other they were prioritizing the interests of Saudi Arabia.

In a statement explaining his decision, Obama expressed sympathy for the victims but argued that the legislation, the Justice Against Sponsors of Terrorism Act (JASTA), was misguided on grounds that it would have allowed U.S. citizens to sue foreign governments and that this, in turn, could be turned against American leaders, thereby jeopardizing national security. If the U.S. citizens could pursue foreign governments for attacks against them on U.S. soil, foreign citizens could pursue similar claims of justice against U.S officials, thereby increasing their liability and exposure to discovery and other legal actions. Perhaps it would have opened the door for Americans to sue their own leaders. One instance might be Obama's authorization of killer drones.

Keeping the Agenda on Track

After leaving the White House in 2012, Messina launched a series of seminars with senior executives from Apple, Facebook, Zynga, Google, Salesforce, Microsoft, among other companies. He was also credited with masterminding Obama's re-election campaign with Google CEO Eric Schmidt. High atop Obama's agenda was keeping globalism on track and promoting the green agenda.

As Chief Analytics Officer for Obama's 2012 re-election campaign, Schmidt was "so close to (Obama), in fact, that he spent election night in November 2012, with (the President)'s data analytics team in the Cave, their disco-ball decorated headquarters in a nondescript office block of Chicago," *GQ* reports. "Many believe it was Schmidt and this crack unit of genius-IQ programmers who ensured Obama's pundit-defying five-million-vote margin of victory - largely due to their ability to predict where campaign resources needed to be targeted before polling booths closed."

Schmidt was Obama's "underappreciated asset," *Bloomberg Businessweek* reports. "He helped recruit talent, choose technology, and coach the campaign manager, Jim Messina, on the finer points of leading a large organization." Schmidt reportedly advised Messina in a way that "abandoned every step of a traditional presidential campaign and merged technology and politics in a way that was both unpredictable and unprecedented."

In addition to donating $5,000 to Barack Obama's 2012 campaign, Schmidt provided strategic vision on digital operations along with opportunities in several start-ups founded by engineers and analysts from the Obama presidential campaign who developed new ways to use campaign data to improve advertising and voter-turnout operations.

∧∧∧

Obama, arguably set the stage for BRICS – that of realigning power away from the United States and towards China – and a global currency that would be controlled by elites.

Right after his election, in November of 2009, Obama attempted to launch the TransPacific Partnership (TPP) at APEC in Singapore, to establish a Free Trade Area of the Asia Pacific (FTAAP) that would eventually link in Communist China and Russia and Pacific Rim economies from China to Chile to the United States through regional and bilateral free trade agreements.

During Obama's engagement of the Asian nations, the idea for crypto-currencies was launched. Digital currencies provided a means to track, trace, and regulate consumer purchases and potentially deny credit based upon a credit score; the idea originated in China and Japan. Schmidt was credited with inventing the Chinese social credit score," while Microsoft CEO Bill Gates was advising China on its technological development.

"The United States must give a "greater voice (to) Asian nations in financial institutions," Obama announced at Suntory Hall in Tokyo, Japan. "Each of us must do what we can do to grow our economies without endangering our planet. (If) we put the right rules in place (to) unleash the creative power of our best scientists, engineers, and entrepreneurs, (information technology) will lead on new jobs, new opportunities, and entirely new industries. And Japan has been at the forefront of this issue."

A global leader in the mining of the digital "bitcoin," Japan established the Tokyo Electric Power (TEPCO) "to power cryptocurrency mining with excess electricity on its grid," the *Coin Republic* reports. "It will involve the deployment of distribution data centers throughout Japan that hybridize surplus electricity from renewable energy." What this development reflects is an effort to establish a currency that is backed by energy that facilitates the endless spending of the dollar – to develop the world. Arguably, cryptos were born of the realization that the petrodollar was on the way out.

Bitcoin entrepreneurs believed they could become instant billionaires by using digital coins to purchase massive amounts of real estate (hard assets) with imaginary money while pricing ordinary people out of markets. As Artificial Intelligence (AI) eliminated jobs, technocrats proposed a guaranteed income tied to a social credit score, ensuring that elites had unassailable power and control over the people – while the elites held all the wealth. According to *Business Insider,* Obama became the first billionaire former President.

In true kleptocratic fashion, Obama made millionaires and billionaires of friends by dropping money in their laps for jobs they arguably could not even perform, like the ill-fates Affordable Care Act website. A number of Obama insiders made out like bandits. Valerie Jarrett's subsidized housing (described by some as "slums") is a notable example of the schemes that have made politically connected insiders wealthy and privileged at the public's expense while providing little discernible or commensurate value for the money received.

Bitcoin was launched during the first year of the Obama Administration. Touted as one of the "world's leading bitcoin mining experts," Michael Long, the Technical Director for FinalHash, said that China was behind the new currency. "Through my personal contacts and clients and some of the stuff we do, (we) are looking at over 50 percent of the mining power of bitcoin in China," he said. "We just recently signed some contracts to move a rather large exchange to China. That's an exchange called Cryptsy. So, they're expanding to China to kind of serve this under-served population that's, you know, a billion and a half people that are hungry for something. So, in China I would say it's a lot of hardware stuff, a lot of financial stuff, and a lot of folks have problems getting into China just because the economies of scale in China are very different than they are virtually anywhere else."

Others were quick to jump on the bandwagon to promote bitcoin and cryptocurrencies, including, for example, *Shark Tank* billionaires Mark Cuban and Kevin O'Leary, NFL star Tom Brady, and sponsored YouTube "influencers," who encouraged people to invest in cryptocurrencies. (A number of influences remarked, privately, on being bankrolled by Saudi Arabia and other private interests.)

Expounding upon bitcoin, Long said: "This is the first time in history that it's truly easy and openly accessible for anybody to do truly global commerce. So, if I wanted to order something from a U.S. company, and I'm in China, outside of customs, regulations, and these kinds of things, you can physically order something real-time, instantaneously without having to go through any kind of regulatory roadblocks. And from a country that's had a full history of full repression economically, financially totalitarianism is a great place to kind of see bitcoin take off. And that coupled with Xi Jinping being – I'm not going to say an extremely lax premier, but he's definitely more open to some new opportunities."

At the time, China, Russia, and other countries were in the process of separating from the U.S. Bretton Woods financial system that had been established after World War II, to launch the Belt and Road Initiative which sought to link Europe, the Middle East and Asia through Israel, essentially recreating the old silk trade routes of merchants aligned with the Rothschilds, Vatican, and Black Nobility.

At the same time, BRICS (Brazil, Russia, India, China, and South Africa) were expanding their economic ties to forge new markets with each other, independent of the United States.

Obama advisor Jim Messina became a key advisor on government relations and policy strategy for a London-based cryptocurrency trading platform, Blockchain.com; he also served on its Board, CNBC reported. Messina advised the company on lobbying the European Parliament on crypto-regulation. "By bringing on Messina, Blockchain.com, (which) does roughly 30 percent of all bitcoin transactions, is trying to become a key player in the onshore market," *Axios* reports.

In 2015, Cryptospace launched a "Bitcoin Embassy" in Houston, backed by FinalHash, to incubate ideas for tech startups. That year, a disabled vet by the name of Marcus Andrade led a "group of programmers and entrepreneurs" to launch an anti-money laundering bitcoin (AMLBitcoin) where he was connected to Jack Abramoff. While exploring bitcoin, Andrade wrote in court documents that he "would address (issues of security and privacy) by ensuring that banks could identify, track, and trace each end user and transaction."

Meanwhile the elites had expressed concerns that globalism was being derailed with the rise of patriotism and nationalism. Obama had sounded the alarm with Renzi, whom Messina had picked up as a client, as strategic advisor. The elites needed to do something – and quick.

Climate Bond Partners

The networks behind the climate change agenda were revealed through the launch, in 2014, of Climate Bond Partners at the World Pensions and Investments Forum in Paris. Under the pretext of climate change, trillions of dollars in public funds could be redirected into private hands to rebuild a new world.

"Our mission is to mobilize trillions from debt capital markets for climate solutions for a rapid transition to a low carbon and climate resilient economy," Climate Bonds Initiative CEO Sean Kidney said. "Growing a large and liquid green bonds and climate bonds market is a key part of that; we're at $50 billion globally, but we need it to be much much larger. We're inviting organizations around the world to join with us to make that happen."

Climate Bond Partners grew out of the Climate Bond Initiative in the UK – the driver behind the global agenda to corral the world's wealth and power into the hands of the few.

Among the first groups to join the group was Sustainable Low Carbon Transport (SLCT) – a multi-stakeholder partnership that promotes development of sustainable transportation policies globally. SLCT Secretary General Cornie Huizenga salivated over "the huge untapped potential in the private sector when it comes to funding sustainable, low carbon transport" – that is, public funds redistributed to the private sector by way of public-private partnership.

The Climate Bonds Initiative launched as an international nonprofit to "mobilize global capital for climate action," specifically targeting "institutional investors, governments, development banks, and large corporations." The group has "transformed the green bond market from a niche concept to a mainstream source of capital for sustainable development."

By its own accounts, Climate Bonds "drives the market with the only certification scheme for sustainable debt globally under the Climate Bonds Standard." The group's advisory panel consists of representatives based in Boston, Brussels, California, Copenhagen, Dublin, Houston, Geneva, Istanbul, Jarkarta, Kuala Lumpar, London, Luxembourg, Madrid, Mumbai, New York, Paris, Seattle, Seoul, Sydney, Toronto, Tokyo, and Washington, DC.

Within the United States, Climate Bonds is represented by Dr. David Woods, Director of the Initiative for Responsible Investment at Harvard University; and Sean Flannery, former Chief Investment Officer, State Street Global Advisors.

Among the original financial backers of Climate Bonds is the Rockefeller Foundation. Its current financial backers are:

> *The Inter-American Development Bank*
> *European Climate Foundation*
> *ClimateWorks Foundation*
> *European Union's 2020*
> *UK Foreign and Commonwealth Office*
> *ADB*
> *German Cooperation*
> *Frederick Mulder Foundation*
> *Laudes Foundation*
> *Gordon and Betty Moore*
> *Children's Investment Fund Foundation*
> *Oak Foundation*

The Children's Investment Fund Foundation of the UK was established by a billionaire hedge fund manager, with over $4 billion in assets. The Oak Foundation seeks to manage the world's seed supply in the event of the Apocalypse. Consider this doomsday scenario depicted on its website:

> *"Beneath the English countryside in the heart of Sussex lies an incredible bank – but the type that may come to mind as you read this is not the one we mean. In sub-zero chambers, in flood-, bomb-, and*

radiation-proof vaults, 2.4 billion seeds, collected from around the world, are stored. This is the Millennium Seed Bank, an insurance policy against the global biodiversity crisis that is threatening plant species with extinction. Conserving seeds is not just about chasing numbers....It's about increasing the genetic diversity of the collections and unlocking their potential to solve some of the biggest challenges we face today, from biodiversity loss to food security to climate change."

A certain Barbara Rothschild serves on the Advisory Board of the Oak Foundation. It could not immediately be determined if this particular Rothschild was a member of the infamous Rothschild family, however, per one report, the Oak Foundation also funds Greenpeace, the Tides Foundation, Soros' Open Society, and Rockefeller family networks – networks that are aligned with <u>the</u> Rothschild family.

Per online records, "Barbara Rothschild" is listed as President of the Palm Beach, Florida-based Rothschild Family Foundation. While "Richard Rothschild" is identified as Vice President, Treasurer, and Director. *(https://projects.propublica.org/nonprofits/organizations/352413378)*

"Richard Rothschild," *is identified in the* 2013 Annual Report for American Friends of the Hebrew University, *which the couple sponsors, as the Vice President of Wells Fargo.*

Meanwhile, "Richard A. Rothschild" was recorded as having patented Covid-19 biometric tests in London in 2013 and 2015. *(https://jdfor2024.com/2021/05/system-and-method-for-testing-for-covid-19_inventor-richard-a-rothschild/)*The method involved sending the data to a cloud – consistent with Google CEO Eric Schmidt's efforts to exploit public health records (in apparent violent of HIPPA laws) to extract, share, and analyze personal data from health records and recommend treatments, as rolled out in Project Nightingale.

The Oak Foundation reportedly spends, on average, $250 million per year on 350 different projects. Its current president is Douglas Griffiths, the Obama Administration's Representative to the UN Human Rights Council in Geneva; its vice president is Heather Graham, *a former program manager at the Bill & Melinda Gates Foundation and a former White House adviser to President George W. Bush.*

Among the leaders of the Oak Foundation is Brigette De Lay, Director of Prevent Child Sexual Abuse Programme (PCSAP), an organization dedicated to "supporting courageous leaders and survivors around the world working to end child sexual abuse in our lifetime."

Per PCSAP's website: "Child sexual abuse is preventable. This fact drives and inspires our support to end child sexual abuse online and offline. Our partners are survivors, advocates, and researchers working to accelerate action at the community, national, and global levels." Its six priority funding areas include: (1) Solution and research; (2) Men and boys; (3) Safe digital environment; (4) Safe sports; (5) Justice for survivors; and (6) Survivor-led organizations.

The main sponsor of the Oak Foundation is "British-born businessman, Alan M. Parker, currently living in Geneva, Switzerland with an estimated net worth of about $2 billion.

The other sponsor is Charles "Chuck" Feeney, founder of Atlantic Philanthropies, a Bermuda-based foundation that bankrolled Health Care for America Now (HCAN), "one of the drivers of the campaign to pass Obamacare," which facilitated the government's takeover of the healthcare system within the United States.

HCAN was created by Arabella Advisors, a consulting firm, established in 2005 by Eric Kessler, a member of the Clinton Global Initiative.

Arabella Advisor, which raked in $635 million in in 2018, sponsors hundreds of "fake groups "via Arabella's in-house nonprofits. "These fake groups are little more than websites designed to look like standalone nonprofits," influencewatch.org reports. "Since the Arabella's network's inception, it has sponsored at least 340 such groups. These fake groups rarely disclose their relationship to Arabella Advisors or its in-house nonprofits. Nevertheless, many of them accept donations from the public, funds which go to Arabella's nonprofits. This system also allows these groups to hide their funds since it's virtually impossible to trace individual grants to Arabella's grants to Arabella's nonprofits to any particular fake group."

Araballa's Hopewell Fund manages the Economic Security Project, which promotes guaranteed basic income – that of providing cash payments to individuals, such as those doled out during the global pandemic lockdown. Among the signatories of the Economic Security

Project was Alicia Garza, the founder of Black Lives Matter and self-described "Marxist."

The co-founder of the Hopewell Fund was Facebook "spokesman and "co-founder" Chris Hughes. Arabella Advisors' former CEO, Sampriti Ganguli, previously worked for JP Morgan Chase.

XII.
Pandemic as Panacea

"There is nothing I dread so much as the division of the republic into two great parties, each arranged under its leader, and concerting measures in opposition to each other This, in my humble apprehension, is to be dreaded as the greatest political evil under our constitution."

President John Adams
American Founding Father

President Barack Obama visited the Saudi Kingdom for the first time in June of 2009. The following month he signed the Car Allowance Rebate System (CARS), billed as the "cash for clunkers," a $3 billion federal program to provide an incentive for the public to turn in their gas guzzlers to purchase more fuel efficient cars. The Obama Administration was lavish in its subsidies of "green energy" projects appropriate for an era of "peak oil," though nobody publicly wanted to acknowledge this element as a reason for the rapidly changing developments on the world stage as the syndicate realized that the petro-dollar was on borrowed time.

In 2014, Obama visited the Ritz Carlton in Riyadh, Saudi Arabia, spending nearly $267,000 in public funds for the trip. The Ritz Carlton, which is owned by Marriott International, has deep ties with intelligence – and the wider syndicate. For example, Saudi arms trafficker and prolific money launderer Adnan Khashoggi negotiated many of his arms deals at the Ritz of Paris, which was monitored by British intelligence and which pandered to the world's elite. Through tracking and surveillance devices, intelligence could monitor high profile assets, their escapades and deals. The Ritz in Russia was the venue where Trump was allegedly filmed with prostitutes. The Ritz of London is a venue frequented by members of the British Monarchy and celebrities, the public relations assets of the Crown.

During this trip, Obama sought to strengthen bilateral ties between the two countries and address Iran's nuclear program, among other matters. Perhaps a coincidence, but in 2014, hackers breached Marriott's Starwood reservation system, stealing the personal data of up to 500 million guests.

The Obama Administration, along with several other countries, negotiated the Joint Comprehensive Plan of Action (JCPOA), commonly known as the Iran nuclear deal. This agreement was reached in July 2015 and aimed at limiting Iran's nuclear program in exchange for sanctions relief. Between January 2014 and July 2015, Iran received $700 million every month from funds previously frozen by U.S. sanctions. Though the total amount granted Iran is in dispute, some put that number at $11.9 billion, with details surrounding the deal "shrouded in mystery."

"Iran may have received as much as $33.6 billion in cash or in gold and other precious metals," according to Mark Dubowitz, executive director at the Foundation for Defense of Democracies.

Between March and April of 2016, Obama met Italian Prime Minister Matteo Renzi at a Nuclear Security Summit in Washington, DC. During this time, according to Maria Zack from Nations in Action, Obama and Renzi discussed shared concerns that populism and nationalism could derail globalism. Together they conceived strategies on how they could keep globalism on track. Zack alleged that money was diverted from Obama's Iran deal to fund such efforts.

Later in April of 2016, Obama visited Saudi Arabia for a summit with Gulf Cooperation Council (GCC) leaders – to address regional security concerns, including the Iran deal.

The following year, Saudi's sovereign fund, the Public Investment Fund launched the Future Investment Initiative Institute, a Saudi nonprofit, to invest in "promising solutions" as part of Saudi Vision 2030. Known as the "Davos of the Desert," the FII was created by Saudi King, Salman bin Abd al-Aziz Al Sau by decree and run by his son, Crown Prince Mohammad bin Salman (MBS), who is Chairman of both the Public Investment Fund – and the Saudi Arabian Economic and Development Council.

Renzi was among the Board Members, thereby aligning the Saudis in opposition to nationalism and populist movements. Among the other Board Members were:

Richard Attias, CEO of the FII Institute and "advisor to international leaders, companies, and nations;" an organizer of the World Economic Forum Annual Meeting at Davos, the Clinton Global Initiative, One Planet Summit, UNESCO NGO Forum, Bloomberg New Economy Forum; and Executive Chairman of of Publicis Events Worldwide.

Yasir Al-Rumayyan, Governor of the Saudi Arabian Public Investment Fund; Chairman of Saudi Aramco, "the world's most valuable listed companies;" and Board Member for Uber Technologies.

Princess Reema Bint Bandar, Saudi Ambassador to the United States; CEO of Alfa International Companry, Ltd., a "multi-brand luxury retail company;" Saudi Deputy Head of Development and Planning; President of the Mass Participation Federation; and Member of the World Bank Advisory Council for Women Entrepreneurs Finance Initiative.

Mohammed Alabbar, Leader of eal estate development companies Emaar Properties and Eagle Hills since 1997 who has stakes in China's leading mobile transport platform, Didi Chuxing; and the popular coffee chain, Luckin Coffee.

Peter Diamand, *Fortune* magazine's "50 Greatest Leaders in the World;" founder of Singularity University, co-founder of BOLD Capital Partners, a $250 million venture fund; and Executive President of XPRIZE Foundation.

Tony Chan, President of KAUST; president of Hong Kong University of Science and Technology; Deputy Director of Mathematics and Physical Sciences for US National Science Foundation.

Adah Almutairi – Director, Center for Excellence in Nanomedicine and Engineering at the University of California's Institute of Engineering in Medicine.

PIF's Advisory Board Members:

Masayoshi Son, CEO of Japan's SoftBank group
Joe Kaeser, President and CEO of Siemens
Stephen Schwarzman, CEO of Blackstone private equity
Mohamed Ali Alabbar, founder and President of Emaar Properties, the largest listed developer in Dubai
Ajay Banga, the President and CEO of Mastercard

Victor Chu, who heads the First Eastern Investment Group
Mellody Hobson, President of Ariel Investments
Arianna Huffington, founder and CEO of Thrive Global
Peter Thiel, Partner of the Founders Fund
Tidjane Thiam, Chief Executive of Credit Suisse
Lubna Olayan, head the Olayan Financing Company

Towards the tail end of the Obama Administration, in 2015, representatives from 196 countries signed off on the Paris Accords, an international treaty which sought to deindustrialize the world to mitigate "climate change." The Saudis signed off on the climate accords, but kept a low profile.

While the Saudis were expected to sabotage the Paris Accords, "in the run up to the Paris summit, the kingdom adopted a more amenable posture," the *Guardian* reports.

As could be expected, the Kingdom raised reasonable concerns about how the transition from fossil fuels would impact its economy; at the same time, the Kingdom invited investors to help the Saudis "diversify" its economy so that it was no longer reliant upon oil.

Even though Saudi Arabia was identified as the largest producer of oil, a number of countries have been exporting their oil to Saudi Arabia including, for example, Russia, the United States, Iraq, Kuwait, United Arab Emirates, Nigeria, Angola, Kazakhstan, Azerbaijan, and Noway. Was oil being moved around the world in a manner similar to the way in which public funds were laundered from one bank, one country, one account to another, and then another, and then another?

Were the elites somehow vested in keeping the illusion of Saudi Arabia's oil fields alive? If so, why? Whatever the case, no one acknowledged publicly that the Saudis were dealing with a peak oil challenge. Rather, the challenge could be inferred through context. "To lessen the dominance of its oil industry by growing its petrochemical and mining sectors among others, (the Saudis needed) financial assistance to compensate for slower economic growth," the *Guardian* reports.

At the same time, the Saudi actions were characterized as "opaque" and "with numerous caveats" when its role, as world development partner, would have warranted transparency.

The Saudis also went out of their way to deny peak oil. Consider, the public statements of Ali al-Naimi, a leader in the global oil industry and Minister of Petroleum and Mineral Resources for Saudi Arabia from 1995 to 2016. As one of the longest-serving Saudi energy ministers in the world, al-Naimi shaped Saudi Arabia's oil policies within OPEC and throughout the global market. His influence extended to the World Bank.

As has been reported, al-Naimi "was often seen as a key architect of Saudi Arabia's strategy in managing oil production levels to influence global oil prices" – prices that were determined by the World Bank.

By 2015, around the time of the Paris Accords, al-Naimi was ready to concede that "the global economy was moving away from fossil fuels, and that Saudi Arabia was prepared to move with it," the *Guardian* reports. "In Saudi Arabia, we recognize that eventually, one of these days, we are not going to need fossil fuels," al-Naimi was quoted as saying. "I don't know when, in 2040, 2050 or thereafter."

Concurrently, "oil analysts (were remarking that) the kingdom also faces enormous domestic pressure to diversity its electricity supply," the *Guardian* reports. "Nearly all of Saudi Arabia's domestic electricity supply comes from oil, and keeping the lights on and air conditioners humming is taking up a growing share of production that would otherwise have been sold for export."

Yet, despite its public image as dominant global oil producer, a Saudi delegate conceded that the Kingdom was "too poor" and had "too many other priorities" that might prevent it from meeting global warming targets. In so many words, the Saudis were demanding a bail out, or protection "from loss of future oil income;" they "sought financial aid to acquire new green energy technology."

Saudi Arabia was assured of getting it – as a key development partner of the World Bank, which advanced the global imperialism of Rothschild dba the U.S. federal government.

The Paris Accords were signed on April 22, 2016 in New York, with support from the Rothschild-controlled Vatican and Crown. President Barack Obama had signed on by way of an Executive Order (EO).

As President, Donald Trump withdrew from the Paris Accords after signing an EO directing the Environmental Protection Agency to review the plan.

Mid-2017, MBS was elevated in stature to Crown Prince, and the Trump Administration's relationship with the Saudis grew tighte. Many recoiled over the Prince's authoritarian tendencies. As critics observed, his leadership style was top down and dictatorial. Those who resisted his demands could wind up fleeced, beaten, imprisoned, or dead.

The United States helped stabilize world oil supplies by fracking. Even though the United States remained a key Saudi ally, plans were underway to decoupled Saudi Arabia from the petro-dollar for the simple reason that the Kingdom did not have enough petro to support the dollar – and by extension, global development. Widespread adoption of fracking began in the 2000s, following the Saudi Gas Initiative, reflecting the changes in priorities.

Trump likely withdrew from the Paris Accords over domestic political considerations, rather than a rejection of globalism. Indeed, given the growing opposition to globalism, allowances were made for countries to determine the extent of their participation in climate schemes.

Within the United States, Republican legislators, who had received campaign donations from Big Oil, signed a letter demanding that Trump withdraw om the Paris Accords. Trump withdrew, therefore, to appease constituents. Among the signatories were representatives of oil-rich states.

Withdrawing was easy since Obama had signed onto the Paris Accords by way of an EO – that bypasses the normal process of checks and balances, as required by the Constitution. As such, whatever is done by EO can be undone just as easily. *Foreign Policy Journal* observes, moreover, that "The Paris Accords did not specifically call for a reduction in petroleum imports from Saudi Arabia. Neither did it call for a reduction in petroleum imports overall. It called for a reduction in the production of greenhouse gasses, which could be achieved in any number of ways that would not necessarily impact petroleum imports."

The Paris Accords fundamentally transformed global climate governance by introducing a new framework based on a bottom-up system of nationally determined contributions (NDCs).

In the past, global climate governance relied on top-down approaches in which countries negotiated their own binding emissions reduction targets and commitments through international treaties such as the Kyoto Protocol or the Paris Agreement.

However, the new bottom-up approach allows each country to determine its own emission reduction targets and strategies based on national priorities. Under this framework, each country outlines emissions reductions targets along with proposed policies and actions. As signatory to the Paris Accords, Saudi Arabia established a goal of avoiding up to 130 million tonnes of carbon dioxide (CO_2) equivalent emissions per year by 2030.

At the start of the new Administration, Ivanka Trump, Senior Advisor to her father, President Donald Trump, leveraged her presidential contacts to secure patents to market her products in the vast Communist Chinese market. She then attempting to rebrand herself as an advocate for women's work, both through a book, *Women Who Work,* which was dismissed as "out of touch" with the realities of America's working women; and through a partnership with the World Bank.

In 2017, Ivanka partnered with the World Bank to create the Women's Entrepreneurs Finance Initiative (We-Fi) to help women in developing countries access loans and grants for their own businesses and development projects. Princess Bandar, an Advisory Board member for the FII – the nonprofit arm of the Saudi sovereign fund controlled by MBS, served as World Bank Advisory Council on this project.

The We-Fi consisted of a partnership among governments, multilateral development banks, and private sector stakeholders. financing the gap faced by women entrepreneurs in developing countries. While noble in its stated intent, the fact is that Americans – both women and men – were losing their jobs to offshoring. At the same time, the federal government was advancing the interests of Wall Street over those of Main Street, making it increasingly difficult for entrepreneurs to succeed.

Given the pattern of World Bank schemes, without a full audit, it is impossible to know whether the money ever reached its intended, or stated, destination – and it raises questions of why the Trump Administration, which had campaigned on an "American First" agenda was redistributing money from struggling Americans to entrepreneurs in developing countries. Wouldn't the money have been better spent at home, to help America's women? It wasn't as if the United States had a budgetary surplus. In fact, the nation's debt was increasing, with Americans left to foot the bill. Taking a cynical view, this was likely just another pretext in which to redistribute public funds into the politically connected and their families, granting them opportunities to become rich by serving the global agenda through public-private partnerships and government contracts.

Ivanka and German Chancellor Angela Merkel took credit for conceiving of the plan – in which Saudi Arabia and the United Arab Emirates pledged a total $100 billion. That year, Trump traveled to Saudi Arabia, this first foreign country he visited as President, followed by trips to Israel (Jerusalem), Rome (The Vatican), and Brussels (the capitol of Rothschild's European Union).

The Saudis were seeking outside funding to "diversify" their economy at the 2017 Saudi-U.S. CEO Forum. As part of that investment, the Saudis offered $40 billion to develop U.S. infrastructure while billionaire Blackstone founder and CEO Stephen Schwarzman, a member of PIF's Advisory Board, entered into a non-binding memorandum. Blackstone holds over $1 trillion assets under management and significant holdings in the global casino industry, some of which are connected to Trump – and the Crown.

In addition to accompanying Trump on a trip to Saudi Arabia, Schwarzman was briefly Chairman of Trump's Strategic and Policy Forum. Among the other members were Citadel founder Ken Griffin; Jamie Dimon, Chairman and CEO of JPMorganChase; Travis Kalanick, CEO of Uber; Doug McMillon, President and CEO of Walmart; Kevin Warsh, former governor of the Federal Reserve; Daniel Yergin, expert on Saudi Arabia and Vice Chairman of IHS Markit; Larry Fink, CEO Of BlackRock; Bob Iger, President and CEO of Disney; Brian Krzanich, CEO of Intel; Rich Lesser, President and CEO of Boston Consulting Group; Ginni Rometty, Chairwoman, CEO and President of IBM; and Jim McNerney, former President and CEO of Boeing.

With a reported net worth of some $32 billion Schwarzman invests in casinos through Blackstone. For example, in 2019, Blackstone acquired the Bellagio Resort and Casino in Las Vegas from MGM Resorts International for approximately $4.25 billion. This acquisition was made through Blackstone's real estate investment trust (REIT) MGM Growth Properties (MGP), which was formed as a joint venture between MGM Resorts International and Blackstone in 2016. MGP was established to acquire properties for MGM Resorts International, providing MGM Resorts with a source of capital. The acquisition of the Bellagio by Blackstone through MGP further solidified the relationship between Blackstone and MGM Resorts International in the real estate sector.

In 2021, MGM Resorts sold its Las Vegas-based Mirage casino to the Seminole Tribe of Florida's Hard Rock International for nearly $1.1 billion.

Like others who run in his charmed circle, Schwarzman owns a Manhattan apartment that features "35 rooms, including a foyer the side of a ballroom, his and hers saunas, a pine-panelled library, 11 fireplaces, and 13 bathrooms," the *Guardian* reports. "Works by Claude Monte and the American abstract artist Cy Twombly adorn the walls of the two-floor, 20,000 square foot Park Avenue residence. In pride of place, according to visitors, is a silver-framed photograph of Schwarzman arm-in-arm with President Bush."

CNBC named Schwarzman "the premier capitalist in America" while *Fortune* "crowned him "Wall Street's Monarch."

In May 2017, President Trump made a deal to sell $110 billion worth of weapons to Saudi Arabia. ABC News reports that the sale included "tanks and helicopters for border security, ships for coastal security, intelligence-gathering aircraft, a missile-defense radar system, and cybersecurity tools." This was part of a 10-year, 350-billion agreement reflecting a "strategic vision" between the two countries. It was unclear how Trump's campaign promise to keep restrain wasteful spending on wars not in the national interest aligned with selling weapons to Saudi Arabia and other countries. However, Trump explained that selling weapons created jobs – while also enriching government contractors.

Previously, the Obama Administration had approved a $115 billion arms deal with the Saudis – an agreement that derailed following reports of human rights violations of the Saudi military campaign against Yemen. As development partner of the World Bank tasked with alleviating poverty and developing the world on behalf of humanity, at least 10,000 lost their lives in this war while over three millions were displaced. Saudi warplanes reportedly targeted hospitals, schools, roads, farms, livestock, and other civilian targets, in the long-standing tradition of the syndicate.

At the same time, Trump couldn't bring himself to criticize the Saudis. "They buy apartments from me," he said at campaign rallies. "They spent $40 million, $50 million. Am I supposed to dislike them? I like them very much." He even told Fox News that he "would want to protect Saudi Arabia, but Saudi Arabia is going to have to help us economically. They were making, before the oil went down....they were making $1 billion per day."

Trump's son-in-law, Jared Kushner reportedly played a key role in the arms deal. In one meeting, a U.S. official brought up the possibility of adding a "sophisticated radar system designed to shoot down ballistic missiles," inspiring comparisons with Reagan's Star Wars or Israel's dome. The Saudis were interested in the radar system.

In a move that was a page out of the syndicate's playbook, in November of 2017, the Crown Prince, Mohammed bin Salman (MBS), rounded up 400 of Saudis' wealthiest people, including princes, tycoons, and ministers, seized their assets, and detained them at the Ritz Carlton Hotel of Riyadh. The pretext given was fighting corruption, not unlike the high minded rhetoric used by Marxists or even the revolutionaries of the rational Enlightenment to justify stealing the assets of the privileged classed in order to consolidate the wealth and power of the syndicate.

Many conspiracy theories surround the events that transpired on September 11, 2001. This book will not explore them since that event is not the focal point of this book. However, it's worth noting that the Saudis were determined to prevent American citizens who lost relatives to the terrorist attacks from proceeding with litigation – and that the federal government sided with the Saudis.

In response to legislation that would seemingly create opportunities to hold the Saudis accountable for the attacks, the Saudis threatened to sell nearly $750 billion in treasury securities and other U.S. assets if the bill passed to prevent the assets from being frozen. The Saudis were key suspects in events of that day.

Essentially the legislation would have removed restrictions for sovereign nations, including Saudi Arabia, to be sued in U.S. courts. As it stands now, sovereigns, like the Queen of England, cannot be sued nor can federally recognized Indian tribes (sovereign nations) unless they agree to be sued.

Chief among Obama's concerns was that if restrictions were lifted for the Saudi government to be held liable for the events of September 11th, 2001, then he could be held liable for events other nations might perceive as war crimes. Perhaps this is a good thing that would prevent leaders the world over from engaging in human rights abuses and other crimes. Perhaps all of Rothschild's puppet leaders could be brought before a court and held accountable for their crimes. The truth is, there would be no warm without the syndicate's funding and bank loans. Wars incur tremendous debt, devastate lives, and are never in the national interests, unless in self-defense. In truth, no sovereign nation has grounds under international law to invade or pre-emptively strike another for the purposes of stealing resources, genociding people, and toppling governments to install puppet regimes. Perhaps if such restrictions were lifted, the public might come to understand, through discovery, how Obama became the first billionaire President.

Obama had his own liability concerns. For example, as the Voice of America reports, in 2013 the Obama Administration "formally formally acknowledged the killing of four Americans in drone strikes" a day or so before delivering a speech about "the legal principles, since 2009, supporting the use of drones against terrorist suspects, and about detention policies." Yet, as the VOA reports, "The use of drone warfare and targeted killings, including of Americans helping al-Qaida or affiliates, stirred major controversy during President Obama's first term and continues in his second."

Obama established a "targeted killing program that has been the cornerstone of U.S. counter-terrorism strategy," Just three days into his Presidency, Obama "authorized his first kinetic military action: two drone strikes, three hours apart, in Waziristan, Pakistan, that killed as many as 20 civilians," the Council on Foreign Affairs reports.

In an interview with Tucker Carlson, former Blackwater CEO Erik Prince said that Americans with guns will be not match for drones with guns, a chilling thought. Prince's company killed innocent civilians in Iraq while "providing security" following the U.S. invasion. His mercenary forces have not only provided security for the Communist Chinese along the Belt and Road Initiative, but he has been authorized to use "lethal force" to maintain security in areas devastated by hurricanes. Erik Prince runs the largest mercenary army in the world, which massacres civilians, smuggles arms, and commits atrocities. Erik Prince accepted a contract to spy on anyone who opposes Monsanto, which lies behind the destruction of 300,000,000 acres of farmland, 290,000 suicides in India, and a host of America's health problems, al Jazeera reports.

All considered, it's time for that legislation to be passed holding all sovereigns accountable for the crimes they commit, particularly since they are being undertaken by a crime syndicate that is demonstrably at war with humanity.

Saudi Political Consultants

Trump has received a lot of criticism for allowing the Saudis to pay for rooms at the Trump Hotel in Washington, DC – the site of the Old Post Office, which Jack Abramoff was in the process of acquiring before the federal investigation felled his career.

According to reports, no Saudis stayed at the hotel or paid money to the Trump Organization. Who did then? The occupants were lobbyists and consultants employed with the U.S. public relations firm, MSL Group -who were retained to petition the U.S. government to repeal the Justice Against Sponsors of Terrorism Act (JASTA) – which would have allowed U.S. citizens to be compensated for the terror attacks of September 11, 2001.

The MSLGroup is a part of the French multinational Publicis Group – which acquired the Sapient Corporation, forming Publicis Sapient, the world's largest digital network, with a presence in 100 countries worldwide.

The Chairman and Supervisory Board of Publicis is Maurice Lévy, who in 2006, was invited to a state dinner hosted by President George W. Bush in honor of the Rothschild-connected French President Nicolas Sarkozy, who alluded to "reconquering" the United States. "You know, I've come to Washington to bear a very simple, straight-forward message, and I bear it on behalf of all Frenchmen and women," he said. "I wish to reconquer the heart of America and I wish to reconquer the heart of America in a lasting fashion."

The event was attended by Secretary of Treasury Henry Paulson and French Minister of Finance Christine Lagarde. As President of the International Monetary Fund (IMF), Lagarde proposed "taking pensions and extending maturities of government debt to prevent redemption," *Armstrong Economics* reports. Lagarde remained IMF President until September of 2019, a month or so before a pandemic struck the world, prompting a global lockdown to curb the spread of the virus – at which point she assumed the Presidency of the European Central Bank.

Among the clientele of Publicis are a who's who of multinationals and elite-corporations – for example: Coca-Cola, Nestlé, L'Oréal,

Renault, McDonald's, Samsung, General Motors, Unilever, Walmart, Pfizer, IBM, Verizon, Heineken, Mars, Incorporated Adidas, Audi, Bayer, Chase, Disney, Fiat Chrysler Automobiles (FCA), GSK (GlaxoSmithKline), HSBC, Johnson & Johnson, Kellogg's, Mercedes-Benz, Nike, PepsiCo, Reckitt Benckiser, Toyota American Express, BMW, Canon, Colgate-Palmolive, Dell, ExxonMobil, Ford, General Mills, Intel, Mastercard, Netflix, Philips, Shell, Sony, Visa 3M, Airbnb, Cisco, eBay, FedEx, Goldman Sachs, Hilton, IBM, LinkedIn, Marriott International, Oracle, Red Bull, Siemens Target, UPS Allianz, Amazon, Boeing, Caterpillar, Chanel, Chevron, Emirates, Facebook, Gucci, Huawei, JPMorgan Chase, Louis Vuitton, Royal Dutch Shell, Siemens, Starbucks, Tesla, Tiffany & Co., Twitter, Volkswagen, Walt Disney Company, Warner Bros., Xerox, Yahoo, YouTube, Zurich Insurance Group, Accenture, Adobe, Bank of America, Barclays, Danone, FedEx, General Electric (GE), American Airlines, Oracle, Spotify, T-Mobile, Visa Inc., Accenture, AT&T, BP, CVS Health, Ferrari, Gap Inc., Hershey Company, Instagram, Kia Motors, Nestlé, Nintendo, PayPal, Ralph Lauren, Subaru, TD Bank Group, Twitter, United Airlines, Verizon, Volkswagen, Volvo, Whole Foods Market, Yum! Brands (owns KFC, Taco Bell, Pizza Hut), Zara, Zurich Insurance Group...

The company has a significant presence in BRICS nations, the United States, and the UK.

Saudi Investments

In March 2016, the ownership of Saudi Aramco was transferred to the Saudi Public Investment Fund (PIF), its sovereign fund – with a goal of listing five percent of its shares by 2017 – and amassing $2 trillion in assets by 2030.

The Saudis pursued strategic acquisitions into the United States. For example, Prince Alwaleed bin Talal, the kingdom's most famous billionaire investor, acquired stakes in Citigroup, Snap, and Twitter. PIF has acquired stakes in Uber and Tesla. In 2008, Sanabil, a subsidiary of PIF, was created with $5.3 billion in seed capital to invest abroad through strategic investments.

Trump, in return, has registered at least eight corporations in Saudi Arabia, including, for example, THC Jeddah Hotel and DT Jeddah Technical Services – corporation established as part of a hotel development project – set up August of 2015 around the time the first primaries were held for the Republican presidential candidates – and when Obama had signed off on the Clean Power Plan – aimed at combating climate change in which each state was assigned a goal of reducing carbon emissions – to be accomplished as each saw fit.

Meanwhile, as the Saudis sought outside investments to diversify their economy. PIF has stakes in a number of global-backed companies, including, for example, Boeing – and the Larry Summers-launched Meta Platforms (Facebook), which interfered in American presidential elections, first to help secure the election of Sen. Barack Obama– and, again, in 2016, on behalf of the Zionist Sen. Ted Cruz – and then, once Cruz conceded, to support Trump.

Saudi Arabia is also supporting China's AI development, as Microsoft's Bill Gates and Henry Kissinger, before his death, advise the Chinese government. A Saudi fund recently became the sole foreign investor in Zhipu AI, a Chinese startup to rival OpenAI – a company led by Sam Altman, with support from Kushner's brother, Microsoft, and Larry Summers. Kissinger had opened up channels to pass U.S. patents and technological advantages to American strategic competitors, creating the current dynamic in which the United States is no longer the market leader, but merely a mark foreign interests have exploited mercilessly for labor, intellectual property, and assets.

Barclay's reports that Russia and Saudi Arabia both have been vying for market share in China. Interestingly, part of Russia's success in China had been attributed to its willingness to accept Chinese yuan denominated currency for oil, reflecting that the petro-dollar is on the way out.

Notably, the PIF acquired ownership of Neom, as a global hub for technology, with Saudi Arabia *overtaking* Silicon Valley. Launched in 2017 by MBS as part of Saudi Arabia's 2030 plan, Neom is a futuristic city development project, located in the northwest of Saudi Arabia, bordering Jordan and Egypt. According to Neom's promotional materials, the project is "envisioned as a high-tech, sustainable city."

Neom aspires to be "a hub for various industries, including renewable energy, biotechnology, robotics, and tourism" while incorporating "cutting-edge technology and sustainable practices to create a city of the future." In a post-oil world, the city will be "powered entirely by renewable energy sources and feature advanced infrastructure, smart technologies, and a high quality of life for its residents."

Despite being the World Bank's "development partner," Saudi Arabia under MBS's leadership is less concerned with the needs of Saudi citizens and the underprivileged, and more focused on positioning the Kingdom as a "global leader in luxury tourism," by way of its strategic investment arm, the Neom Investment Fund.

MBS has already received criticism internationally over his human rights abuses – that include mass executions for those who hold an unpopular opinion or who are "terrorists." Reflecting indifference, if not callous disregard for the poor, in Jeddah, the Saudi government reportedly displaced at least 500,000 locals to build luxury apartments and hotels to attract foreigners for investment.

Yet the strategies Neom employs to achieve its economic goals are vintage syndicate – that is, destroying the lives of anyone who gets in their way of profits and development. MBS cleared over 6,000 individuals from villages connected to the Huwaitat tribe for a Neom project. The Kingdom denied the evictions took place, stating in a letter that "the process of population relocation passed through a number of phases beginning with consultation sessions, followed by citizens' reception and then the provision of development interventions," *Dezzem* reports.

The UN Human Rights Council condemned the genocide of at least three men who protested the alleged evictions, *Dezzem* reports. In a letter from its Permanent Mission to the United Nations, the Saudi Kingdom denied that three men were sentenced to death for criticizing the evictions to clear land for a Neom project, and promptly characterized them as terrorists affiliated with Daesh and al-Qaeda.

The BBC reports that Saudi forces were cleared to use "lethal force" to remove anyone who refused to relocate to clear land for a mega city connected to the Neom project. "Whoever continues to resist (eviction) should be killed, so it licensed the use of lethal force against whoever stayed in their home," Col. Rabih Alenezii told the BBC, which conceded that it was unable to independently confirm his allegations.

Neom is one of 14 giga projects being developed in Saudi Arabia as part of the Saudi Vision 2030 plan to shift the country's economy from its reliance on oil. Neom is reportedly the linchpin in MBS's Vision 2030, the BBC reports, adding that the Prince "will will let nothing stand in the way of the building of Neom," reflecting that development is fueled by greed, rather than the public interest.

MBS has been merciless in eliminating critics – by way of censorship, arrests, and even assassination, as demonstrated most notably in the murder of *Washington Post* reporter Jamal Khashoggi, a relative of Adnan Khashoggi who were murdered and dismembered by the Saudis after publicly criticizing the Saudi leadership.

As the Council on Foreign Relations' Richard Haas writes:

"A large part of the truth is undeniable: Khashoggi was murdered by individuals with close ties to the Saudi government and its *de facto* leader, Crown Prince Mohammed bin Salman (widely known as MBS). Weeks of official Saudi denials and lies only reinforced the conclusion – now also the reported judgment of the CIA – that the murder was premeditated and approved at the top. MBS's direct role may not be 100% proven, but most observers familiar with Saudi Arabia harbor little doubt. This is not a system that tolerates much freelancing.

"What makes the truth inconvenient is Saudi Arabia's strategic importance. The Kingdom still accounts for over 10% of global oil output. Its sovereign wealth fund sits on an estimated $500 billion. Israel, too, has indicated support for MBS, owing to his willingness to move in the direction of normalizing relations and, more important, the two countries' shared interest in countering Iranian influence in the region. And U.S. President Donald Trump's administration is standing by its man, so far refusing to acknowledge his role in Khashoggi's murder and resisting calls for sanctions against Saudi Arabia.

"What, then, should be done? Former US Secretary of State James A. Baker recently drew a parallel to U.S. policy toward China in 1989, at the time of the massacre of protesting students in Beijing's Tiananmen Square. George H.W. Bush's administration (of which I was a part) worked hard to thread the needle: introducing sanctions to convey displeasure with the Chinese government, but limiting the punishment and keeping lines of communication open."

Worse, the Trump Administration expressed little concern for Saudi Arabia's vicious silencing and murder of a journalist. As the Jewish *Forward* reports, "Jared Kushner reportedly argued that the firestorm over journalist Jamal Khashoggi's murder 'will pass, just as it did after other

Saudi errors like the kidnapping of the Prime Minister of Lebanon and the killing of a busload of children in Yemen'."

The Washington Post reports that Khashoggi was alarmed over the American media's fawning coverage of MBS. "America is being brainwashed," he told colleagues.

"In 2018, Saudi Crown Prince Mohammed bin Salman traveled to the United States to sell himself to the American public," the *Washington Post* reports. "The idea behind the visit — during which MBS, as the Crown Prince is known, met with everyone from President Donald Trump to Oprah Winfrey, with stops at media outlets, including *The Post* — was to present MBS as the modern, youthful face of reform in Saudi Arabia. But as he smiled for the cameras and dined in the Hollywood hills, Saudi Arabia was jailing critics, had started a destabilizing spat with Qatar, and was bombing Yemen."

"The Khashoggi murder fixed a view of the Crown Prince as brutish, thin-skinned, and psychopathic," *The Atlantic* reports.

In 2017, the year the Crown Prince hosted the Future Investment Initiative, he rounded up hundreds of wealthy Saudis and imprisoned them in Riyadh's Ritz-Carlton hotel on informal charges of corruption and then stripped them of their assets – a reported $100 billion in total. The arrests had been decreed by the monarch, King Salman, and expedited by MBS. Taking a page out of syndicate's playbook, the wealth of Saudi's ruling elite were seized by MBS, with some of the detained claimed to have been beaten and coerced.

The Ritz Carlton is a wholly owned subsidiary of the Marriott – and is connected to the Royal families, arms traffickers, intelligence, and essentially the crime syndicate leading back to Rothschild.

In another instance reported by the *Daily Mail*, an American citizen, 72-year-old Saad al-Madi, was imprisoned in Saudi Arabia over old tweets critical of MBS.

This same year, Saudi Arabia granted citizenship to a humanoid robot by the name of Sophia. Meanwhile an agenda was afoot to merge man with machine. In 2023, in a discussion with Israeli Prime Minister Bibi Netanyahu, OpenAI President Greg Brockman said that he believes that 2029 will witness the emergence of artificial general intelligence (AGI) – that is, artificial intelligence that far surpasses human level intelligence – and that in 2030, man will finally merge with machine. The panel discussion included Elon Musk and MIT physicist Max Tegmark.

In this discussion, the speakers explored two possible future scenarios for mankind – one of extinction – or one of "heaven" in which AGI eliminates poverty, hunger, and sickness by merging with machines, thereby finally achieving singularity.

Towards a New Normal

In 2019, before the first instance of covid was reported, Saudi Aramco launched its IPO for which its raised nearly $30 billion. MBS had hoped to drive up its valuation to $2 trillion. "Since the IPO, Aramco has remained a cash cow for the Saudi government, financing a mammoth economic drive to end the kingdom's 'oil addiction,' as the Crown Prince once called it."

In 2020, when covid was spreading throughout the world, Saudi Arabia assumed the Presidency of the G-20, or Group of 20, an international forum of the governments, central bank governors, and the European Union. The G20 countries represent the world's leading economies and account for a significant portion of global GDP, trade, and population. While originally planned for Riyadh, the capital city of Saudi Arabia, the G20 Leaders Summit was held remotely to accommodate the "safe distancing" requirements of the pandemic.

The G-20 leaders discussed the need for a coordinated global response to the pandemic, including efforts to develop vaccines and support economic recovery. They also spoke to debt relief to low-income countries – by way of the Debt Service Suspension Initiative (DSSI) and appealed for the IMF and World Bank to address debt sustainability. This latter agenda was critical given that global planners were relying upon the petro-dollar to develop the Third Word. Now they needed a fall back plan.

The 26th UN Climate Change Conference of the Parties was convened in Glasgow, Scotland, bringing together the representatives of governments international organizations, civil society, and the private sector to forge strategies on global climate action while Saudi Arabia strengthened its leadership role.

Saudi Arabia's Minister of Energy Prince Abdulaziz bin Salman highlighted the Kingdom's contribution to climate change, including the Saudi Green Initiative and Middle East Green Initiative championed by MBS, with a view towards achieving net zero carbon emissions by 2060 –

and establishing a center for climate technologies in the Middle East and North Africa.

Global planners emphasized the need for collective action to reduce the effects of climate change, and to provide facilities for the least developed countries to use clean fuel to provide food.

In remarks to the G20 Riyadh Summit, Saudi King Salman bin Abzulaziz stressed the need for "equitable" access to the tools needed to combat the coronavirus pandemic, including vaccines. "We have expressed our commitment ... to urgently mobilize resources – at the onset of the crisis, $21 billion to support global efforts to respond to the pandemic; and to distribute $11 trillion to support individuals and businesses," he said.

The pandemic also presented the opportunity to "expand our safety nets" to protect "those prone to losing their jobs or source of income" while the transition to the "New Normal" took place. To this end, the G-20 provided "emergency support to developing countries, including the G-20 Debt Service Suspension Initiative to the low-income countries."

At the same time, the G-20 announced that "we must prepare better for any future pandemic," implying that there were more to come; the "global economy" must be supported by "reopening our economies and borders to facilitate the mobility of trade and people." He also appealed to "coordination" to "support" for developing companies (to establish public-funded enterprises to "maintain the development already achieved over the past decades."

He also recommended creating "the conditions for a more sustainable economy" by way of a "Circulate Carbon Economy to achieve "our climate goals" and "affordable energy system."

The Circular Carbon Economy (CCE) refers to an approach to reduce carbon emissions and mitigate climate change by managing carbon resources more efficiently throughout the life cycle by reusing, recycling, and repurposing carbon-based materials and adopting sustainable practices to minimize carbon waste.

"Realizing that trade is a key driver of economic recovery," the Saudis adopted the Riyadh Initiative on the Future of the (World Trade Organization), "with the aim of making the multilateral trading system more capable to face any present or future challenge."

The G20 met for the first time in November of 2008 in Washington at the peak of the global financial crisis. "The outcomes achieved (since then) are ample proof that the G-20 is the most prominent forum for international cooperation and for tackling global crises," Saudi King Salman said. "Today, we are working together again to face another, deeper global crisis, that has ravaged people and economies."

Another conference – for the Future Investment Initiative sought to "invest in humanity." The Future Investment Initiative Institute (or FII Institute) is a nonprofit organization run by the Public Investment Fund, Saudi Arabia's main sovereign fund.

Yasir al-Rumayyan, chairman of the FII Institute board of trustees, reaffirmed the need for public-private partnerships to address global challenges. "By leveraging the enormous economic opportunities that will lie ahead in the post-covid era, we will catalyze the changes needed to achieve an equitable, prosperous future for all," Rumayyan said.

Saudi Aramco similarly aspires to achieve net zero emissions by 2050. *Arab News* reports Saudi Arabia has already invested $20 billion to "lead the world in artificial intelligence."

Trump campaigned on a $1 trillion infrastructure plan with promises to "fix our inner cities and rebuild our highways, bridges, tunnels, airports, schools, and hospitals." However, he never delivered. "The $1 trillion (later $1.5 trillion) package boiled down to a series of White House budget sketches, proposing to use $200 billion as an incentive for private investors, states, and localities to put up the remaining $800 billion," *Bloomberg* reports. But "the president's building vows never came to pass."

In 2019, Jared Kushner, a Senior Advisor in the Trump Administration and son-in-law to the President, attempted to launch a U.S. digital dollar. While the Federal Reserve was being merged into the Department of Treasury, Kushner thought it would be a good idea for the Fed to have its own central bank digital currency, or CBDC.

According to the Bank of International Settlements – the central bank for the central banks, no fewer than 86 percent of the central banks have researched the potential for digital currencies while about 60 percent are experimenting with this technology.

The Secretary of Treasury (which was then Steven Mnuchin) is the U.S. Governor and U.S. Executive Director of the International

Monetary Fund (IMF), an organization of 189 member countries which fosters global monetary cooperation and ultimately answers to Rothschild. The Treasury Secretary, therefore, is one of 24 directors who can exercise voting rights over the strategic direction of the IMF, with the United States ranking as its largest shareholder. The digital coin could potentially be used as a global currency to replace the dollar.

On May 29, 2019, under the Subject line, "Digital U.S. Dollar," Kushner emailed Mnuchin with a suggestion to assemble a group to "have a brainstorm" about the topic of a U.S. digital currency. "My sense is it could make sense, and also be something that could ultimately change the way we pay out entitlements as well as saving us a ton in waste, fraud, and also in transaction costs," Kushner wrote.

The email included a link to a blog written by OpenAI CEI Sam Altman in which Altman declared that the United States could "create the (cryptocurrency) winner."

Altman promoted a WorldCoin for global use – along with a universal basic income, or guaranteed income, anticipating a loss of jobs to automation.

In March of 2020, the Treasury Department held a crypto-summit that brought together "high ranking government officials from the Treasury, FinCEN, the FBI, and other agencies to meet face-to-face with crypto bigwigs from such firms as Coinbase, Xapo, Square, and Fidelity," according to emails acquired by CoinD

While working on a digital dollar, Kushner expressed interest in accepting bitcoin for real estate. In 2021, Ivanka Trump's luxury Miami apartments accepted crypto payments for condos from newly minted crypto millionaires and billionaires. According to local reports, the condo actively pursued "crypto millionaires and billionaires attracted by Miami's bitcoin-friendly reputation."

The Mayor of Miami had even met with Dogecoin (and Tesla) CEO Elon Musk, Twitter CEO Jack Dorsey, and Google CEO Eric Schmidt to convince them to set up shop there. "We're positioning ourselves for a future where half the world's billionaires are crypto billionaires, which will happen once bitcoin reaches $200,000," said Alex Sapir, the Chairman of Sapir Corp. "With cryptocurrencies already creating incredible worldwide wealth, it is real estate that will sustain that wealth and provide buyers with a legacy."

Kushner was "ahead of the curve in contemplating a digital dollar," *CoinDesk* reports. "Discussions for a central bank digital currency (CBDC) didn't pick up broadly until late 2019, after the announcement of Facebook's Libra project (received) ferocious backlash, and China got serious about its digital yuan."

According to *CoinDesk*, "Much of the push for a U.S. CBDC came from the private sector."

In February of 2023, Rothschild & Co expanded its North America reach with a new Miami office as the digital currency inched along. The Blockchain Association engaged Mnuchin through Kirkland & Ellis, the firm with a presence in Miami that represented Jeffrey Epstein and which had employed Alexander Acosta – the U.S. Attorney who provided the pedophile a "sweetheart deal," Ken Starr, the Trump/Epstein defense attorney; and Bill Barr, Trump Attorney General who intervened on behalf of Epstein.

The Rothschild Investment Fund, which was established by Lord Jacob Rothschild, announced plans to dump the U.S. dollar as the global reserve currency" and pursue gold-backed cryptocurrencies. Rothschild's Capital Partners then announced a prospective Kraken crypto-exchange. A note Rothschild sent to investors reflected that the Coinbase crypto-exchange earned $1.8 billion in the first quarter of 2021.

Vanity Fair reports that in 2018 Trump offered Bill Gates a job in the White House. "In an interview, (Gates) revealed he'd broached the topic of a universal flu shot with Trump, and that the President was uncharacteristically excited, so excited, in fact, that he asked Gates whether he wanted a job at the White House."

He then invited Gates to be his science advisor – an opportunity the Microsoft CEO rejected on rounds that it was not a good use of his time. However, the pandemic set off the agenda that benefited the Saudis Agenda 2030.

Google CEO Eric Schmidt worked with Kushner on a coronavirus track-and-trace surveillance system to give the government a near real-time view of the spread of coronavirus.

At Kushner's direction, the federal government attempted to compile a "national database of potentially sensitive health information," with critics drawing comparisons with the USA Patriot Act, that rolled back privacy protections and facilitated data harvesting. Kushner's company, Oscar Health, was reportedly given the contract to build the federal governments coronavirus website with help from Google.

Eric Schmidt, who is worth a reported $22 billion, invested $375 million in Kushner's AI healthcare group while Salar Kamangar, a longtime Google executive and former CEO of YouTube, joined the Oscar Board.

Linda Yaccarino, who played a key role in managing the Trump Administration's response to the coronavirus pandemic by way of reinforcing channels of communication with Big Business, NBC Universal, and the federal government. worked with the World Economic Forum, which promoted stakeholder capitalism, a cause celebre of Lynn Forester de Rothschild. Once Musk acquired Twitter (renamed X), she assumed a leadership role there.

Reports emerged that Trump and Texas Gov. Greg Abbott helped finalize the sale of the U.S. largest oil refinery, at Port Arthur, to Saudi Aramco in 2017. This sale gave the Saudis "complete control over the refinery," CNN reports. "They could then likely bring more of their own crude oil into the U.S. for refining and selling in the North American market."

Perhaps in gratitude for his efforts at the White House, in 2021, the PIF invested $2 billion into a private equity firm, Affinity Partners, that was established by Kushner. That same year, the Saudi sovereign fund injected $1 billion in the investment fund established by Mnuchin. In May 2022, it was reported that Kushner's firm, Affinity, Partners was planning to invest in Israel. With Kushner's help, the Saudi sovereign fund will also for the first time invest in Zionist state.

PIF has been characterized as among the least transparent sovereign wealth funds in the world. In 2016, *The Wall Street Journal* observed that none of the fund's investments were named – a curious dynamic given that Saudi's role as development partner of the World Bank. The governance structure of PIF has been called into question, specifically with respect to how much control MBS holds on decision making at PIF.

Yasir al-Rumayyan, the Governor of the PIF, raised concerns over MBS's plans to invest tens of billions of dollars buying international stock at the beginning of 2020, when covid was making its way around the globe. Perhaps he expected stocks to tank due to restricted commerce, allowing him to buy up corporate assets for pennies on the dollar with the expectation of a dramatic increase in value once the global economy reopened, transforming him into one of the wealthiest men on Earth. This strategy is reminiscent of that which the Rothschilds pursued during the Battle of Waterloo, which transformed them into the richest family in Europe.

Prince Alwaleed bin Talal has backed The Giving Pledge, led by Bill Gates and Warren Buffett, to give away most of what his own. However, far from being generous, this scheme allows the syndicate, under the cover of pseudo-philanthropy, to invest the public's money in ways that advance the Rothschild's wider objectives. It should be clear by now that a significant portion of the wealth obtained by so-called billionaires was acquired by way of public-private partnerships and other schemes which have redistributed the public's wealth to themselves.

Saudi Arabia and Qatar have established a 2.5 billion fund, backed by the Bill and Melinda Gates Foundation and the Islamic Development Bank. To "tackle problems that we all care about in countries we all care about," said Hassan Al-Damluji, head of Middle East Relations at the Gates Foundation. How about returning some of that money to the U.S. treasury to offset taxes for the overburdened American citizens, pay down the national debt, reinforce America's infrastructure, providing quality, affordable health care and affordable housing. Why is money being stripped from Americans, shipped overseas, and then invested in ways that do not directly help Americans?

Saudi Arabia was heavily aligned with corporate America. *Business Insider* wrote in 2020 that Saudi Arabia had invested billions of dollars purchasing stocks in Boeing, Disney, and Facebook.

In 2020, Saudi Arabia's sovereign wealth fund quadrupled the value of its U.S. stock portfolio to $9.8 billion, Business Insider reported. Its $300 billion Public Investment fund revealed stakes valued at over $500 million Boeing, Cisco, Disney, Facebook, Berkshire Hathaway, Starbucks, and other U.S. companies.

In October 2021, Golf Saudi, a division of the PIF, bankrolled the establishment of LIV Golf Investments, with world-renowned Australia golfer Greg Norman as its CEO. Norman, in turn, owns an estate on Jupiter Island, the center of the National Security State apparatus.

Norman also advised on golf courses in Saipan where Asian women were trafficked during Abramoff's representation of the

Commonwealth of Northern Mariana Islands as lobbyist for Preston Gates.

In 2014, the Imperial Pacific was granted a 25-year license to construct a casino in Saipan, with a proposed budget of $7.1 billion to accommodate 42,00 hotel rooms and 1,600 gaming tables, with a view to becoming "the most expensive integrated resort project ever."

The vision for the resort was laid out in a press release: "Imperial Pacific's plans for Saipan include at least a half dozen major hotel/casinos, private villas and other resort properties, shopping malls (for duty free shoppers) a huge conference center, world class golf courses ... and the world's largest winter park. The company is also investing millions of dollars to upgrade Saipan's airport and terminal facilities, build docks, and marinas for ultra large yachts and cruise ships, and improve access to the island's offshore coral reefs, which provide perhaps the best diving in the world."

Bloomberg reports that according to renderings, the resort was *to* "resemble a $1.5 million square foot mashup of the Forbidden City (in China) and Palace of Versailles (in France), with a 100 foot glass sculpture of an undulating dragon in the lobby reached via hallways drenched in golden filigree."

Imperial Pacific's CEO was Mark Brown, a "trusted Trump advisor," whom Trump had recruited to serve as CEO of his casinos in Atlantic City during the "Golden Age of gaming."

Critics wondered how the casino would ever show a profit in a part of the world where incomes were so depressed. Ever optimistic, Brown said in a released statement that he was "expecting fantastic results" and that the he was "already accepting bookings from China and Japan when this very special facility opens for business in the auspicious Chinese Year of the Chicken."

It would not be long before the FBI began investigating allegations of money laundering due to its high transaction volume connected to "high rollers, including Chinese who sometimes bet millions of dollars at a time."

In September of 2016, Imperial Pacific reported $3.9 billion in bets, "meaning that the 100 or so high rollers whom it says come through its doors monthly waged an average of $39 million," Bloomberg reports. "The story of how Saipan's casino came to enjoy such dazzling success is a tale of money and political intrigue that stretches across the Pacific, connecting it to top power brokers in Washington and New York....Above all, it links the island with the burgeoning ranks of China's super-rich and fathomless wealth obtained legitimately or otherwise that they're moving around the world."

Serving as Board Members of the new casino project were prominent Democratic and Republican luminaries, including James Woolsey,who ran the CIA for President Bill Clinton and provided national security advice to the Trump presidential campaign; Louis Freeh, an FBI Director for Presidents Bush and Clinton; Former DNC Chair Ed Rendell, and former RNC Chair and Abramoff rival Haley Barbour.

After his inauguration, Trump tapped casino rival and fellow billionaire Steve Wynn to serve as finance chairman for the Republican National Committee, giving him a leading role in raising money for the GOP to elect (and re-elect) leaders who would support Trump. Among Wynn's notable accomplishment was selling his company, Mirage Resorts to MGM Grand, resulting in the formation of MGM Mirage, which is in business with the Seminoles.

The CNMI's "world class" golf courses were designed by Australian golf legend Greg Norman, a friend of Presidents Bill Clinton who has designed golf courses for Trump.

In 2015, the Beijing office of a prominent Chinese law firm, Decheng (大成) was appointed legal adviser to the Metallurgical Corporation of China, a company "carrying out the integrated resort construction project for Imperial Pacific" in Saipan, "conducting a civil infrastructure construction project" and laying the foundation to "undertake projects in developed countries such as the United States and the Europe (sic) in the future."

That year, Dentons, a prominent U.S. firm which counts the most elite financial, pharmaceutical, defense contractors, oil companies, and global corporations as its clients, merged with Decheng and was retained in 2016 as the CNMI's registered lobbyist.

As President of the United States, Trump appointed a Dentons partner to handle all compliance and ethics matters for the White House, raising possible conflicts of interests surrounding Trump and related interests overseas. With offices in Riyadh and Jeddah, Dentons is one of Saudi Arabia's leading law firms.. Having advised the Kingdom for over 40 years, Dentons "understands the strategic framework and objectives of Vision 2030."

The New York Times reports that "Saudi Arabia has already launched a hostile takeover of professional golf. It has invested billions of dollars in world soccer. Now it wants to own professional boxing too." Does this sound like the Saudis are interested in mitigating world poverty or in owning the world?

In 2023, Kirkland & Ellis, the firm that vigorously defended Jeffrey Epstein in pedophile matters, opened an office in Riyadh. "The Kingdom is one of the fastest growing economies and a rapidly modernizing country that is quickly becoming increasingly significant for Kirkland's client case," the firm announced in a public statement. "Saudi Arabia recently amended its rules allowing foreign law firms to operate independently in the country. Kirkland is the world's largest law firm, generating $6.5 billion in revenue in 2022.

The Next Pandemic, Permanent Lockdowns

Based in the Bahamas, Sam Bankman-Fried (SBF) was marketed as an eccentric tech prodigy whose genius and work ethic were such that he slept on beanbags and played video games in important meetings while effortlessly building a crypto-exchange that transformed him into a tech billionaire. The networks, agenda, and dynamics surrounding the failed FTX exchange and its disgraced founder are all too familiar. He was released on $250 million bail after his first court appearance facing fraud charges concerning the collapse of FTX, the cyptocurrency exchange he "co-founded."

For the purposes of this book, the focus will turn its attention to SBF's younger brother, Gabe Bankman-Fried (GBF), who worked for Guarding Against Pandemics (GAP) – an organization into which SBF invested some $22 million in 2021. "We need all Americans to work together to stop the next pandemic before it starts," GAP's website implores. "That's why GAP is pushing Congress to include a $30 billion investment in the upcoming budget reconciliation bill – less than one percent of the total cost of the bill – to prevent the next pandemic."

With great prescience, GAP professed to "already know what diseases may cause the next pandemic" and so positioned itself to "develop, approve, and manufacture therapeutics and vaccines so we can save millions of lives." As GAP discerned, pandemics were good for businesses. "The next pandemic will likely be spread primarily indoors," GAB writes. "We need to pandemic-proof our buildings."

The most "effective way to curb pandemics," according to GAP, is to "test everyone as frequently as possible. We need to develop tests for possible pathogens in advance and be ready to scale them up and distribute them immediately."

GAP determined that the pandemic had inflicted $16 trillion worth of damage to the United States – or what amounted to 90 percent of the annual gross domestic product. Reminiscent of the World Wars, society was being destroyed and rebuilt by corrupt, self-interested parties for the purposes of reorganizing the world's wealth and power under themselves by way of public-private partnerships

For guidance on the financial aspects of the pandemic, GAP looked to David Cutler and economist Larry Summers, reflecting a familiar network and agenda at play. Far from being independent analysts, Summers has partnered with Rothschild on business deals, such as Genie Energy for which Summers, "Lord" Jacob Rothschild, Vice President Dick Cheney, former CIA Director James Woolsey, and Gov. Bill Richardson served as Advisors.

Cutler was on the payroll of the Pharmaceutical Research and Manufacturers of America (PhRMA) a former client of the Alexander Strategy Group, which dedicated $150 million to an advertising campaign to promote President Barack Obama's Affordable Care Act (ACA) in which the Bush-aligned pharmaceutical company, Eli Lilly, is a dues-paying member. (Former CIA Director and President George H.W. Bush served on Eli Lilly's Board of Directors; Mitch Daniels, former Director of President George W. Bush's Office of Management and Budget, was an Eli Lilly Vice President; Sidney Taurel, an Advisory Council Member of President George W. Bush's Department of Homeland Security, was Eli Lilly CEO.)

Eli Lilly has sponsored retreats for ministers through its foundation, helping to convince pastors to carry water for the pharmaceutical company.

By 2020, covid posed "the greatest threat to prosperity and well being the United States has encountered since the Great Depression," Summers and Cutler wrote. "This viewpoint aggregates *mortality, morbidity, mental health conditions, and direct economic losses."* They assigned the *"statistical life"* of every American a *"conservative value"* of seven million dollars a piece.

The solutions this group offered were consistent with what Senior Trump Advisor Jared Kushner – and Eric Schmidt were proposing – that of contact tracing and covid testing, citing a Rockefeller Foundation report that predicted that 30 million weekly covid tests could generate $75 billion in revenue while contact tracing could produce $100 billion, with the government financing the products and services and bypassing the democratic process to eliminate individual choice.

Among the solutions promoted by Cutler and Summers were "<u>isolation established permanently</u> and not dismantled when concerns about covid-19 begin to recede," or what they billed at the time as "the new normal" – that of a top-down imposed technocracy connecting people, employers, banks, transportation, education, and service providers into an "Internet of things" controlled through automation.

With 15-minute Smart cities in which gas-fueled cars were reduced in number, until eliminated altogether, people were being forced to rely upon electric cars and have their homes and lives completely automated through 5G, with their every expenditure monitored, taxed, and rationed, based upon and driven by social credit scores tied to bank accounts and determined by the whims of the gatekeepers and controllers, like Summers and the Rothschilds, who stood to profit handsomely through the new system they were creating.

The agenda was neither Republican nor Democratic, but technocratic. Reflecting an agenda overlapping both political parties, GBS donated money to the head of President Trump's Operation Warp Speed – who happened to be the former head of the vaccine department at the Rothschild-backed GlaxoSmithKline (GSK) which was awarded $2.1 billion to develop and manufacture a coronavirus vaccine while its chief scientist advised Trump and was paid by Bankman-Fried, who took guidance from Summers.

When funding was being disbursed during the Coronavirus Aid, Relief, and Economic Security (CARES) Act, Schmidt joined the Hamilton Project, alongside Carlyle Consulting founder David Rubenstein and a host of Obama Administration officials to advise the Trump Administration on how the federal government should spend the public's money to respond to the covid threat.

Prior to the GAP, GBF worked for Civis Analytics, a data analytics firm founded by Obama staffers and bankrolled by Schmidt. In 2021, Civis raised $30.7 million from Silicon Valley Bank, whose investors included Chinese and Israeli tech companies and Peter Thiel.

Once SVB collapsed, its London branch was acquired by the Jeffrey Epstein-connected Hong Kong and Shanghai Banking Corporation (HSBC) Bank for £1. The Vice President of Research at Civis was Maeve Ward, the Deputy Director of Public Engagements for the Bill & Melinda Gates Foundation which helped plan and fund the global response to the pandemic and whose trustee was Berkshire Hathaway billionaire Warren Buffett.

The CEO of Civis is Dan Wagner, a member of the Aspen Institute and Council on Foreign Relations who used analytics to optimize voter targeting to garner the greatest return on investment in campaign ads for Obama while receiving strategic guidance from Schmidt. A division of the Aspen Institute is Aspen Digital, whose sponsors include Schmidt Futures – an organization founded by Eric Schmidt. According to Schmidt's website, the world is "much better (since) more than 70 percent of the world's population has now received a dose of a Covid-19 vaccine."

Rothschild's RIT Capital Partners funds Aspen Digital, a division of the Aspen Institute that is behind an online platform intended to serve as a single portal that manages crypto-investments and which receives backing from such entities as Google, Amazon, AT&T, and Schmidt Futures. Aspen Digital has partnered with Liberty City Ventures, a venture capital firm based in New York that invests in blockchain, e-commerce, and the "Internet of Things," which is leading efforts to create Smart, 15-minute cities.

The Aspen Institute established a Henry Crown Fellows program to "develop the next generation of leaders" through the Aspen Global Leadership Network (http://www.aspeninstitute.org/crown), whose fellows include a who's who of technocrats. Crown was a billionaire American industrialist who established a company that merged with General Dynamics and owned the Empire State Building, which sits in the real estate portfolio of Leona Helmsley, who funds Vatican conferences featuring technocrats and representatives of Big Pharma. The Helmsley building in New York houses Burson-Marsteller, the agent for the Saudi Basic Industries Corporation (SABIC).

According to Schmidt Futures, the world can be made "much better (by) reimagining the basic meaning of life and death, (giving) more people access to the opportunity through electrification, and (harnessing) technologies from artificial intelligence to biology for good."

To this end, the Schmidt-backed organization is "seeding" a taskforce for "the next wave of innovation in synthetic biology and a bio-economy," in which bodies, genders, identities can be re-imagined through trans-humanism overseen by an AI God.

With aspirations for a "net zero carbon economy," Schmidt is exploring genome editing, artificial intelligence, automation, and miniaturization to "accelerate the U.S. bio-economy towards $4 trillion over the next 10 to 20 years."

Schmidt partners with the Rhodes Trust, which was established by Cecil Rhodes on behalf of the Rothschilds for the purpose of consolidating the world's wealth and power into the hands of the few and restoring the United States to the status of a British colony.

Among the MTG's most well-heeled contributors were Schmidt, LinkedIn Co-Founder Allen Blue; Chris Vargas, the founder of Emerging Cities; Facebook co-founder Dustin Moskovitz; Jill Parker of Planned Parenthood; and venture capitalist Russell Siegelman, a Partner of Kleiner Perkins, an early investor in a number of prominent technology and bio-tech firms including Amazon, America Online, Beyond Meat, Google, Netscape, Sun Microsolutions, Twitter, among many others.

Building on the electronic election system backed by Rothschild, MTG sought to "empower private political donors to strengthen our democracy by providing them with evidence-based guidance on the electoral strategies, tactics, and programs that are likely to achieve the greatest impact in a given election."

At the same time, they have flooded the political process with money that has undermined and corrupted, not strengthened, the nation's democracy.

While launching Guarding Against Pandemics, GBF worked as a congressional aide to Rep. Sean Casten (D-IL), who helped establish the Regional Greenhouse Gas Initiative, with the goal of zero carbon emissions by 2050. As always, Summers was leading the way. A reminder of his credentials and affiliations:

Senior Economist, World Bank

Multiple roles, Department of Treasury, Clinton Administration
President, Harvard University
Member, G-30
Director, Teach for America, backed by the Bill & Melinda Gates Foundation
Member, Global Development Advisory Panel, Gates Foundation
Chair, Policy Board, Harvard AIDS Institute
Board, Brookings Institution
Board, Center on Global Development
Board, Institute for International Economics
Board, Global Fund for Children's Vaccines
Board, Partnership for Public Service
Member, Council on Foreign Relations
Member, Trilateral Commission
Members, Bretton Woods Committee
Member, Council on Competitiveness
Member, UNCTAD Panel of Eminent Persons

Hamilton's Technocrats

In 2006, former Clinton Administration officials established the Hamilton Project, an economic policy initiative with the Brooking Institution. According to its literature, the official purpose of the Hamilton Project is to "advance America's promise of opportunity, prosperity, and growth." The group reportedly closed shop in 2009 so its members could work in the Obama Administration to advance the global green agenda. The group was relaunched in 2010, with Michael Greenstone, an MIT Environmental Economics Professor as its new director. Greenstone went on to advise the Secretary of Energy within the Trump Administration and serve as co-director of a member of the advisory board to the London School of Economics-directed IGC Climate Change, Environment and Natural Resources Research program. Hamilton advised the Trump Administration on budgetary priorities during the covid lockdown. The following is a list of current members of the Hamilton Advisory Council and their affiliations:

Roger Altman

Founder and Sr. Chair of Evercore – the "most active" independent banking advisory firm, with more than $14 billion assets under management – and whose investment advisory arm holds $1.5 trillion in "announced transactions."
Clinton Administration Deputy Secretary of the Treasury
Facilitated the passage of the North Atlantic Free Trade Agreement (NAFTA)
Considered for replacement of Larry Summers as National Economic Council Director in Obama Administration
Advised on AstraZeneca's $39 billion acquisition of Alexion Pharmaceuticals
MIT Trustee
Recipient, 2001 Nobel Prize in Economics

Karen Anderson

Managing Director, Hamilton Project
Chief of Staff, Council of Economic Advisers, Obama Administration
Regional Coordinator, White House Office of Political Affairs, Clinton Administration
Vice President of State and Local Government Relations for Citigroup, which advised on Saudi Arabia's first international multi-billion dollar bond sale.

Larry Summers

Secretary of Treasury, Clinton Administration
Director, National Economic Council, Obama Administration
Vice President, Development Economics and Chief Economist, World Bank
Professor Emeritus, Harvard University

Eric Schwartz

Professor, Harvard University

CEO, Global Equities and Investment Management Divisions, Goldman Sachs
Co-head, Partnership Committee, Goldman Sachs – to supervise and promote partners around the world
Chair, City Harvest – largest "food rescue and redistribution non-profit" in the United States whose partners include the Starr Foundation (established by AIG founder CV Starr whose nephew is Ken Starr), Credit Suisse (The credit side off the Swiss Banking Industry for which "Bilderbergers" are reportedly representative shareholders), Warburg Pincus, American Express, Citi, Leona Hemsley Charitable Trusts, Blackstone, BlackRock, Feeding America, Mandarin Oriental)

Joshua L. Steiner

Partner, SSW (private investment firm)
Senior Adviser and Head of Industry Vertical and Bloomberg,
Co-founder and Vice President, Quadrangle Group, LLC (private equity and asset management firm)
Managing Director, Lazard Frères & Co. LLC.
Chief of Staff, U.S. Department of Treasury, Clinton Administration
Policy Advisor, Economics, Obama Administration
Board Member, Yale University, International Rescue Committee

Tom Steyer

Founder, Farallon Capital Management, a multi-strategy global investment business ($36 billion assets under management)
Partner, Member of Investment Committee, Hellman & Friedman, multi-billion dollar private equity firm.
Passionate climate activist
Co-founder, Beneficial State Bank, founded with over $1 billion in assets
Founder, NextGen America, "the largest youth voter mobilization organization in American history"
220 Democratic Presidential Candidate

Co-Chair, California Gov. Gavin Newsom's Business and Jobs Recovery Task Force
Co-Chair, Vice President Biden's Climate Engagement Advisory Council to mobilize climate voters.

Ralph Schlosstein

Chairman Emeritus, Co-Chair of Board of Directors, and co-CEO, Evercore, which caters to "high net worth individuals"
CEO, HighView Investment Group
Co-founder and Director, BlackRock
Managing Director, Investment Banking, Lehman Brothers (started the firm's interest rate swap business and led the mortgage and savings institutions group)
Deputy Assistant Secretary of the Treasury
Associate Director, White House Domestic Policy Staff
Economist, Congressional Joint Economic Committee
Member, Council on Foreign Relations
Director, Pulte Corp., the nation's largest homebuilder
Member, Visiting Board of Overseers, John F. Kennedy School of Government, Harvard University

Eric Schmidt

CEO and Chairman, Google
Founder, Schmidt Futures ("A philanthropic initiative that bets early on exceptional people making the world better")
Founder, Special Competitive Studies Project (Non-profit initiative focused on strengthening America's long-term AI and technological competitiveness in national security, the economy, and society)

Howard Marks

Co-founder and Co-Chairman, Oaktree Capital Management
Group leader and Chief Investment Officer, TCW Group – responsible for investments in distressed debt, high yield bonds, and convertible securities

Vice President and Senior Portfolio Manager, Citicorp Investment Management

Kriston Alford McIntosh

Chief Communications and Marketing Officer, ACLU

Glenn Hutchins

Chair, North Island Ventures
Co-Founder of Silver Lake
Board of Director, AT&T
Chair of CARE
Vice Chair, Obama Foundation
Member, Investment Board and International Advisory Board of GIC Private Limited – sovereign wealth fund of Singapore
Director, Nasdaq
Director, Audit/Risk Committee, Federal Reserve Bank of New York
Special Advisor, Economic and Healthcare Policy, Clinton Administration
Director, Harvard Management Co.
Co-Chair, Harvard University's capital campaign
Founder, Hutchins Family Foundation – to support construction of Obama Presidential Center
Founder, Hutchins Center for African & African American Research, Harvard University
Founder, Hutchins Center on Fiscal and Monetary Policy, Brookings Institution

Suzanne Nora Johnson

Vice Chair, Goldman Sachs Group
Chair, Global Markets Institute
Attorney, Simpson, Thacher & Barlett (Firm represented underwriters of Google's $2.7 billion IPO and its $1.65 billion acquisition of YouTube; JPMorganChase; Tesla in its IPO;Facebook, which the firm "launched" by assisting the underwriters of its $16 billion IPO;

Alibaba Group Holding, Ltd. - China's Amazon – in its IPO; Microsoft in its $26 billion acquisition of LinkedIn and in its $7.5 billion acquisition of GitHub. Challenge anti-semitic incidents at elite law schools, warning that an escalation of incidents targeting Jewish students would have corporate hiring consequences.)
Board Member, AIG, Intuit, Inc., Pfizer, Visa, Broad Foudnation, Brokings Institute, Carnegie Institution for Science, Markle Foundation; University of Southern California.
Chair, Global Agenda Councils, World Economic Forum
Henry Crown Fellow, Aspen Institute

Lawrence Katz

Professor, Harvard University
Research Associate, National Bureau of Economic Research
Author, Race between Education and Technology
"Wage inequality" expert

Melissa S. Kearney

Director, Aspen Economic Strategy Group
Co-Chair, MIT's J-PAL State and Local Innovation Initiative
"Poverty, inequality, and social policy expert"

Timothy F. Geithner

Chair, Warburg Pincus, Warburg Pincus, a global private equity firm
Secretary of Treasury, Obama Administration
President and CEO, Federal Reserve Bank of New York
Undersecretary for International Affairs under Secretaries Robert Rubin and Larry Summers
Chair, Program on Financial Stability, Yale University School of Management
Co-chair, Board of Directors, International Rescue Committee (https://www.rescue.org-- which is facilitating international migration of refugees due to "climate change" and covid.)
Co-chair, Aspen Economic Strategy Group.

Member, Group of Thirty (G30) - an international body of financiers and academics which aims to deepen understanding of economic and financial issues and to examine consequences of decisions made in the public and private sector
Author, Stress Test: Reflections on Financial Crises
Co-edited, First Responders, *with Ben S. Bernanke and Henry M. Paulson, Jr.(Explores working on the frontlines of the 2007-8 financial crisis)*

Bob Greenstein

Founder and President Emeritus, Center on Budget and Policy Priorities
Recipient, Heinz Award for Public Policy for "improving the economic outlook of many of America's Member, Policy Translation Working Group of NASI's COVID-19 Task Force
Member, Advisory Committee, Harvard University's John F. Kennedy School of Government
Administrator, Food and Nutrition Service, U.S. Department of Agriculture, Carter Administration – directed agency that operated federal food assistance programs, like food stamp
Designed Food Stamp Act of 1977
Member, Commission on Entitlement and Tax Reform, Clinton Administration
Chief Economist, President's Council of Economic Advisers, Obama Administration – where he co-led the development of the U.S. Government's "social cost of carbon."
Professor of Economics, MIT
Director, Hamilton Project
Influences policy within the United States and globally, focusing on "the global energy challenge that requires all societies to balance the needs for inexpensive and reliable energy, protection of the public's health from air pollution, and minimizing the damages from climate change. Recently, his research has helped lead to the United States Government quadrupling its estimate of the damages from climate change, the adoption of pollution markets in India, and the use of machine learning techniques to target environmental inspections.

Co-Director, Climate Impact Lab
Creator, Air Quality Life Index – converted air pollution concentrations into their impact on life expectancy
Co-founder, Climate Vault – uses markets to allow institutions and people to reduce their carbon footprint and foster innovation in carbon dioxide removal.

Ben Harris

Assistant Secretary of Economic Policy and Chief Economist U.S. Treasury Department
Executive Director, Kellogg Public-Private Initiative
Chief Economist, Vice President Joe Biden
Senior Economist, White House Council of Economic Advisers
Senior Economist, Budget Committee in the U.S. House of Representatives
Fulbright Scholar

Michael Froman

President, Council on Foreign Relations
Vice Chair, Mastercard
Chairman, Mastercard Center for Inclusive Growth
U.S. Trade Representative, Obama Administration – concluded the Trans-Pacific Partnership agreement in the Asia Pacific and negotiations toward a Transatlantic Trade and Investment Partnership with the European Union; the negotiation of agreements on trade facilitation, agriculture and information technology products at the World Trade Organization; the monitoring and enforcement of U.S. trade rights; and congressional passage of Trade Promotion Authority, the African Growth and Opportunity Act, the Generalized System of Preferences program, and the Trade Facilitation and Trade Enforcement Act.
Assistant to President, Obama Administration
Deputy National Security Advisor, International Economic Affairs – responsible for coordinating policy on international trade, finance, energy, climate change, and development issues.

"U.S. sherpa" (Tibetan-style gofer?) for the Group of Twenty and Group of Eight Summits
Staffed, APEC Leaders Meetings
Co-chaired, Major Economies Forum on Energy and Climate, the Transatlantic Economic Council, the U.S.-India CEO Forum, and the U.S.-Brazil CEO Forum.
Played leading role in the launch of several of the Obama administration's development initiatives, including Power Africa and Trade Africa.
CEO, various divisions, Citigroup
Senior Fellow, Council on Foreign Relations
Resident Fellow, German Marshall Fund
Deputy Assistant Secretary, Eurasia and Middle East, U.S. Department of Treasury
Director, International Economic Affairs, National Security Council and National Economic Council

Jason Furman

Professor, Harvard University
Senior Fellow, Peterson Institute for International Economics
Chairman, Council of Economic Advisors, Obama Administration
Member, Council on Foreign Relations, G30, and Economic Strategy Group
Trustee, Russell Sage Foundation (supports Yale's Skull & Bones)

Mark Gallogly

Co-Founder, Three Cairns Group – a social impact firm focused on climate through venture investing, philanthropy, and public policy.
Senior Advisor, Special Presidential Envoy for Climate John Kerry, U.S. Department of State
Co-founder, Centerbridge Partners, an investment firm with over $30 billion of assets under management that deploys capital in private equity, real estate, and credit investing.
Blackstone Group

Member, Council on Jobs and Competitiveness, Obama Administration

Douglas W. Elmendorf

Professor, Harvard University
Director, Congressional Budget Office, Obama Administration
Senior Economist, White House's Council of Advisers
Deputy Assistant Secretary for Economic Policy, Treasury Department
Assistant Director of Division of Research and Statistics, Federal Reserve Board
Concentrations: budget policy, health care issues, the macroeconomic effects of fiscal policy, Social Security, income security programs, financial markets, macroeconomic analysis and forecasting

William C. Dudley

Chairs, Bretton Woods Committee
Co-leader, Digital Team
Member, G-30 and Council on Foreign Relations
President and CEO, Federal Reserve Bank of New York
Vice Chair, Federal Open Marekt Committeet
Executive Vice President, Markets Group, Federal Reserve of New York
Managing Director and Partner, Goldman Sachs (chief U.S. economist for a decade)
Vice President, Morgan Guaranty Trust Company (which financed Bolshevik Revolution)

Blair Effron

Co-founder, Centerview Partners, a leading independent investment banking and advisory firm with offices in New York, Chicago, London, Los Angeles, Palo Alto, Paris, and San Francisco. Since its founding in 2006, firm has advised on over $3 trillion in transactions and ranks among the most active firms globally in strategic advisory. (Rahm

Emanuel headed of Centerview's Chicago Office; former Secretary of Treasury Robin Rubin is counselor to the firm)
Board of Trustees, Council on Foreign Relations

Judy Feder

Promoted healthcare reform as Staff Director, Congressional Pepper Commission (Chaired by Sen. John D. Rockefeller, IV)
Deputy Assistant Secretary, Department of Health and Human Services, Clinton Administration

Ray Dalio

Global marco investor for more than 50 years
Founder, Bridgewater Associates – largest hedge fund in the world

Brian Deese

Current Innovation Fellow, MIT and Center for Energy and Environmental Policy Research – focusing on climate change and promoting sustainable economic growth
Director, White House National Economic Council, Biden Administration, coordinating economic agenda
Senior Advisor, Obama Administration
<u>Negotiated Paris Climate Agreement</u>
Global Head of Sustainable Investing, BlackRock, focusing on climate and sustainable risk in investment portfolios, "creating investment strategies to help accelerate low carbon transition."
Acting Director, Office of Management and Budget
Deputy Director, National Economic Council

Steven A. Denning

Chairman Emeritus, General Atlantic, LLC, global private equity firm, with over $20 billion of assets under management
Director, Engility Corp.
McKinsey & Co.

Chairman of the Board of Trustees, Stanford University
Co-chair, Board of Directors, The Nature Conservancy
Board of Directors Council on Foreign Relations
Emeritus Director, National Parks Conservation Association
Board, Bridgespan Group, McKinsey Investment Group, Investment Office Advisory Council

John Deutsch

Professor, MIT
Director, CIA
Deputy Secretary of Defense
Acting Assistant Secretary, Department of Energy
President's Commission on Reducing and Protecting Government Secrecy
Chairman, Commission to Assess the Organization of the Federal Government to Combat the Proliferation of Weapons of Mass Destruction
Director, American Natural Resources, Citigroup, CMS Energy, Raytheon, SAIC....
Trustee, Center for American Progress
Board, Council on Foreign Relation

George Akerlof

Recipient, Nobel Prize in Economist
Co-author (with Janet Yellen), Efficiency Wage Models of the Labor Market

Alan Blinder

Columnist, Wall Street Journal
Vice Chairman, Board of Governors, Federal Reserve System
Member, Council of Economic Advisers, Clinton Administration
Economic Adviser, Al Gore, John Kerry, and Hillary Clinton, members of Congress, and various office holders

Co-Director, Center for Economic Policy Studies, Princeton University

    Through the The Coronavirus Aid, Relief, and Economic Security (CARES) Act, "the top one percent of Americans have taken $50 trillion from the bottom 90 percent." Time *magazine reports of the $2.2 trillion economic stimulus signed by President Donald trump in March of 2020 in response to the economic fallout of the covid-19 pandemic in the United States.*

XIII.
Building BRICs for the New Abnormal

> "Our Constitution was made only for a moral and religious people. It is wholly inadequate to the government of any other."
>
> **President John Adams**
> *American Founding Father*

BRICS, linking the emerging markets of Brazil, Russia, India, China – and later, South Africa into a common market, were two decades in the making. The group did not emerge overnight nor is it even close to being realized. While the petro-dollar is a relic of the past, ending June 9, 2024, the dollar remains a strong reserve currency that is used the world over, and far from being rendered obsolete. Global planners are simply reorganizing the chess board to keep development targets on track.

That the petro-dollar was on borrowed time was acknowledged at the end of the Clinton Administration – coinciding with the rise of China. Among the proponents of China's entry into the World Trade Organization was Treasury Secretary Larry Summers, a principal architect of the U.S. financial system (and arguably, not for the better).

Speaking before a Closed Plenary Session of the China-U.S. Joint Economic Committee in October of 2000, Summers said, "This year we have opened a new chapter in the relationship between our two countries -- and in China's relations with the rest of the global economy. (In 1999,) questions of Chinese entry into the World Trade Organization, and the changes that it would bring, were also very much on all our minds. One year on, with the signing of our bilateral agreement for Chinese entry into the World Trade Organization, and the passage of legislation here in the U.S. to grant China Permanent Normal Trading Relations status, China is closer than ever to becoming an integral member of the world trading community." China had been allowed to join the world trading community without any attempts to ensure its compliance with Western standards and mode of conduct. Congressman Tom DeLay predicted that China would become more like West. Instead the West has become more like China.

With concerns that the overproduction of Saudi oil fields precluded the availability of cheap gas, the United States would eventually be unable to rely upon the Saudis to purchase its U.S. treasuries or support the petro-dollar – for the purposes of developing the world.

Saudi Arabia was the World Bank's key development partner through which the hi-jacked United States, under Rothschild control, was projecting its hegemony and "developing the world" – that is, establishing a global monopoly for Rothschild-backed corporations. The world needed to change course to keep Rothschild's New World Order on track. The solution was provided by the City of London.

On November 30, 2001, a little over a week before China was inducted as a member of the WTO, Jim O'Neill, the Head of Global Economic Research for Goldman Sachs in London, published a paper, *Building Better Global Economic BRIC*, providing the conceptual framework for what would become BRICS.

In an article written for the IMF, O'Neill sought to "make a case for changing the framework for global economic governance, not necessarily the inevitable future growth of these countries." In other papers, he "laid out what the world *could* look like, in the highly unlikely event that the countries we studied reached their potential."

"Because of their population size, the associated size of their workforce, and the scope for productivity catch-up, it was quite easy to show that the potential growth rates of BRICs were higher than those of most advanced economies," he writes. "What our analysis was *not* meant to show was that all these countries would persistently grow at their potential. That frankly is not realistic, and not what we intended as our message. *My primary goal was to make a case for changing the framework for global economic governance.*"

Some BRICS countries he conceded recently, "need to diversify their economies away from commodities and grow the role of the private sector. In contrast, the ongoing strength of the Chinese economy suggests that it is fully achieving its potential. China's GDP, in excess of $14 trillion (as of 2019), is more than twice that of the other BRICS in aggregate. The sheer scale of China means that the BRICS economies combined are now larger than that of the European Union and are approaching the size of the United States."

It should be clear from the outset that BRICS is a creation of the financial interests surrounding the City of London, and just another manifestation of Rothschild's efforts to corral the world's wealth and power into the hands of the few. When one strategy runs its course, another is conceived, possibly going in a different direction in order to arrive at the final, intended destination Consider the background and affiliations of O'Neill:

Commercial Secretary to the Treasury to Prime Minister David Cameron, a client of Jim Messina, who was aligned with the technocrats, rigging election outcomes, and engaging Italian Prime Minister Matteo Renzi to keep globalism on track, with particular emphasis placed upon neutralizing nationalists who were causing globalism to derail. Cameron necessarily took direction from Rothschild as UK Prime Minister, with O'Neill playing a key financial advisory role within his Administration.

Chairman of Chatham House (Royal Institute of International Affairs), which the *Executive Intelligence Review* identified as a key center of operations for international money laundering and drug trafficking operations; this is the center through which the syndicate plans and executes its global imperialist designs.

Worked for **Bank of America** (institutional partner of the World Economic Forum) and **Marine Midland Bank** which was acquired by **HSBC**, the bank associated with Jeffrey Epstein and the Clinton Foundation.

Chief of Global Research at Swiss Bank Corporation, one of the original private banking firms in Basel, Switzerland. SBC became the **Union Bank of Switzerland,** the largest Bank in Europe, the second largest bank in the world – and one implicated in drug trafficking, money laundering, and tax evasion.

"Union Bank of Switzerland was … caught up in the biggest drugs money laundering case in Swiss history," the *Independent* reports.
O'Neill, however brilliant, was the Rothschild's man.
More than likely, the idea for BRICs was bandied about in British elite circles, and somehow O'Neill was the first to put pen to paper, to give it life. "Although China's real GDP growth rate will slow beginning in 2021, given its increasing demographic challenge, that will not stop it from overtaking the United States as the world's biggest economy,"

O'Neill writes, with the City of London essentially having orchestrated this outcome.

He also linked vaccines to the post-covid economic recovery. "Obviously, an immediate strong post–COVID-19 recovery almost exclusively depends on developing and distributing vaccines and treatments to eradicate this pandemic," he writes. "In my judgment, the multiplier benefits of the required $20–$30 billion from donors are such that it would represent the *biggest* no-brainer *economic stimulus* any generation has had the chance to agree to, dwarfing the *potential benefits* of 2008–09."

In both instances – the former having been orchestrated by Larry Summers, who advocated "permanent lockdowns" as "the new normal," wealth was being redistributed from the public to the corporate elite while smaller businesses (and a number of families) were wiped out financially. Meanwhile, the financial elite continued to consolidate their wealth and power, fulfilling Rothschild's long-term agenda.

Reflecting the role played by these Rothschild-created global institutions, O'Neill writes: "The IMF must play an active role in encouraging this stimulus and - in addition to its newfound focus on climate change - *must enter the arena of health systems and integrate analysis of health spending in its surveillance work*."

To this end, he recommends "aligning with finance ministers to support the Access to COVID-19 Tools (ACT) Accelerator," which was launched by the World Health Organization and its partners to support "the fastest, most coordinated, and successful global efforts in history to fight a disease." The Accelerator tools were *advanced through public-private partnerships* to "deploy the tests, treatments, and vaccines the world needs," making a windfall for Big Pharma, and yet what did O'Neill know about health care? He is an economist.

ACT was launched in April of 2020 at an event co-hosted by the Director General of the World Health Organization, the President of France, the President of the European Commission, and the Bill & Melinda Gates Foundation to bring together "governments, scientists, businesses, civil society, and philanthropists, and global health organizations (like the Bill & Melinda Gates Foundation, CEPI, FIND, Gavi, The Global Fund, Unitaid, Wellcome, the WHO, and World Bank)."

With the launch of ACT and UNICEF became delivery partners for COVAX, the vaccine pillar. O'Neill led the British government's independent Review on Antimicrobial Resistance. "Trying to strengthen the links between economics, finance, and health should be at the forefront of our emerging ideas," he writes.

In the aftermath of covid, the federal government should *"prioritize public investment,"* he writes. "To be specific, the time has come to truly distinguish between government investment spending and consumption spending; the former is likely to have a positive multiplier effect and should not be treated from an accounting perspective the same as government expenditures on consumption. Tackling climate change and future health threats requires such investments. *Emerging market economies' achievement of their growth potential depends on such investment*, which is arguably more important for economic growth than financial conditions."

And with that, he reveals the agenda behind BRICS – and the pandemic lockdown – keeping development of the world, specifically the Third Word – and China on track in a post-petro-dollar age: *"A ramework for smarter fiscal policy will almost definitely require stronger domestic financial systems. Continued dependence on a monetary system based on the U.S. dollar (petro-dollar) makes this difficult.* Despite the relatively smooth but ongoing slow relative decline of the share of the U.S. economy in the world, the dollar-based monetary system remains as dominant, broadly speaking, as it was when I started my financial career in 1982. This means that the world must ride the cyclical roller-coaster of the Federal Reserve's monetary policy, its consequence for the United States, and the global financial conditions that follow. *As the Fed tightens, by and large, financial conditions for emerging markets tighten* —often chaotically. As the Fed eases, the reverse happens. T*here is a way out, and one day, this change will take place*. T*he monetary system needs to evolve to be more reflective of the changing dynamics of the world*, and until it does, *emerging market nations' ability to reach their growth potential* will remain challenging, albeit perhaps not quite as challenging as other domestic initiatives such as health and education systems."

Ultimately, the syndicate was concerned with its continued survival and ability to develop the world with public funding to secure a global monopoly on commerce, power, and wealth.

Whatever was going on with BRICS, the media and indeed the political establishment were not being upfront with the American people, who were fed a steady dose of doom and gloom, that they were on the cusp of losing their country to forces unseen, that the dollar was on the way out.

In January of 2024, Saudi Arabia joined BRICS, signaling to many an end to the Bretton Wood system. Having become enriched through U.S. technical, financial, and strategic support, the syndicate, which had exploited the United States for wholly self-serving reasons, was now moving on. Was Saudi Arabia friend or foe?

The BRICS bloc included Brazil, Russia, India, China, and South Africa, with other countries joining, including Saudi Arabia, United Arab Emirates, Egypt, Iran, and Ethiopia. China was suddenly Saudi Arabia's biggest oil customer and America's greatest strategic competitor. American media and politicians complained about China, then sent oil to the Chinese. Somehow Saudi Arabia was cultivating strong ties with China too. American governors and other politicians, both at the state and national level, were cutting deals with China and Saudi Arabia – most notably in the area of AI and "sustainable food production," with the Saudis leading both.

The United States was somehow at war with Russia in the Ukraine, having poured billions into that country with no end in sight – and with limited oversight and accountability. Yet, Saudi sovereign fund was investing in the Russian Direct Investment Fund (RDIF), the sovereign fund of Russia, America's enemy. Yet, as an enemy of the United States, Russia had invested in American tech. "U.S. startups ... have secured large funding rounds led by Russian-based investors," Crunchbase.com reports.

In 2015, the Russian and Saudi sovereign funds established a long-term strategic partnership to invest in projects in Russian territory, worth $10 billion. Meanwhile, every OPEC country has been incorporated into the Chinese Belt and Road Initiative, Communist China's global infrastructure project, challenging U.S. hegemony.

Saudi Arabia joined the BRICS and the Shanghai Cooperation Organization - the largest regional financial and military organization on the planet while the United States continued to sell the Saudis weapons. A BRICS New Development Bank (NDB) was launched in 2015 based in Shanghai as an alternative to the U.S.-dominated World Bank. Like its soon-to-be predecessor, the NDB was geared at mobilizing resources for infrastructure and sustainable development – this time throughout BRICS, having seemingly absconded with America's wealth.

The NDB's first Chairman was Kundapur Vaman Kamath, who had previously presided over Infosys Ltd, India's second largest IT services company and one which partnered with the Saudis for business in the Kingdom. Revealing possible, if unrealistic plans to replace the World Bank, the NDB has opened its doors to *all* members to the United Nations.

Stranger still, among the NDB's Board of Governors, the highest decision-making authority of the bank, is Anton Siluanov, Russia's Minister of Finance for Russia. In 2014, the International Monetary Fund, which receives money from the United States, provided a $18 billion bailout to the provisional government of the Ukraine that was established after the Ukrainian revolution. As the largest contributor, the United States has provided in excess of $155 billion to the IMF as of 2018. Meanwhile, Congress has approved $113 billion to the Ukraine – an amount that continues to grow.

As is the syndicate's pattern, Ukraine is being destroyed and rebuilt with government contract while the politically-connected are shoring up markets and becoming impossibly rich off taxpayers. The war has provided an opportunity to rebuild the country with modern technology and showcase new and emerging tech, as Palantir's Peter Thiel expressed at the World Economic Forum.

Russia – the alleged antagonist in this war – has contributed billions to the IMF, in addition to receiving billions from the United States. Given that Russia is in a position to contribute billions to the the IMF, why hasn't it paid the United States back and why does the United States give money to a country that is in a position to give it to someone else. Looks like a global money laundering scheme.

Recently, Russia sought to transform $24 billion in IMF reserves to cash to fund its war effort. At the same time, *Time* magazine has reported that the IMF is promoting Russian propaganda, certifying, for example, "Vladimir Putin's unsupported rosy economic forecasts, inexplicably doubling its forecast of Russian GDP growth which …far exceeds that of much of Europe."

"The IMF has become a source of data distortion and policy confusion either as an unwittingly naive tool of Putin's propaganda machine due to incompetence and laziness, or perhaps something more sinister," *Times* reports.

China and Saudi Arabia have signed a comprehensive strategic partnership agreements, linking Saudi Arabia's Vision 2030 with China's Belt and Road Initiative to encourage investment. While OPEC is scaling back oil supply (probably due to scarcity prompted by overproduction), China, Saudi Arabia's largest trading partner is its greatest purchaser of oil. Yet, the United States is curtailing its own oil production. At the same time, both the Biden and Trump Administrations have tapped U.S. Strategic Petroleum Reserves to sell oil to China, a strategic competitor of the United States, reflecting priorities of of a hijacked government.

China has proposed buying Saudi oil in yuan while Russia seeks to pursue oil transactions in the ruble, revealing that the push to discard the petrodollar is motivated by a desire to keep moving money around the world without interference from the United States. The Russian collusion delusion that dogged much of the Trump Administration was prompted by efforts of Russian oligarchs to circumvent or repeal the Magnitsky Act, which allowed the federal government to freeze their assets over human rights abuses. A petro-yuan or petro-ruble would ensure that even if the U.S. did freeze the assets of a human rights abuser, pedophile, oligarch, drug runner, or global thief, their global transactions could proceed through another, fall-back currency.

O'Neill calls their bluff, stating that the mere idea of a BRICS currency is "ridiculous," stating that the BRICS nations have "never achieved anything since they first started meeting."

In an interview with the *Financial Times*, he remarked, "They're going to create a BRICS central bank? How would you do that? It's embarrassing, almost."

He also explained why efforts were being made to weaken U.S. dominance within the global financial system: it was simply not strong enough to support the development of emerging economies. "The dollar's role is not ideal for the way the world has evolved," he said. "You're got all these economies who live on this cyclical never-ending twist of whatever the Fed decides to do in the interests of the United States."

Ironically, the Federal Reserve is controlled by the financial interests surrounding the City of London. The Fed also needs to manage the U.S. economy – and is somehow struggling to do this while remaining the global reserve currency, given the unsustainability of U.S. debt, which is compounded by the weakened (now, non-existent) petro-dollar, fueled by Saudi Arabia's dwindling oil supply. This, in turn, has led bankers to seek new types of currency to keep the development agenda on track – for example, by way of crypto-currencies created by "mined energy" or a gold-backed currency based upon the purloined global gold supplies.

When asked if foreign currencies will overtake the dollar, O'Neill tells the *FT*, "None of these things will ever happen until those countries want to have their currencies used by people in other parts of the world." It's unlikely that Americans will begin trading in rubles or yuan anytime soon.

At a global level, an international reserve currency helps investors and sovereign governments settle payments for exports and imports of goods and services between nations, pursue global portfolio investments, borrow funds, and set prices for commodities such as oil or gold. International reserve currencies are the linchpin of both world trade and the global financial system. Any commercial or financial transaction between two or more parties is always conducted by exchanging money.

The currency that is widely accepted as the medium of exchange in all transactions is called an international reserve currency. That is still the dollar. All international prices, international contracts, and financial transactions are quoted in terms of reserve currency units. Since World War II, the U.S. dollar has served as the international reserve currency.

Investors, governments, and sovereign wealth funds typically view reserve currencies as a safe haven to protect their assets during periods of heightened uncertainty. This is the "store of value" characteristic of international reserve currencies.

The dollar will therefore likely remain a global reserve currency for a long time to come. Why? For one, the United States is a strong sovereign nation, perhaps accounting for persistent efforts by China and Russian to weaken it. The United States is a functioning republic, though less so, with each passing day. The world – and its financial markets – take comfort in the relative stability and calm of the United States – and its property rights. Global finance revolves around the dollar. This will not change overnight.

The United States is being compromised by foreign interference in its political process and economy attempting to bend the nation to its will. During the first year of the Biden Administration, "Saudi foreign agents disclosed more than $25 million in payments for foreign influence operations and lobbying targeting the United States," the Center for Responsive Politics reports. This amount "exceeds any prior year other than the unprecedented sum of about $39 million it spent in 2018, the bulk of which came as foreign agents worked to rehabilitate Saudi Arabia's image in the weeks after *Washington Post* journalist Jamal Khashoggi was killed at Saudi Arabia's consulate in Turkey on Oct. 2, 2018."

According to Saudi foreign registration filings, Saudi Arabia's investment in the American political process peaked in 2018 at $40 million – and then ballooned up to nearly $92 million in 2023. In contrast, in 2017 and 2018, the Saudis spent $19 million and $17.8 million respectively.

In 2023, Microsoft announced plans to establish a cloud data center and to invest in infrastructure in the Kingdom – thereby placing itself in a position to exploit the country's data for commercial use. The effort was described in the media as "part of (Microsoft's) continued efforts to empower public and private organizations around the world with intelligent, trusted, enterprise-grade cloud services to realize their digital transformation ambitions."

Microsoft's partner ecosystem reportedly expects to earn $8 for every $1 of Microsoft cloud-generated revenue by 2026, bringing opportunities for partners in the Kingdom to grow *their* revenues, local content contributions, and customer bases.

It should be remembered that despite the self-serving agenda of the criminal elite, international law enshrines the right for Americans to pursue to self-determination. They fought the American Revolution to be freed from British (and, in general, foreign) meddling in their affairs. The American people had expressed their desire to establish their own Republic and constitutional framework that enshrined a Bill of Rights for the people and which restrained the branches of government through checks and balances.

They specifically and consistently erected barriers to insulate governing process from the money trust. The intent of the people, and its leaders, was to be freed from the meddling of these international financial interests, with a desire to be self-governing. "Self-determination denotes the legal right of people to decide their own destiny in the international order," Cornell Law School's Legal Information Institute affirms. "Self-determination is a core principle of international law, arising from customary international law, but also recognized as a general principle of law, and enshrined in a number of international treaties, including the United Nations Charter and the International Covenant on Civil and Political Rights."

Reflecting the influence Saudi Arabia wields. Consider that Aramco has acquired exclusive right to sell Shell-branded gasoline and diesel in a number of U.S. states. In a 2024 Shell Energy Transition Plan, Shell announced, "Our target to become a net-zero emissions energy business by 2050. ...We believe this target supports the more ambitious goal of the Paris Agreement....We aim to grow our public charging network vehicles and remain one of the world's largest blenders of biofuelds. As the energy transition progresses, we expect to sell more low-carbon products and solutions and less oil products including petro and diesel....The world needs a balanced and orderly transition away from fossil fuels to maintain secure energy supplies while accelerating the transition to affordable low-carbon solutions."

The recurring theme has been the need to maintain "secure and affordable energy supplies" for the purposes of "developing the world." To achieve this goal, global planners have sought to restrict movement and freedoms, keep people in place and build an infrastructure around them from, with elites regulating, restraining, and harvesting the assets, energy, labor, and expenditures of the people to enrich themselves.

At the same time, the United States selected an Indian-born American to preside over the World Bank to leverage India's IT to development the world by way of public-private partnerships. The new head, Ajaypal Singh Banga, was Chairman of the U.S.-India Business Council, representing more than 300 of the largest international companies invested in China. He also chaired the International Chamber of Commerce – and Mastercard.

The Biden Administration tapped him to preside over the public-private Partnership for Central America with Vice President Kamala Harris – to develop the Northern Triangle of Central American, which seeks to address economic issues associated with migration while promoting job creation and social programs. This program was launched in 2021 with Harris to support a White House "Call to Action to the Private Sector to Deepen Investment in the Northern Triangle."

Yet, little attention has been given to America's homeless and jobless problems, with priority given to recent immigrants for housing subsidies and employment. Among the 75 "strategic partners" of this partnership are Tent Partnership for Refugees, Harvard's T.H. Chan School of Public Health, Mastercard, Microsoft, Aisa, the Inter-American Development Bank, and the World Bank.

Consider Banga's other affiliations:

Member, Obama's Advisory Committee for Trade Policy and Negotiations.
ember of Board of Governors, American Red Cross
Vice Chair of the Board, Economic Club of New York.
Member of the Trilateral Commission
Member, Board of Directors, Peterson Institute of International Economics
Member, Trilateral Commission
Co-Chair, and Board of Directors, American India Foundation
Member of the Board, National Urban League
Member of the Board of Trustees, World Economic Forum

He is a global planner through and through. In November 2022, PCA, the World Bank, and the United Nations World Food Programme launched the "Disaster Risk Insurance and Finance in Central America Consortium to support climate-related agricultural insurance solutions for two million smallholder farmers in Guatemala, El Salvador, and Honduras to increase their food security and financial resilience.

Meanwhile, Americans increasingly cannot afford their grocery bills. The plan of the global planners is not working out for we, the people. Something needs to change. The American people need to speak up and lobby for their own interests so that they can get a better deal and protect what is theirs. They must demand that America's represent their interests and not those of the City of London. The global agenda does not align with America's

IX.
Solutions: Let's End this Madness!

"Liberty once lost, is lost forever."

President John Adams
American Founding Father

When I first embarked upon the Abramoff investigation in 2006, I had no idea what I was getting myself into or what I would uncover. After a moment of prayer, an inner voice prompting me, "the truth surrounding Jack Abramoff will set the country free." I didn't really know who Jack Abramoff was then, beyond reading a few articles about him in the newspaper and seeing him briefly on TV. I had already decided that Capitol Hill was too corrupt for my tastes and that I needed to forge a life outside of it.

I think I am very much like many Americans. I descended from the Pilgrims and Founding Fathers. I was raised as a Christian, to believe that integrity was the greatest attribute one could possess, and without character and the trust of others, what else was there? "Too much is given, much is expected," I was told growing up, believing that leaders served the public interest and that it is good to share one's good fortune with others, to give as God prompted. I believed that the United States offered unlimited opportunities to pursue one's God-given talents and that people were fundamentally good, decent, and kind. The fact was, I had never encountered anyone in my young adult years who wasn't morally above reproach. Everyone I knew, with few exceptions, had integrity. This background made me naive and ill equipped for the treachery I encountered on Capitol Hill.

I had always dreamed of covering the White House and State Department as a journalist. Upon arriving, I couldn't leave fast enough. Wading into the swamp devastated me on many levels, but I believe God has a purpose in everything.

When I made my discoveries about the truth surrounding the Abramoff investigation in 2006, I received a bona fide offer from a major publisher, but politics intervened to block publication. Actually there was great interest in what I had to say. Somebody needed to expose the truth behind the swamp – and through Abramoff, I had ventured into the belly of the beast. He opened his Rolodex to me – though I was able to forge my own access into the impenetrable federally recognized Indian tribes, track down hundreds of high placed contacts who generously granted me interviews and supplied me with paperwork. I read voraciously, explored public records, and methodically pieced together the most extensive corruption probe to grace Capitol Hill, one whose tentacles reached clear across the globe. Through serendipity, I attended meetings where secrets were disclosed that would break the case wide open. New insights led to new discoveries, and then, clarity!

How far down did the corruption go, how far did it extend, I wondered. Where was the beginning? Where was the end? The mission to discovery was a fool's errand. When I wanted to give up, an inner voice prompted me again, "the truth will set the nation free." The further down the road I ventured, the more I realized that unless America corrected course, the country would be lost forever, and I loved my country too much to allow this to happen. If not me, who? Had I not worked with Jack Abramoff, I never would have understood the peril the country faced. I concluded I had a duty of conscience to come forward with what I knew, as much as I preferred to keep my own counsel.

As much as I explored, there was more still, and then the pieces began to come together, allowing me to see the proverbial Deep State in its entirely. I remember when my grandfather, Judge William C. Dixon, a deeply honorable man, discovered it. He was asked to throw a case – and upon refusing to do so, forces began to act against him. After successfully prosecuting Standard Oil et al before the U.S. Supreme Court as leading federal anti-trust attorney, the defendants were fined all of $1, a mere slap on the wrist. Many good men and women before and after him have seen and experienced different sides of the darkness within America – as I ultimately did.

I suppose from the start, I prayed to understand the dark forces behind the country so that I could set things right. And so here I am. I believe I now have a deep understanding of how the country was lost, who did it, and why, and now I would like to set things right – as would millions of other Americans.

So what can be done? I am asked this frequently, and I am at a loss for words. Who am I to offer a solution to the problems that have plagued the United States for over a century now? As much as I have endeavored to learn, there is always more to learn still. At times like these, I wish I had a law degree, an accounting degree, the power of the media at my disposal, and a Rolodex of powerful contacts I could consult.

So, I put the matter to the American people. Let's put our heads together and find a way forward. The good news is that there is a way. I believe the agenda and method through which it has been achieved are clear. There is also a growing consensus that the criminals are acting under color of law – and have done so since at least the Civil War.

The American people can stand up, in unison, and demand an end to this deception. That the so-called elites were prepared to sacrifice millions, if not billions of people at the altar of greed and power – and have advanced along this path, strips them of any legitimacy to power that they may claim through their color-of-law institutions. Their outright criminality and lawlessness, proliferation of war, genocide of people, assassinations of leaders, denigration of the food supply, disruption of the healthcare and educational systems, corruption of governments, media, and institutions worldwide, and their vicious abuse of young and old alike strips them of any legitimacy they could possibly have. They have broken the contract between governed and government.

Neither nations nor people are obligated to accommodate their psychopathy, entitlement, or delusions of grandeur. They are not worthy of the positions they hold nor the wealth they have obtained – most of which has come through illicit means.

OK, so what can be done? For one, do not allow them to divide us. We must stand in unity as we, the people, as one humanity – and take back our power to restore God's kingdom on Earth.

A starting point is understanding the problem in all of its complexities – and then forging solutions based upon them. One solution may be to restore the original confederation of states, legitimate governments – under a functioning Republic based upon the Constitution and the Bill of Rights, with checks and balances restored.

We must also challenge and eliminate debt. Dr. Eric Toussaint, Spokesman for the Committee for the Abolition of Illegitimate Debt, has made this case and demonstrated that colonies have successfully rejected the debt burden placed upon them by their colonizers. Make no mistake, the United States has been colonized by the City of London and its many proxies.

The Federal Reserve came into being, not through an act of Congress – but through an act of deception. The founders, along with generations of Americans, have rejected the central bank and the money trust. Indeed our Constitutions restricts the right to print money to Congress. If self-appointed elites have violated our Constitution and corrupted our government to the point where it cannot function properly as intended, then we must start again and build from the ground up. Our representatives must serve the people first and foremost. America was not built upon greed but upon a love of freedom and devotion to God. A free society is only possible with a righteous people. In fact, our Constitution and system of government was created with this vision and these principles in mind. Therefore we must restore our churches, separating our society from Godless materialism and spread the Gospel of Jesus Christ. We must not only work to restore our national sovereignty and integrity to our governments, but we must help other nations do the same – and welcome their help in return.

We should have absolutely no tolerance for the lawlessness of our colonizers – nor abide by their deceptions. The truth should be our guiding light. The era of darkness is slowly being extinguished in the majesty of light that is spreading worldwide.

I'd like to see the pirates return what has been taken from us – and to come clean so we can set things right. As viciously evil as they are, we must take the high road and create a new society, one envisioned by our founders, not based on retribution or vengeance, but on God's law.

We will figure it out as we go.

In God we trust,
Susan Bradford

Printed in Great Britain
by Amazon